The Life Elysian

Leaves from the autobiography
of Fredric Winterleigh,
A soul in Paradise

Originally recorded & published
for the Author in 1905
By
Robert James Lees

Volume Two

Also in this series, Vol 1 "Through the Mists"
and Vol 3 "The Gate of Heaven"

This paperback edition published 2009
By

Sanders & Co UK Ltd
5 Artizan Road, Northampton NN1 4HU
England

CONTENTS

TITLE PAGE		i
RECORDED PREFACE		iii
CHAPTER 1	THE OPEN SEPULCHRE	3
CHAPTER 2	THE FAMILY IN PARADISE	15
CHAPTER 3	THE LOVE OF GOD	27
CHAPTER 4	THE RESURRECTION AND ITS BODY	41
CHAPTER 5	THE ANGEL OF DEATH	53
CHAPTER 6	THE BONDAGE OF SIN	65
CHAPTER 7	THE GATE TO HELL	81
CHAPTER 8	ANGELS AND ANGELS	97
CHAPTER 9	WHO RULES IN HELL?	113
CHAPTER 10	NEARER TO THEE	127
CHAPTER 11	A LESSON IN CREATION	135
CHAPTER 12	CUSHNA AT HOME	147
CHAPTER 13	"CAN THIS BE DEATH?"	157
CHAPTER 14	THE MANY MANSIONS	171
CHAPTER 15	I BREAK DEATH'S SILENCE	187
CHAPTER 16	"THEY WILL HEAR HIM"	199
CHAPTER 17	THE HALLELUJAH STRAND	207
CHAPTER 18	LIFE'S MOSAICS	217
CHAPTER 19	THE GOD OF MEN	231
CHAPTER 20	THE MEN OF GOD	241
CHAPTER 21	THE COMING OF THE CHRIST	251
CHAPTER 22	THE WORK AND TEACHING OF THE CHRIST	263
CHAPTER 23	THE COMMUNION OF SAINTS	287
CHAPTER 24	THE MISSION OF PAIN	303
CHAPTER 25	AU REVOIR	315
THE LIFE ELYSIAN		325
A BRIEF BIOGRAPHY OF ROBERT JAMES LEES		327
PRINTING HISTORY		328

The Life Elysian

This extract is taken from 'The Gate of Heaven', the third volume in the Trilogy by Robert James Lees. It illustrates every stage of a soul's journey through Physical & Spiritual lives to reach the ultimate goal of 'Heaven'. I believe it to be such a clear explanation, that I felt it was worthwhile including it in this volume and hope that Fred will forgive me! *Bill Sanders* Publisher

THE HEAVEN and EARTH SECTIONAL DIAGRAM

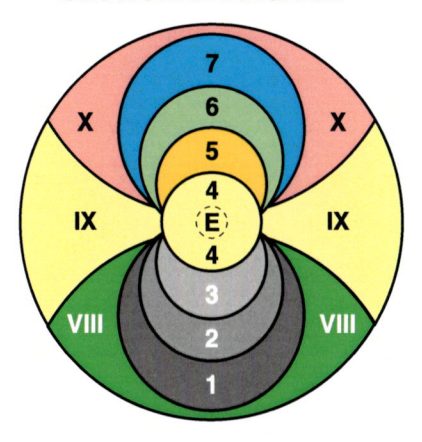

EXPLANATION OF THE DIAGRAM

The outer circle indicates the position of the Psychic Sphere. The 'firmament' or heaven of (Gen. i, 8). This, as described in the following pages, embraces every provision for the reception and maturing of the newly-born soul until it reaches the Spiritual condition of a son of God.

E - The Earth. Its position in the Physical indicated by the dotted circle.

1-7 - The Seven Spheres, or Intermediate State. The Schoolroom where the youth of the soul is passed in Spiritual preparation.

VIII - The location of the uncultured, or "nations that forget God," in which they are suitably instructed and prepared.

IX - The Sleep State, where the sleep-life is spent by all mankind in communion with the departed. (Job xxxiii, 14-18)

X - The Great Nursery, where children who pass away prior to birth, or before they "know to refuse the evil, and choose the good" (Isa. vii, 16), are developed and educated.

All these states are Psychic or Intermediary between the Physical and Spiritual, as the twilight divides the light from the darkness in the natural world. The first Spiritual Sphere lies beyond this circle and is attained by "the Second Birth" (John iii, 3) as set forth in the following pages.

RECORDER'S PREFACE

This book is not a novel, neither have I any more claim to its authorship than the publisher, compositor or binder who will presently do their part in handing it forward to the public!

This disclaimer naturally demands an explanation and my present object is to furnish the same as briefly and simply as possible. But the task is by no means an ordinary one, for the affidavit it necessitates, and which I reverently make in the presence of God, is of such a nature as probably to constitute it unique in the annals of literature.

We live in an age of marvels, with almost every edition of the newspaper bringing reports of some new wonder, but I have one to place on record, the portentous significance of which is sufficient to shake the foundations of earth in its proclamation!

If any man has been summoned to step with unshod feet upon holy ground, I also have heard the call and have had laid upon me the awful responsibility of publishing the things I have seen and heard.

The voice said, "Write the things which thou hast seen, and the things which are, and the things which shall be hereafter." How shall I escape if I refuse him that speaketh? Therefore I obey, not fearing any consequences which may result, but rather weighed down with a sense of my own unworthiness of the mission to which God has called me.

Let me try to make myself and mission understood by a necessary but brief reference to my past.

On the maternal side I come of a line of prophets-using the word in the sense it is employed in the following pages-and from both parents inherit a strain of Puritan blood. 'Psychic invasions,' as F. W. H. Myers would call them, have been my companions from the cradle, I am informed, but I am personally aware that as a child I cried at being left in the darkness unless I saw a mysterious, and to others invisible, kilted Highlander who remained beside me talking or singing till I fell asleep. And even now, after a lapse of half a century, the vivid memory of his strong but kindly face is as freshly recalled as if he had sat beside me while this new year was born.

When about thirteen years of age, I entered upon a second and vastly different series of psychic experiences, the invasions taking the form of a change of consciousness, and for several years I was associated with the Spiritualistic movement in Birmingham, where I was brought into connection with D. D. Home and many of the early pioneers. This is neither the time nor place for me to dwell upon the accepted evidences of the continuity of existence after death which were given through my lips during these periods of hypnotic oblivion. I merely wish to indicate the way by which the guiding hand of God has brought me to the present.

Before reaching my twentieth year, I was removed from the sphere of my activities into a most determined seclusion, having previously declared, during an entrancement, that the life I was pursuing in connection with promiscuous séances was unfitting me for some special work I had to do in the future. And now followed a period of very active doubt and agnosticism as to the source from which these truly remarkable phenomena sprang.

While the pillars of cloud and fire stood still, though my faith was shaken, my interest never for a moment abated, and several years were spent in a very close study of the subject while I retained an unshakable faith in Christ as the anchor of my soul.

In this inquiry, of course, the Bible-read by itself, as I would read another book, and for itself, to see what it really had to say-formed a very important part of my quest; and it was from the pages of that book that the newer after-light first broke upon me. I began to read it in the desire that it would strengthen my agnosticism into certainty, but to my great surprise it spake with another voice, charging me to bless where I had sought for a mandate to condemn.

Then I married, and with one beside me who has ever been as

Recorders Preface

the angel of a holier presence-without whose patient suffering and encouraging assurances all must have been so different to what it is-I entered upon the third and more memorable epoch of my life. The old phenomena and many I had not hitherto experienced were quietly and almost imperceptibly re-insinuated into recognition with so definite a confirmation of their origin as to finally compel acknowledgement. It would be an easy matter to fill volumes with the unanswerable evidences which came upon us at this time like a flood, were this the place to do so.

I have said the old phenomena were revived, but this scarcely represents what actually did occur, for while they might have been the same in kind, the latter were in every way far greater and the communications they transmitted were incomparably more reliable than the former. The why and wherefore of this was presently explained to me, and in the counsel which accompanied it, a sharp and definite dividing line was drawn, which has from that time separated myself from the ordinary spiritualist. If I was to fulfil the mission opening out to me, I was to hold no séances, but rather to live a life which would supply an ever-present condition for the operation of a spiritual ministry.

Unquestionably assured of the bona fides of these angelic visitors, we naturally grew into a compact of service in which each mutually waited upon the other, and striking evidences of their nature, fidelity and power began to multiply. Then as the months went on, shadowy forms from the invisible began to make their appearance, which presently and gradually increased in density until I became able to touch, handle and speak to them, and the whisper of musical voices was heard in reply; still the development went on, until now for years past they have assumed such solid shape as to be able to use my books and sit with me for hours in the full light of day!

I can see you start-almost catch the emphatic exclamation with which you are tempted to throw the book aside and read no more. But 'yield not to temptation.' 'I am not mad . . . but speak forth the words of truth and soberness.' I am saying no more than James, John and Peter might have told their companions after coming down from the Mount of Transfiguration. I proclaim no more than the gospel of the Lord Jesus Christ- that gospel which has been given to bind up the broken-hearted. It only sounds incredible because we have lost the evidences of this vital part of it. I bear this testimony calmly, reverently and thankfully, in the presence of that God whose angels aforetime were entertained by Abraham, wrestled with Jacob, closed the mouths of the lions for Daniel, liberated Peter from prison and rolled away the stone from the door of the sepulchre. He is still the same God, invariable, 'without the shadow of a turning,' and 'whatsoever He doeth it shall be for ever.'

It is now a quarter of a century since this last stage of my career began, during which, so far as their particular work is concerned, I have been kept very much to myself, while they have been working towards some goal they see, but which I, at present, do not understand. But the years have not been fruitless. The evidences of their ministry lie thickly strewn along the way, and many to-day rejoice at the blessings these angels of God have bestowed in their passing by.

But to the book!

With few exceptions, I spend two or three hours every day in the companionship of these visitors from across the border. Some years since they suggested at one of our conferences, that in answer to many earnest solicitations for some definite record of life as they enjoy it, I should assist them in writing a volume which might prove to be a helpful illustration and clear up some of the many mysteries of existence. The proposal was taken up with eagerness; Myhanene foreseeing a valuable aid therein to the work he had in hand; a choice was made of one to direct the undertaking, with many promises of assistance from his fellow-labourers, and myself to act as amanuensis. We commenced our labours at once, but the task of translating ideas even from one language to another entails much sacrifice for which no adequate recompense can be supplied. What then was the loss we found to be involved in representing the Life Elysian in the gross and unmusical jargon of earth? Many times and oft did we come to a stand, doubtful of our success, but in the end, with many regrets and misgivings at what he called 'the sorry achievement,' Aphraar gave me permission, some six years ago, to publish the volume entitled "Through the Mists". Never did a book leave the hands of its creator with a clearer consciousness and acknowledgement of its failure to represent the ideal aimed at, a deficiency far more clearly recognized by its Author than its critics appear to have discovered.

But sown in fears it has produced a most unexpected harvest of thankfulness, and the grateful recognitions of the help it has afforded has led Aphraar to redeem his conditional promise, and throughout the whole year which has just closed, we have laboured together in the production of this second volume now sent forth upon its errand of consolation and revelation.

Of the subjects discussed herein, it must be left to deeper minds than my own to express any opinion. Whoever reads will find that it treats of some of life's great mysteries with a frank familiarity and certain composure which suggests more than speculation, and to my mind the harmonious completion towards which every various subject is found to contribute its individual part, savours more of truth than otherwise. But I may be prejudiced in my opinion by the reverent affection they one and all inspire in their more than human tenderness and consideration for my many shortcomings, therefore I will leave any suggestion as to its relative value as a revelation to minds better qualified to judge.

It will now be understood, I trust, why I penned the above disclaimer; but let me, in closing, say with what unspeakable gratitude I acknowledge the honour of being called to the service I have here so inadequately rendered. I know, more than my readers will discover, how much my own limitations have prevented the ideals of the Author from being realized, and am humbled at the knowledge, but since he approves, I send it forth as the joint effort of hands clasped across the tomb, hoping by the blessing of God that it may be the means of helping many homeward, even more so than was granted to its predecessor.

Engelburg, Ilfracombe Robert James Lees
New Year's Day, 1905

* * *

THE LIFE ELYSIAN

CHAPTER 1

THE OPEN SEPULCHRE

Behold, there went out a sower to sow. The eloquent silences of Christ often speak to the sympathetic disciple with more divine inspiration than His utterances. For instance, when He spake His parables, did He not wish us to take cognizance of the fact that He found His analogues for spiritual life in the kingdom of nature, and thereby teach us that the law of the lower is carried upward into the higher? To suggest that this is not so is also to suggest that He is unsafe to follow beyond the limitations of the letter, and since He never wrote a word, we cannot be certain as to what He said, therefore the Christ, for us, does not exist.

If anyone wishes to assume such a position, I have no right to interfere with his resolves, but it will be necessary for us at once to part company; since my knowledge, experience and purpose all lie in the other direction.

I am not, however, anxious to enter the lists of controversy just now. It may be that my ministry will carry my feet soon enough on to debatable ground in the exposition of the truth as I have found it. My reference to the parable of the sower was suggested, rather by its allusion to the certainty of the harvest of futurity, than the analogy between nature and grace.

Some time ago I ventured—at the instance of the agony I was all too conscious of—to make an effort to return to earth in the hope of being able to sow some few seeds of consolation in hearts broken and crushed by the universal catastrophe called death. I wished to tell simply and faithfully what I had experienced in that supposed unreachable beyond, confident that the truth would prove to be a solace. I was not altogether unacquainted with the existing ideas, teachings, even prejudices which earth entertains against such a discredited communion, and was quite prepared for the cold incredulity I was certain to arouse on one side, as well as an exclamation of pious horror on the other. But I had, in my new condition, discovered something far otherwise than I anticipated; God was so much better than I had been led to imagine; the afterlife was so inexpressibly different to my expectations that, as a man, I could not keep silent when I found that silence was not forced upon me, and common sympathy for humanity as well as gratitude to God would not allow me to rest until I had done my best to make known how generously He has provided, infinitely above all we could ever ask, think, or conceive, in the life which lies just beyond the softened twilight of absence from the body. The God before whose judgement-seat I had been expecting to stand, with more of doubt and misgiving than filial anticipation, was found so far to out-father the best of fathers, transcending even him who met the prodigal of whom Christ spake, that woe would have fallen me had I kept silence, and in relation to the agony of earth I should have played the part of a demon rather than a man.

I did not keep silent. So soon as I had found that return was possible and the natural obstacles were overcome, I answered my heart's desire and scattered over the world the gospel of my former message,[1] and it is the almost incredible harvest of thankful acknowledgement from that imperfect effort that fills me with surprise at the moderation with which the Christ estimated His results in the parable.

How I wish I could cull a few expressions of thankfulness from the hundreds of letters lying before me as I take the now familiar seat to redeem my promise, that if my initial effort served its purpose, I should be glad to come again and continue the record of my experiences in the life to which you are all hastening on. But such letters have come to me through my Recorder, in confidence —or so I choose to regard them in the absence of permission—

[1] Volume One - "Through the Mists"

Chapter 1   The Open Sepulchre

and therefore I can do no more than ask you to accept my assurance and read on until, that which I have now to say, falls like the holier balm of God's better Gilead into your own wounded heart, and you experience, for yourself, the power of truth as it is in Jesus, to minister to those who fall crushed beneath the avalanche of the world's greatest suffering.

Still, though my success has been far beyond my most sanguine expectations, I cannot forget that I have only been able to touch the merest fringe of the garment of sorrow, and, while I rejoice for what has been done, my heart still goes out in sympathy to those who weep disconsolately beneath the cypress trees. "Comfort ye, comfort ye, my people, saith your God, speak ye comfortably" to the children of men. It is like our God to issue such commanding encouragements, for is He not a Father who ever pities His children, not expecting too much from them and always remembering they are but dust? Surely,

"If all the world my Saviour knew,
Then all the world would love Him too"

This is the hope, aim, desire of all the ministering legions sent forth to minister, for when this is accomplished, sin will cease and the effects of sin will shortly come to an end.

There is far more cause for hope than despair in the world if men would only quietly consider it. How often have we heard the aphorism that even 'the Devil is not as black as he is painted.' If therefore the night is not hopelessly black, and we are standing with our faces toward the daybreak, why not dry our tears and look hopefully for the coming glory? Let me ask you, my unknown but sorrowing friend, to sit with me for a while beside the tomb—not the one at Macpelah, nor that in the valley over against Bethpoer, nor yet again that over which the disconsolate Psalmist declares 'the dead know not anything'—all these are buried too deep under the debris of ignorance and prejudice—but I will invite you to commune for a while beside that most sacred of all tombs to be found in Joseph's garden. Most sacred because most normal, fulfilling all but never exceeding the slightest duty for which the tomb was called into existence; the one tomb at which we may sit and learn all that the office was designed to teach—hope, joy, victory and a horizonless beyond!

Thrice sacred are the scenes of decisive victories, but when the battle was the all-important one in the history of a universe, then the spot becomes a thousand times more sacred. This is such a place. Here He, who is our life, lay. (Sad for us if He does not hold this position, for we are poor indeed.) Here He did single-handed combat with the king of terrors, and broke the tyrant's power; here He closed with the world's despair and tore His bands asunder; here love captured hope from the grasp of ignorance; truth triumphed over error, righteousness defeated sin, and life cast death into the bottomless pit! See, the stone is still rolled away! The sepulchre did not open its door to be closed again with a spring! The victory of Easter morning was not a demonstration for the moment only! It was a conquest by the Lord of Hosts; and whatsoever the Lord doeth, it shall be for ever. The Lord is risen! and in His rising He hath set before us an open door, which none can shut again. He carried away with Him through the everlasting doors the keys of death and hell, and holds them still in His hands before the throne, while the angel of the resurrection keeps guard before the open tomb and sits upon the stone that once for all has been rolled away.

Do we understand what all this means? If only earth would listen to the full chorus of the evangel of the risen Lord! Dry your tears; lift your eyes—

"There is no death! What seems so is transition;
This life of mortal breath
Is but a suburb of the life Elysian,
Whose portal we call death."

Do you wonder I ask you to sit with me here—you whose life has been embittered by the failure to recognize the unmeasured fullness of the gospel, and I who also have drunk the cup of bitterness to its dregs? Listen! Jesus came back—is ever coming back. He wishes to make the pilgrimage of life a journey to Emmaus, if we will, but He does not come alone; they that are His also come with Him. With Him—in Him—we 'come to Mount Zion, and unto the city of the living God, the heavenly Jerusalem, and to an innumerable company of angels; to the general assembly and church of the first-born...and to the spirits of just men made perfect.'

All the loved ones you have lost for the time are present with the Master. They follow Him wheresoever He goeth. If He come again to redeem the promise, 'Lo! I am with thee,' shall not they too come with Him? Would they not gladly come? Do you think their love, their interest and concern for your welfare has perished? Strong as you have believed death to be, do you think it is strong enough to crush their old affection? I speak to you as men and women.

Is the hope I would inspire too large—too good to be true? Thomas once thought so till the risen living Jesus stood before him. Are you not as precious in the eyes of the Father—who is no respecter of persons—as Thomas was? Is He not still able to answer the same incredulous hope, the staggering commonsense love, as ever? If death has once for all been swallowed up in life, is it not time the truth was known, and the balm of its divine gospel freely poured out for the healing of the brokenhearted? Mighty minds wield mighty forces; is not our Christ travelling in the greatness of His strength—the mighty to save? What if the hour has come 'in the which all that are in the graves shall hear His voice, and shall come forth'? Nothing is impossible with God, who sent Samuel, Moses and Elias back again even before the victory of Christ, and my own return bears witness that He is still the same unchanging God.

Come, let us commune together, and I will speak of Him and the visions my eyes have seen beyond the veil.

I know whereof I speak—know also the weakness as well as the yearning of the flesh to know that the things I intimate are true. In the blackness of a mourner's despair, I groped 'for the touch of a vanished hand,' in the silence of death I strained my ears for 'the sound of the voice that was still.' My mother was lost before I knew her, and I was compelled to tread life's pilgrimage the victim of a hunger earth had no power to satisfy. Nor father, sister, friend, art, literature nor employment could fill the void I knew, and the ordinary pleasures of others served to further isolate me from my fellows.

I was never conscious of one single unclouded pleasure; hence I can deeply sympathize with the souls with whom death has claimed an enforced kinship. The nearest approach to happiness I am able to recall was of a negative character momentary cessation of misery. I had stolen away from the family and friends who were uncongenial to me by reason of their enjoyment, and in my solitude was mechanically turning over the pages of a magazine lying upon the library table when my eye caught the headline of three verses which instantly aroused my attention. Then I read—

LONGINGS

"I shall rest when the earth life is over,
And to-morrow itself shall be dead;
When dread shall no more be prophetic,
Of agony waiting ahead.
How calmly the ocean is sleeping to-night!
But the morning may break with the storm at its height.

I shall sing when my heart ceases aching,
And my head is not weary with pain.

Chapter 1

The Open Sepulchre

My smiles only mask the fierce anguish
My heart cannot bury again.
The face of the ocean is smiling with rest,
But the break on the shore heaves the moans from its breast.

How I pray while my heart-strings are breaking,
How I count all the days as they come!
I watch in my sleep for my mother,
In my dreams I sigh for her home;
Two words, oh, how sweet! Earth, earth! let me go!
In their music is heaven—all the heaven I can know!"

The name of the author was not given, but the fact that someone lived who could so sympathetically voice my own sorrow touched and soothed my grief for the moment. The verses breathed a faint hope into the region of my despair that somewhere, some day I might be satisfied. Then the gloom closed over me again, and I sighed more deeply to atone for the throb I had stifled. In my gratitude, however, I cut the verses out, and for days they became my meat and drink, until their every word was burned into my hungry soul, and the paper they were printed on fell to pieces. Even then I reverently gathered the fragments together and treasured them with a lock of hair I wore above my heart.

I shall discover and meet the author sometime and tell him how his cry of sorrow ministered to my own, in which acknowledgement he will find the harvest of the seed he sowed in tears.

So Heaven gathers up all fragments that nothing is lost.

Through such a school of mourning the Father saw it was best to bring me, therefore I am able to sympathize with whosoever sit in darkness and in the valley of the shadow of death.

For those whose acquaintance I am newly making, let me now say that my sympathy is not based upon speculative philosophies concerning the hereafter. We meet at the open door of the sepulchre, but I return from within; you, for the present, are from without. My feet have already forded the Jordan, from beyond which I have come back to speak with you of the things I have seen and heard. I have already stood upon the mountain side, where the light of God is falling, have seen in the shadowless land the pathway Christ Himself once trod, and am able to offer the ministry of guidance by which His divine footprints may be safely followed. Let me ask you to listen before, in your incredulity, you draw back and treat my statement as the blasphemy of a deceiver. Equally pious souls with yourself have made serious mistakes in the past in that direction. From before the time of Christ the heretics who were martyred yesterday have become the recognized saints of the morrow, chief of whom is Christ Himself. I know the gospel I proclaim is an impossible one from your point of view, but is your position one to warrant a reliable judgement? Have you a full and perfect knowledge of the ways and purposes of God? If nothing is impossible with Him, can you imagine anything more God-like than the ordination of such a dispensation as the crowning demonstration of the work of Jesus Christ? I know not. Therefore for the sake of yourselves and the comfort my message is empowered to confer, I counsel you to hear, then judge me by the fruit our communion bears.

To those who know me through my former message, I have no need to do more than extend my greeting, since I am here by their earnest wish to redeem a promise I will proceed to ratify.

Pardon me for a moment in gathering up the thread of my experiences, if I ask you to turn your mind backward in review, not that I wish to summarize what has been already said, but I am anxious to make it clear that on throwing aside the body every soul receives personal treatment and is dealt with individually as it enters Paradise. Everyone goes to his own place. Dissolution works no transforming miracle, but as the man leaves earth he enters upon—or rather continues—his spiritual condition. There are no magical formulas or processes by which, however repentant the soul may be, the evil-doer becomes a saint in the interval of transition. 'God will render to every man according to his deeds.' 'Whatsoever a man soweth that shall he also reap.' The faith that produces works is the only witness available for testimony in that assize,' and the work is estimated by the quality of its fruitfulness.

I am led to make this necessary reminder just here, because in several of the letters lying before me there is some expression of regret and even surprise that in my last I said so little about the Master. In view of the law I have just referred to, this may easily be understood of the time covered by the experiences recounted in *Through the Mists*. In leaving the earth, I carried with me no great love, but rather an aversion for all forms of orthodox religion. I had not been a church-goer, and had no warm admiration for the method of salvation or the Christ I could never satisfactorily understand. I had some little sympathy and human feeling for the multitudes of unfortunates, herding like animals in the purlieus of London, some few of whom I did, occasionally, a little to help, but the one desire and wish of life was, if possible, to find my mother. She was far more to me than God or religion; hence, when the change came, it was my mother I first desired to see—the one heaven I wished to reach —and my aspiration was granted. I had my reward; and that explains why I was so silent in reference to the Master.

Others of my correspondents hope that in resuming my experiences, I shall be able to refer to the reunion. Why not? Like every other feature of my new life, it abounds with lessons andcorrections of vain anticipations; therefore I will commence my present message at that point and deal with those things which are of general interest concerning our meeting.

I concluded with the arrival at my first spirit home, over which Myhanene conducted me, pointing out its chief features and the relationship everything bore to the life I had lived. How patiently he lingered while I traced the connection of its appointments with a

hundred incidents I had wholly or in part forgotten! After this he led me to the roof-garden from which I was able to study its delightful surroundings, then back again to that closely-curtained doorway, hiding that face—how well I knew it; what need to tell me—which, unseen and all unknown,
had been the load-star of my life, and at that moment was more than all in earth or Heaven to me!

I understood his generous and silent intimation, as he passed on and left me all alone, conscious that the gates of Heaven were about to open and let me in. From the time of my arrival until that instant, the old earth-hunger had been restrained—held in check by the engrossing series of surprises which had been afforded me, but now it came back with a vigour and force for which I had been prepared by the ministry of the friends who had so divinely led me, by a way I had not known, towards the heavenly consummation. I thanked God that the meeting had not come sooner! How my soul ached to clasp her, and yet I dared not thrust the curtain aside.

In the old days it had been a favourite employment of less melancholy moments to plan what I would do—if there was really an after-life—when I met my mother. How many times did I reconstruct and revise the plans, which unfolded and enlarged with the years, until they became a whole series of programmes with only the mother-thread to hold them together. It may be that the oft-recurring effort served to turn me into a soothing by-path wherein I escaped a lurking stab of pain, and if so they served a truly beneficent purpose, but that was all. To plan on earth what we will do in Paradise is a thousand times more futile than for a child to boast of the valour of his manhood. The new life is so crowded with overwhelming surprises, so fruitful of charming distractions, so beautifully bewildering with unimagined pleasures, so tender in its diverting sympathies, that even earth's purest conceptions are certain to be shattered and carried away, and the perfect God-design leads us gently forward into the fullness of our unanticipated joy.

Chapter 1 — The Open Sepulchre

You are impatient, my reader, and wonder why I do not dash that curtain aside and fall into the arms of my mother. Ah! Why indeed? These perplexingly welcome pauses which intervened and temporarily postponed action at such crises as those I have mentioned were beyond my comprehension at the time, but I understand them better now. Where the mind of Father and Child are working together to do His will, God is never late, but rather before the moment, for which we needs must wait. In that slight pause the fullness of the meted measure of bliss is reached. When God throws the portal open we find ourselves in Heaven; man forces it, and lo! He stands in hell!

The waiting is never long. It was a simultaneous action to draw the curtain. We met upon the threshold and fell upon each other's necks. There was not much to say: "My mother?—my son." That was all. Then we were silent.

* * *

CHAPTER 2

THE FAMILY IN PARADISE

In that first embrace I was ever conscious of, I tasted something of the sweetness to be found in the compensation Heaven bestows upon those whose happiness has been deferred by the untoward circumstances of earth. If it is possible, do not murmur at thy lot, poor, unloved, benighted, and lonely one—I am speaking after having passed through the ordeal, after bearing the burden, after refusing to be comforted, and I tell you, you will be the envied one by and by. Thousands who have revelled in love of the type recognized on earth will presently regret that your lot has not been their own. As the buttercup is to the rose and the daisy to the lily so is the love of earth in its holiest, sweetest form—to the ravishing dream which descends from Heaven and lingers undisturbed by time in Paradise. It passeth understanding, defies expression in its entrancement, is voided by everything base and ignoble, pure as Heaven can keep it, strong to the healing of every wound, without a shade of estrangement free from limitation, and opens a career of sacred evolution which confidently leads to God.

How long we lingered in the silence of that divine ecstasy I do not know—never shall know. Time limits for us are now measurements of the past, and the only standards we are subject to are those of fullness—complete, pressed down and running over. We have waited long, what if our greeting was long? Heaven is generous, and ordains that every soul shall be satisfied.

Dismissing then all question of the duration and nature of our greeting, let me at once pass to the first question of closer interest which will rise in the mind of every reader as to whether I knew my mother when we met.

The subject of the recognition of friends in the after-life is one of never waning interest; preacher, poet, teacher, parent, child and friend are ever speculating in hope, doubt and fear respecting it. Shall we meet again—and if so, shall we be able to recognize each other after so long a separation? Such, and a thousand other questions are asked with breaking heart over the silent corpse from which no answer is expected. In this hopelessly regarded quest the heart is far more loyal to God and truth than is the intellect—the one lingers on and on around the inquiry hoping against hope if only for a suggestion of some response, while the other with cold unsympathetic harshness declares the thing impossible, and bids affection to accept fate's stern decree. But even in the minds of those who refuse to accept the conclusion of reason, there is an equally cheerless uncertainty as to the condition in which those who have gone before will be restored. Will the beautiful prediction of Longfellow be upheld?

> *"Not as a child shall we again behold her,*
> *For when with raptures wild;*
> *In our embraces we again enfold her*
> *She will not be a child.*
> *But a fair maiden in her Father's mansion,*
> *Clothed with celestial grace;*
> *And beautiful with all the soul's expansion*
> *Shall we behold her face."*

Or will the desire of the mother who breathed the following pathetic response to his poetic dream be realized?

> *"Oh say not so! how shall I know my darling*
> *If changed her form and veiled with shining hair?*
> *If, since her flight, has grown my starling,*
> *How shall I know her there?*
> *On memory's page by viewless fingers painted,*
> *I see the features of my angel child;*
> *She passed away ere vice her life had tainted—*
> *Pass'd to the undefiled.*

Chapter 2 — The Family in Paradise

Oh, say not so! for I would clasp her, even
As when below she lay upon my breast;
I would dream of her as a bud in heaven
Amid the blossoms blest.
My little one she was a folded lily,
Sweeter than any on the azure wave;
But night came down, a starless night and chilly,
Alas! we could not save.

Yes, as a child, serene and noble poet—
Oh, heaven were dark were children wanting there;
I hope to clasp my bud, as when I wore it,
A dimpled baby fair.
Though years have flown, toward my blue-eyed daughter
My heart yearns ofttimes with a mother's love;
Its never-dying tendrils now enfold her,
E'en as a child above.

E'en as a babe my little dove-eyed daughter,
Nestle and coo upon my heart again;
Wait for thy mother by the river water,
It shall not be in vain.
Wait as a child. How shall I know my darling
If changed her form, and veil'd with shining hair;
If since her flight has grown my little starling,
How shall I know her there?"

It would be easy for me to continue the enumeration of nebulous ideas that exist with luxuriant uncertainty in the minds of men and women upon this point of recognition in Paradise, if such were the purpose of my writing. But it is not so. My aim is, so far as possible, to set these doubts at rest, by recording my own experience as an illustration of what God has mercifully provided as an answer to this universal prayer of affection.

The Life Elysian

I may be wrong—everyone naturally regards his own case as the best suited for the purpose—but I am disposed to think that my experience is one singularly designed to throw light upon this deeply pathetic inquiry, and for that reason I am willing to dwell upon the incident longer than I should otherwise elect, hoping that by doing so I may be able to relieve some burden of doubt.

Did I, then, know my mother when I first looked upon her face after a lapse of nearly forty years? Yes—perfectly. Not only so, but I was certain it would be so even before I saw her, while yet the curtain falling between us had not been drawn aside. How this was so I cannot explain, whether by a reciprocated out-reach and embrace of mutual affection or by some new power of recognition flashing into existence as our spiritual spheres blended with each other, I do not know; but I knew that I should know her as certainly as she would know me, and when the veil was thrown aside I threw my arms around and pressed her to my heart before my eyes had caught a glimpse of her dear face. It was not until the heart was satisfied that any claim for sight was recognized.

Then I raised her head with both my hands to take a first look into her love-lit eyes. A first look, did I say? So I thought. But as our eyes met, the fountain of my memory opened and one of the most beneficent tender mercies of God flashed upon me.

"Vaone!"—I gasped.

"Aphraar," she murmured, and the head fell back again upon my breast, while I drank of a deeper, sweeter cup than before.

Fear not, poor timid anxious soul, lest the child of your affection may be changed when to your embraces you again enfold her. What if she has become a fair maiden, beautiful with all the soul's expansion, when at length your feet shall cross the threshold of immortality. In her development she will not be unknown—will not be estranged. In that first flash of my mother's eyes I remembered—the memory came back to me— that during all the days of my sorrowing for her absence, the great majority of the hours of sleep had been spent in her company in that scarcely known boundary land between the physical and spiritual worlds, which God has mercifully located for the solace of sorrowing souls, and the new name with which I greeted her was the familiar one by which she had been known to me in my sleep-life all along.

Long, long ago God promised through the mouth of Hosea (xiii. l4) a consolation to mankind of which this almost unrecognized possibility may well be considered a fulfilment:—'I will ransom them from the power of the grave; I will redeem them from death; O death, I will be thy plague; O grave, I will be thy destruction.' Why has earth not learned to rejoice in these richly-provided ministrations? Where are the God-appointed teachers of men that these things have not yet been proclaimed from the mountain tops, that their healing virtues have not been applied to broken hearts?

The pioneers of physical science have long since discovered and affirmed that matter is indestructible; where are the prophets and seers of spiritual science who have so far failed even to understand the significant inference established by materialistic inquirers, that if the instrument is indestructible, the artist behind, who has power to control the same, must, at least, be equally eternal? Life is more than dust, and mind superior to chemical constituents. Matter may change its form and life its envelope and sphere of operation, but just as the one cannot be destroyed, the other cannot die. The noon never can become midnight; it may by gradual progress give place, but when the midnight comes upon us, the noon is still in as active opposition as ever, performing its appointed vocation though in another sphere. So life is always death's antithesis. It cannot die—for life there is no death—'God is not the God of the dead, but of the living, for all live unto Him.' That which has lived still lives— must live—since life is God and must live in Him.

If this is so—and who is able to deny it?—how beautiful and full of hope is the living parable of the plant buried in a dismal dungeon but struggling, climbing and reaching out to send its shoots into the sunshine. Is the plant more true in its affection than the loved ones for whom earth mourns? If the plant will find its way through all opposition, if the seed sown deep in its grave of earth will conquer and triumph over its tomb, will not the love of the absent ones be equally true? Have plant and seed more of power and individuality, more of continuity and strength of affection for the sun than mother for her child, or friend for friend? 'O ye of little faith!'

The soul has possession of mighty and all-important secrets; it would whisper to mankind if the gates of memory were only wide enough to let them through—secrets that would leave few of our cherished conceptions of God, religion and futurity unshaken.

But these truths are wide, high, deep, requiring portals through which earth might pass with the freedom of a child's marble through a city's gate, and the midget systems of men would vanish in their presence like the shadowy foundations of a dream. So for the system's sake the Needle's Eye remains in spite of inconvenience, agony, and unfaithfulness to God. Men built the gates; if God made the truth too large to pass through, what is to be done—is it not better to reduce the truth rather than remodel the architecture? So the architects argue, and the contention still proceeds.

But the tree of life is sending its shoots through the crannies of the obstructing wall; already serious fissures are discernible running in every direction, and the growth still goes on. Love must and will find a way back to earth in order to make known the truth concerning the beyond; God sanctions the return, sleep is a daily disembodiment of every soul, and in the sleep vestibule of Heaven, the parted meet again and exult in the triumph of life over the impotence of death. Once grasp this great truth, then turn your face hopefully towards the remembrance of it, and the shadow of the tomb will soon be swallowed up in victory.

I can understand some of my critics turning upon me with the inquiry—"How is it, if this is as you say, that the truth of such a provision has not been demonstrated to the world before?" I reply that it has been declared by the teaching and resurrection of

Jesus, but the interests of an ecclesiastical theology have demanded that the former should be ignored and the latter treated as an exception rather than the exposition of an abiding law. The inconsistencies and contradictions which arise and perplex mankind by the decision are not for me to consider or explain. I point them out and pass on, remarking that human ignorance respecting a natural law is no argument against its truth; wireless telegraphy and telepathy—not to mention a dozen other recent discoveries—were accessible possibilities centuries ago, had man been in a position to enter into their possession. All the great gifts of God—the yet undreamed-of discoveries of science—lie accessible along the path of development for whosoever will go forward and seek them. God does not throw His richest treasures into the lap of indolence—they that seek find. Conceited ignorance is never a trustworthy steward, but the secrets of the Lord are with those who wait to do His will and daily fear Him. It is not always safe to judge the value of a man by the coat he wears, nor estimate truth by the tinsel lavished upon its wrappers. Things are not invariably what they seem. The matrix of a gem is seldom of prepossessing appearance. Some flowers bloom late, but they are not always least beautiful. So if this truth I now declare has been neglected and opposed so long, it is still redolent with its original virtue, priestly intolerance notwithstanding.

Where every step in our journey, however, will be thus fruitful of inquiry, lesson, surprise and unsuspected development, it will be impossible for us to tarry indefinitely. We are treading the path of life in which the studies of eternity are strewn around. What wonder if we should find it necessary to return again and again, to find where we are standing to-day the roots of subjects that will first attract our interest in some distant futurity. We shall never exhaust the inexhaustible; let us therefore gather such thoughts as may be helpful in the present and leave the rest until some more convenient season.

Another point of some importance for the moment here forces

itself upon my attention, to which I must now turn my mind. It arises from the names with which we greeted each other when I raised my mother's head—

"Vaone—Aphraar!"

I have already pointed out how certain events act like springs which, being touched, release a host of memories hitherto unsuspected. The lifting of that dear head so acted upon another point of recollection for me that I remembered the names so long familiar to us in our sleep-communion— those new names we all expect to receive as one of the gifts of immortality. But more than this was made known to me in that recovered memory; I had for the last time called her "Mother!" With all the other earth distinctions and differentiations, that sweetest and most cherished of all epithets had now been cast aside. There is no such relationship as mother and child recognized in immortality.

Such an assertion may at first appear as a startling absurdity; but let us consider what it means before we hastily come to a conclusion, then we shall find that if a cherished superstition has to be unwillingly relinquished, in the truth by which it will be replaced, we shall receive something far better and more greatly to be prized.

Truth and sentiment are not always inseparably united, nor is the stamp of antiquity any guarantee of genuineness; hence it behooves men to make sure whether their opinions rest upon the certain basis of ascertained law or merely upon the superstitions of atmospheric unreliability. Paul, following the teaching of the Christ, has once for all declared the law that flesh and blood cannot inherit the Kingdom of God, and if so, surely the peculiar limitations of the flesh are also excluded from the region of the spirit, that wide and diviner forces may be set in harmonious operation.

Still the anticipation of a reunited family has been such a cherished belief through all the ages as to demand reverent and sympathetic consideration, and I would so deal with it in the inquiry truth demands me to make.

Now, on earth this supposed ideal of an exclusive and unbroken family circle is far more of a poetic fancy than a practical reality. It is an impossible conception no sane man or woman would attempt to realize. Do we resent the enlargement of the family circle to admit the successive arrivals by which it is increased? When the lads are growing up how often is it necessary to send one away to a distant city or even a foreign land, to remove him from the influence of companions or temptation. The exigencies of education, business and success make further inroads. Financial and other troubles or some golden opportunity make it desirable that a daughter shall go away; or again, the inevitable lover comes along for whom the girl is willing to leave father, mother and home. In all these and many other circumstances tending to the breaking up of the family circle is the cherished ideal put forward a demand for respect? NO! Not for one moment after the necessity of the situation is recognized. There is a sigh—frequently a tear—then the admission that such is only natural, sometimes desirable, and at once the whole family begin to assist in bringing about the consummation.

Marriage carries one away, and to form the new circle, two already existing ones have to be broken, never to be reunited without shattering the third, which fact at once brings us face to face with the problem as to how it is possible for any one family to be complete in Heaven. It could only be partially realized by each individual group being left parentless, which two members would be necessarily separated to complete the circles from which they had each been drawn. Would this be an ideal realization of a reunited family?

Outside these physically disintegrating forces we have others of a far greater separating character lying in the domain of taste, morals, intellect, art, science, and every other department of civilized life. In all these departments, circles of interests are formed which frequently exert a stronger influence for weal or woe upon the individual than that of blood relationship. Yet the necessity for the existence of many of them is recognized and defended even though the effect is seen in an ever-widening division from other members of the family. The idea of a united circle never suggests itself where such a restriction would wreck a promising career.

Thus where natural law would be violated or intellectual evolution hindered by the continuance of the circle unbroken, man is always ready to sacrifice the latter that the former may be served.

But we have another and even higher stage to consider. The spiritual relationship of soul to soul is far above that attainable by flesh and blood. We are no longer in the region of limitation when we ascend to where eternal affinities are found. In this existence God is the universal Father, and all nations of men are equally sons and daughters, so that the 'whole family of earth and Heaven are one.' In comparison with this Fatherhood no other parental claim can stand. The accident of a moment cannot urge a weightier claim than the eternal laws; nor can the deputed authority for an hour in and for the service of God take precedence in the soul's divine fidelity. There can only be one family in Heaven in which all humanity, of every clime, colour, tongue and nation, will rank as brethren and God the Father of all.

Blood relationships, with every other earthly distinction and limitation, are left far behind in custody of the customs-house of the tomb, but every spiritual kinship will be preserved, and every fraction of memory as to the relationship which bound us together, not as mother and child—such a recognition would keep us too far apart—but in the more holy union of soul with soul, which bond can never be broken since the blessing of God binds all true love that naught can put it asunder.

When, therefore, we reasonably consider this sentimental idea of a united family, even in its earthly aspects, we at once discover how impractical and impossible it is, but when we carry it farther and try to imagine it under the vastly changed conditions of a purely spiritual life, one can only wonder how the question was ever allowed to be seriously accepted. The idea of an undivided family is ever subordinated to individual interests. This is a fundamental working axiom which is recognized on earth and will never be disturbed; hence nothing that will tend to well-being will ever be lost. It is when men postulate the continuance of physical limitations as the rule and law of spiritual conditions that incongruities arise, and it is from this error our family misconception comes in. Parental love has a necessary function to perform on earth, which from being vital in the outset, gradually shades away until the child learns to act for himself—even to the resisting and defiance of parental authority—and then himself assumes the parental role. In the spiritual realm, when the child is born, he becomes a son of God, and Fatherhood is assumed by the Eternal in whose great human family circles of nearer or more distant unions will be formed until the whole race becomes one in Him.

We lose nothing in this but an artificial bond which is seldom more than superficial and often both inconvenient and irksome, but we gain much. The bond between Vaone and myself is closer, much than that of mother and son. We shall never forget all we have been to each other, but the physical barrier has disappeared. As the love we know is greater, sweeter, stronger than I had hitherto conceived, so is my cup larger and more satisfying than I had earned a mother's love could be. So if Paradise has taken away—or rather if I have found one cherished illusion has faded—I have also been rewarded by the discovery that the anticipation I formed was altogether unworthy of the reality 'which God has prepared for those who love Him.'

These two lessons I learned and understood in the joy of reunion with her for whom I had sorrowed and sought so long.

* * *

CHAPTER 3

THE LOVE OF GOD

Have I disappointed and disheartened you at the outset of our communion by touching and attempting to destroy one of your cherished idols? If so—and I have little doubt about it—let me ask you to bear it for the moment as best you may. I know something of the tenderness of the subject on which I have been constrained to speak, can understand how the heart shrinks at the thought of relinquishing the hope I assert to be an illusion, but is not the history of the past strewn with fragments of the erroneous ideas truth has compelled our ignorance to cast aside?

The surgeon who drives his scalpel deep is not necessarily the enemy of our well-being, but rather our true—if painful— friend; it is the foreign and dangerous growth he removes that necessitates the operation he performs. So in our spiritual unfoldment the foes to truth and health must needs be cut away before we shall be allowed to tread the inner courts of the Father's house. I am not altogether unprepared for the angry exclamations and hard accusations that are ejaculated during the operation, but I also know that in the coming days you will discover that, in the language of a well-known hymn, the—

"Bitter is sweet, the medicine is food."

and I can wait until that time to hear your calm and grateful opinion.

"If we but knew the beauty of the flower
That hides potential in the uncouth seed—
Its shape, its perfume, and its brilliant glow,
How should we prize it? But, behold we heed

> *It not; we treat it with disdain,*
> *Because we had imagined it would be*
> *Exactly in the seed as in the flower,*
> *And we should now its rich perfection see!*
> *Not so, my child, 'tis but experienced eyes*
> *Can trace in seed the flower we shall so prize."*

If eye hath not seen, how is it possible for us to conceive? The few who have hitherto returned have had so much to tell, I do not wonder at the prevalence of misconception, especially when I review my own experiences. But now that the true significance of the resurrection of Jesus is being so clearly understood and its ministry established we shall gradually clear away these errors and make the truth of God known. Nor shall we do this by the force of anathemas, but rather by an appeal to reason. If you cannot accept our message, we shall follow the example of the Christ—turn away. The future will decide the question of truth, and by that decision we shall all be acquitted or condemned to penalty.

Nor would I have you misunderstand me when I speak of penalties. God's ways are higher than the ways of men, and the forfeitures He will exact will in every instance be those which are the just sequence of the offence. All sins and sinners do not merit the same punishment. Hence I make no threat of hell because you may honestly doubt what I say.

When the truth is made known to you by experience, you will then understand as I now understand, and if by reason of refusing to consider what I have here advanced you have rejected it, you will have lost the help and assistance it had power to render, and find yourself so far behind where you had the opportunity to be, and the regret at what might have been will form the penalty Paradise will exact. God is love, not revengeful. Let me throw this ray of brightness across the temporary disappointment of the truth I have declared.

I will now proceed with my actual experiences.

Having spoken of a hallucination which had been dispelled, I would fain recount what unanticipated joy came to me in its place, but how shall I accomplish my desire? The silver-tongued Isaiah, in the partial vision vouchsafed to him, could only exclaim, "Since the beginning of the world men have not heard, nor perceived by the ear, neither hath the eye seen...what (God) hath prepared for him that waiteth for Him"; and Paul, who had been caught up to behold the glory, when comparing the experiences of earth with the reward in reserve, declared, "Our light affliction, which is but for a moment, worketh for us a far more exceeding and eternal weight of glory"; how then can I expect to paint or describe the more than fullness into which I entered?

I had lost something. Yes. I had lost the shadow from the sunshine, the husk from the wheat, the thorn from the rose, the possibility of a discord in the music, the uncertainty lest a fear might linger in the bosom of the joy, the doubt whether the hurried holiness was perfect or partial, the wonder whether God was strictly just. All these I had lost—lost completely and for ever. Death shook the last vestige of every doubt and mystery concerning these away, and when the mental earthquake had spent itself, I opened my eyes upon 'a new Heaven and a new earth in which dwelleth righteousness.' Righteousness established upon a basis of law, not dwarfed and fashioned to suit the limitations of man, while my own powers, conception and understanding were all enlarged to comprehend something of the illimitable scheme as designed by God. I say something, but it was only a wee, wee part of the magnificent, stupendous love, which in length and breadth and height reached far beyond my ken. But above, beneath, around, all was harmony, peace and rest. I stood on the threshold of the eternal and shadowless calm.

Far, far away within the awful depths of that profoundly divine solitude, my poor earth-ideal of Heaven had reached the Father's heart. Its clumsy model spoke eloquently to Him of impotence; it was more rough to His conception than a savage effort to mould a deity, but it told of a heart's dear wish, of a great desire yearning to be satisfied, of the Heaven that would supply all the happiness I had power to conceive. Now for the wonder of my existence; He took my plan—the model I had built in the incompetence of my ignorance, and, retaining its outline, Love worked upon it, and from its imperfections prepared the rest into which He had given me entrance. It was my Heaven, enlarged, completed and furnished by the love of God, and just as it transcended all that I could ask or think, so must I fail to convey the overflowing fullness of joy which it inspired.

It was more than this, for when He had so far enlarged my Heaven, He afterwards so far extended the powers of my enjoyment that I might the more appreciate and enter into its glory.

Was the gain greater than the loss? Yes! as God is greater than a man.

So inexpressibly beyond my conception was the mansion of the soul into which I was welcomed. It gave to me the three great desires of my heart—Mother, home and Heaven—beyond all expectation.

Companionship has much to do with the measure of happiness attained in Paradise. When Myhanene stood beside me on the roof of my new home, I was enchanted with the beauty of the scene which lay unrolled before me, but gracious as he was, and tender with truly divine affection, the sense of his condition awed me until I felt something as Peter must have felt when he prayed the Lord to leave him. It was afterwards when I stood or sat beside Vaone in those surroundings that I entered into the full enjoyment of the sweet repose. The magnificence and beauty I saw when Myhanene was present throbbed with life and love in the closer sympathy of the nearer and dearer one. In the heights and depths of Myhanene's meditations I was lost, but Vaone and I wandered hand in hand, soul vibrating in sympathy with soul, and the music heard by one echoed through the other.

With Myhanene I stood near the centre of a mountainlocked

valley stretching into the distance in every direction, but the man was more fascinating to me than the landscape; he saw visions to which I was blind, heard music which could not reach my heavy ears, held communion I could not understand. Across his mobile face passed lights of inspiration I could not read, and through him throbbed a presence I longed to love but feared to meet. He was innocent of this, I am sure, or in his royal condescension he would have stooped to my estate, but I would not have him so. Rather far would I be with him as he is, for though I almost fear to see him, when he leaves, there lingers with me a hopeful aspiration to rise and reach him, where I shall be so much nearer to the Christ he loves so well.

With Vaone everything was different. Sitting side by side we reposed in calm content, while the panorama before us became instinct with life—life free from doubt, uncertainty and care. The scene before me was one of indescribable loveliness, but its charm was increased a hundredfold by the strong, inherent assurance that all was—and must ever remain—well. The world within and the world without, for the first time in my experience, were in perfect unison; they were not even so far divided as to produce harmony—it was unison complete. I knew instinctively that God ruled, and that all that existed lived, moved and ministered in rhythmic harmony with His loving will.

This deep-seated consciousness inspired rest—the rest that remaineth, a rest synchronizing with the peace of Christ which the world can neither give nor take away, because the world is finite, the rest and peace infinite, hence it remains awaiting us as the exceeding great and eternal compensation for the momentary light affliction earth imposes.

In the sweet solace of these almost unbroken communings, now with Vaone and then with myself, a problem once propounded itself to my mind which I long pondered without being able at the time to find a satisfactory reply. I understand it now, and since it touches a point I shall mention again, I will refer to it that you may see how sensitive the soul becomes even to the minutest detail. The most luxurious and carefully considered rest the earth affords is never quite perfect. When we have done our utmost, when sympathy and consideration have been exhausted, there always remains something wanting, some unattainable trifle for which we sigh. This was not so in my experience of Paradise; on the contrary, I was at that time— here is the fact I wish to be noted— somewhat impressed with the sense that, if anything, the rest was overdone! It was too complete, almost tending towards an indolent content unless resisted.

I have conjectured that Myhanene saw visions as he looked over the Elysian landscape visible from the roof of our home. On more than one occasion I have been so favoured, and here I would like to recall one of my earliest, as it illustrates how close the bond may be drawn between the earth and Paradise.

I was listening to a sweet duet which the silence and glow of colour clothing the distant mountains were singing. Vaone stood beside me entranced with the soft, melodious colour tones. The whole valley was equally in repose, when I became conscious of an interspherence creeping over the scene. Every familiar point in the prospect remained distinctly visible, to which a pleasurable something was being added, and with an increase of joy I watched to see what would develop. It was a strange, almost weird, but by no means unwelcome effect, creeping over the whole landscape like a pleasant, but yet invisible, phantom asserting itself. Vaone saw it, and by the gentle pressure of her hand counselled me to watch. I did so, and presently wondered to see well-known faces taking shape beneath the trees, by the river-side, and somewhat familiar forms passing to and fro around me. The outlines of an illlighted, sparsely furnished mission hall took shape and blended with the details of the valley. How strange and yet harmoniously incongruous was the effect! Knowing as I did the little Zion, where I had spent so many nights in my sympathy with the care-burdened congregation, what a magical transformation it

Chapter 3 — The Love of God

underwent to stretch its confines to fill the whole scene in its interblending! But it did so, and for the time the two became one, not only one in the outlines of its inanimate features, but the men (alas! there were but few of these among the visitors), the women and the children intermingled, and the music we had so far been listening to died away, as the ending of a prelude introducing a favourite mission hymn:

> *"Beautiful valley of Eden!*
> *Sweet is thy noontide calm;*
> *Over the hearts of the weary*
> *Breathing thy waves of balm.*
>
> *Beautiful valley of Eden!*
> *Home of the pure and blest;*
> *How often amid the wild billows*
> *I dream of thy rest—sweet rest!"*

Nothing in all my experiences had hitherto touched me with the pathos of that song. God knows I would gladly have shouldered my earthly cross again if by so doing that under-fed, scantily clothed and weary congregation could have laid their burdens down and taken my place. For the moment the regret almost appeared to cast a shadow across the scene, but a gentle voice whispered from the height of the immensity within me "They shall be Mine in the day when I make up my jewels," and in confidence that the promise was sure the cloud withdrew. I was satisfied.

I shall leave the song to suggest its own description of the place. Any attempt to amplify would only spoil it. Such pleasures cannot be detailed—they are experiences. You cannot conceive, but must enter into them. We are told that 'angels fold their wings and rest' in the lovely dells of Killarney—and who can wonder at it after lingering in the enchanting spot? But Killarney is not Eden, where every detail of the place is fragrant with a holier presence:—

> *"This is an angel-home, not angel-rest,*
> *Furnished and ready, all in order laid*
> *To entertain our God in passing by,*
> *For He will tarry in such sacred glade."*

Someone will ask me how far removed from earth is such a home. The thought of it, with all the blessings it includes, makes the heart hunger, and the soul cry with the Psalmist, "Oh, that I had wings like a dove! For then would I fly away and be at rest."

Let me answer you. In the things whereof I speak, near or distant does not consist in geographical miles but in condition. I have carefully refrained from any elaborate analysis of my spiritual development in the earth-life, while not neglecting to give such hints and suggestions in the course of my narrative as will readily assist you in forming a tolerable estimate of the position I occupied. But what I was (on earth) determines what I am (in spirit), and the where I was naturalized me for where I am. Spiritually considered, I am but two steps removed from earth, but the intervening stage I reserve for closer consideration presently.

This should at once inspire hope, and I speak with the full confidence of doing so. I am not portraying a stage of life beyond the tomb, high and difficult to attain to. It would be a mockery to do so, handicapped and misdirected as the great majority of my fellows are. I speak of that which is easily attainable by any man however circumstanced, if he will but accept the golden rule and honestly do his best to put it into practice. Beyond me there are stages of indescribable splendour reserved for those who so follow the Christ-life as to be worthy to enter upon them, but of these also I do not now propose to speak. The majority of men have no serious thought of this life (spirit) which, to them, lies in a very doubtful beyond, having discovered that the men who proclaim it (priests) know no better than themselves. My one object is to arouse this sleeping interest by the simple narration of my own experiences. Truth is mighty to the pulling down of the stronghold of error, and the result of my former effort convinces me that humanity is not indifferent to the consideration of a future life which combines intelligence with spirituality.

The vision faded, but the lessons it enforced are with me still, have had much to do with the message I have already delivered, with the one upon which I am now engaged. I was not so far away from my old-time friends, after all, and the vision was a pathetic plea to be remembered in my new and happier home. It stimulated me to action, raised the question as to whether among the family group within the valley there were others who had passed homeward through the doors of that Little Zion, and sent me out to make a closer acquaintance with my neighbours than I had hitherto essayed. Yes, yes! There were others I had known, and many I had not met before who had come from that and other obscure corners of God's great vineyard. This again gave home an additional charm, and more zest to the work I had determined to engage in if possible.

On another occasion as I meditated on the beauties surrounding me, I inquired of my beloved:

"I wonder if this was the particular Heaven into which Paul was caught up."

"Why do you ask?"

"Because it so completely seems to answer to what he wrote concerning it: 'Eye hath not seen, nor ear heard, neither hath it entered into the heart of man the things which God hath prepared.'"

"Go on," she murmured. "Why do you not finish the quotation?"

"I prefer to leave it unfinished. But surely this must have been the place he saw."

"I think not. He called his the third Heaven, this is only the first."

"Yet if he had seen what I have seen he would have found it equally impossible to tell. But if this is only the first, what will the third be like?"

"That cannot enter into our minds to conceive at present. Let us be content and satisfied until we have enjoyed the full extent of this. But tell me why you did not finish Paul's quotation?"

"Simply that for my purpose it naturally ended where I left it. I am not so competent to speak of the love of God as the Rabbi-apostle."

"And why not, Aphraar?"

"Because men have dressed it in so many fantastic garbs, and surrounded it with such complexity of conditions and adaptations, that I altogether failed to know what was true or false concerning it, and turned away from any profession of following after it."

"Are you quite sure of that?" she asked tenderly. "Do you remember the vision, when you almost wished you could exchange places with those you have left behind?"

"Ah, Vaone; if you understood the suffering of those lonely overburdened souls you also would wish it."

"But when you were with them did you not do what you could to assist them?"

"I did a little occasionally, not nearly what I might—nothing compared to what I wish I had done."

"Still you did something, and however little that something may be it will equally serve my purpose to show you that it was done for God. Even 'a cup of cold water given in My Name shall in no wise lose its reward.' "

"But what I did was neither in the Name of Jesus nor in the Name of God. I had no thought of either. It was for humanity's sake alone. No, no! Vaone, don't credit me with intentions or motives that never once crossed my mind."

"'Inasmuch as ye did it to one of the least of these My brethren, Ye did it unto Me.' Is not that sufficient?" she inquired, and the confident gleam of her soft loving eyes shone upon me with the light of another revelation.

"Can God so generously interpret such an insignificant effort?" I asked.

"He does. Did you imagine you could gauge His goodness by

Chapter 3   The Love of God

any possible earth conception? Listen to me, Aphraar, and let your experience bear evidence to what I say; the fallacies and misconceptions of the lower life concerning God and immortality are all based upon inverted arguments—men build their conceptions of Him upon themselves, rather than first learning to know something of Him and forming their ideas of man in accordance with Divine sonship."

"My opinion has always been that an ancient council established itself, in its corporate capacity, as a divine regency, with God subservient to its decisions, after which the leaders of factions quarrelled to gain the ascendancy, splitting up the Church and leaving an authority in a wrecked condition, from which it has never recovered. But for you and me all this is now of the past, and I would know of those things concerning our present lives. Tell me; in the generous interpretation you have placed upon the trivial acts you have referred to, may you not have formed an erroneous conclusion?"

"No!" Her reply was made in dreamy confidence, as if her voice had been used as the instrument of an invisible authority. Then she continued: "Mistakes may and do arise in the courts of Ignorance, but God reigns here. His law is perfect. His justice acts with automatic precision. Righteousness is natural while error can only be secured by effort. Do you understand?"

"Scarcely."

"Perhaps not," she replied in the same abstracted tone. "You are scarcely free from the last of the earth influences at present, and you unconsciously carry old habits of thought into your new environment."

"I feel you are right in that," I replied. "Everything seems so strange to me because I am so mentally unprepared for it, that I frequently feel as if I wanted to go back again in order to understand."

"That is due in a great measure to the manner of your translation."

"Ah!" I exclaimed, catching at the hope her words inspired.

"Tell me something about that. I know so little, and all is so confused. Why was I and the child I brought with me left alone upon the slope with no one near, when I awoke, from whom I could ask for information? Why were we not carried to one of the reception homes, such as I have seen, and allowed to sleep until all these earthly influences were broken?"

"The almost numberless methods by which the process of discarnation is affected," she replied, "are perfectly natural, and determined solely by preceding circumstances. Those who sleep do so from one of three causes; a lingering illness which leaves a sense of exhaustion on the soul; the desire for life producing something analogous to hysteria for the time; or uncontrollable grief in those who remain behind tending to draw the newlyreleased one back again to earth. For all such cases a period of sleep is provided during which the soul is adjusted to its new life. But with you none of these causes existed. You came by accident, as earth would say, were quite healthy, and, what was much more to your advantage, had no very strong desire to continue in the body. Your one great attraction," and she looked fondly into my eyes, "was already here, so the separation was willingly consented to, and there was no occasion for more than the briefest pause to recover from the shock. As for the rest—well, can you imagine how it might have been better arranged?"

"No! That I most gratefully admit. It is the confusing perfection and considerate adaptability of everything that perplexes me. It is too good. I am not worthy of it, and for that reason I fail to understand it."

"Now I have to turn you back again from a termination you have often reached before," she tenderly answered. "Perhaps it is too good, but it must always be so because it is of God. You remember the old illustration—the prodigal would have been content to become a hired servant, but the Father said, 'Bring hither the best robe, and put it upon him; put a ring on his hand and shoes on his feet.' In the old life you were able to cover your head and shut out all thought of God, but here you must walk with Him and know Him as He really is."

Yes, she understood my ever-present consciousness, and was overjoyed to find each new experience prove how completely I was hedged around.

Turning my thoughts in another direction, I inquired:

"Will you tell me something about yourself? My father—do you ever see him?"

I half-regretted asking the latter question, but she instantly divined my thought, and taking a seat, indicated her wish for me to sit beside her. The sweetness of her face was not clouded, it rather softened as the smile vanished and gave precedence to a look of quiet, restful content.

"Why would you recall your inquiry?" she asked.

"I cannot say. Perhaps I was—shall I say, half-afraid I had no right to make it?"

"You have every right, if you have the interest, to inquire into a relationship from which your existence sprang. I have seen your father once, in the sleep-state. He failed to recognize me, so we did not speak. It was better that it should be so, since our association had been nothing more than a cool friendship, and was always irksome. Our marriage was one of opportune convenience by which my father was saved from some unpleasantness— an arrangement which I was never allowed to forget. When your sister was born she was at once removed from my control, and then you came and I had scarcely time to kiss you before all my trouble ended. There is nothing more concerning that part of my life that need be told."

"But your own friends?" I inquired.

"There again I was equally unfortunate. My mother's aversion to children was very deep-seated, and though I was her only child, she never forgave my intrusion. She passed away when I was but a few years old, and my memory of her is more tinctured with fear than with love. You will not be surprised to hear, therefore, that I have made no effort to find them since my arrival. I could easily do so, but in the absence of love and sympathy, I am assured it is better not to attempt it for the present. We shall be brought together when our development overcomes the difficulties which lie between us, and until then I am content to wait."

"And have you, then, been all alone?"

She laughed merrily at my solicitude.

"Loneliness in Paradise, Aphraar, would be as impossible as summer without the sun. Look at the multitude of friends by whom I am surrounded, at the innumerable visitors ever coming and going, and the excursions to which I am frequently invited. In addition to this, have you not been with me a large share of the time? No, no! I have never known anything of loneliness."

That was one of the most welcome declarations I had heard. Thank God, her experience had not been a similar one to my own. In my gratitude I was silent for a while, reflecting on the difference of life in the two conditions, and when I had set the contrast clearly before me, I was about to speak again, but something restrained me.

"Why did you not say it, Aphraar?" she inquired.

"What did I wish to say?" I asked, wondering how much of my thought was known to her.

"Shall I tell you?"

"Yes."

"It was something like this," she replied. "It matters not where I go, what I see, or upon what subject I speak, everything here moves harmoniously, in narrow circles, all of which turn to a common centre—the wonderful and ever-present love of God."

"You are right," I answered. "It was so, and so it must ever, be."

* * *

CHAPTER 4

THE RESURRECTION AND ITS BODY

Let me introduce an explanation I am bound to make by saying how grateful I am for the considerate treatment my former message received at the hands of my reviewers. I was advocate for a cause which has hitherto suffered most by the indiscretion of its friends and the fraudulent practices of its professed adherents. The ill-advised seekers after curiosity and gain have profaned the sacred associations of the tomb without regard to decency or feeling, have arrogantly assumed the right to tear the veil in twain and make the spirit-life an addition to drawing-room amusements. Such desecrations rightly merit the treatment accorded by the Press, which should always stand as one of the great bulwarks of defence in the sacred cause of reason, law and order.

I naturally anticipated that the title-page of my book would attract that onslaught of adverse criticism which, until recently, the Press has directed against the subject generally. The treatment I received not only surprised, but also assured me that the ears of our reviewers are open to listen with candid consideration to subjects lying far apart from ordinary tracks, if only such questions can be presented with some respect to logical consistency. Still, to say that I ran the gauntlet unscathed and unopposed would be untrue. To be able to boast of an absence of objection would be most serious misfortune, but to acknowledge the moderate terms in which the objection was expressed is an entirely different matter, and it is to the main point thus raised that I wish now to direct my attention briefly.

Some few of my friends, not only reviewers, but among my correspondents also, take exception to what they call my materialistic descriptions of the life and surroundings of Paradise.

More than one earnestly beg of me to remember what Paul says of the general resurrection, "The Lord Himself shall descend from Heaven with a shout, with the voice of the archangel and with the trump of God; and the dead in Christ shall rise first: then we which are alive and remain shall be caught up together with them in the clouds to meet the Lord in the air, and so shall we ever be with the Lord." The particular point urged upon me is the inspired declaration of Heaven being 'in the air', or 'in the clouds', which at once renders buildings, trees and other material objects an impossibility.

Now, I reply to this with the frank admission that my statements were made not as a Biblical commentator, nor as a dogmatic theologian, but rather from personal observation and experience. I never was a Bible scholar, and 'orthodoxy' was a word I always looked upon as possessing the attributes of a literary chameleon, therefore, as I have more than once pointed out, I avoided it. I may hence be excused if my justification is not formulated exactly upon the lines of the schoolmen.

So far as I understand the plain meaning of words, this quotation from Paul is entirely out of place in the connection in which my friends use it here. Paul does not assert that Heaven is either in the air or clouds, but rather that "the Lord will descend from Heaven" into the air to meet His saints, and if this is so it is impossible to draw any inference from this passage as to what Paul's idea of Heaven was. Further, even though I am wrong, according to the theologians in making this comment, Paul's inspiration when writing the passage, appears to be the reverse of infallible, because he says, "we that are alive and remain" at the time of the descent, as if he were under the impression that the second coming would take place in his own lifetime. Of course my idea may be all wrong from an orthodox standpoint, so I shall not press it further.

I knew all through my message that I was not wording it upon generally accepted lines, but at the same time I was not altogether

Chapter 4 — The Resurrection and its Body

unscriptural, and without further controversy let me reply to this charge of gross material conception of the after-life by a scriptural Portrayal of the Heavenly Jerusalem, with which I am quite willing to consider the objection answered:

"And there came unto me one of the seven angels which had the seven vials full of the seven last plagues, and talked with me, saying, Come hither, I will shew thee the bride, the Lamb's wife.

"And he carried me away in the spirit to a great and high mountain, and shewed me that great city, the holy Jerusalem, descending out of Heaven from God.

"Having the glory of God; and her light was like unto a stone most precious, even like a jasper stone, clear as crystal;

"And had a wall great and high, and had twelve gates, and at the gates twelve angels, and names written thereon, which are the names of the twelve tribes of the children of Israel;

"On the east three gates; on the north three gates; on the south three gates; and on the west three gates.

"And the wall of the city had twelve foundations, and in them the names of the twelve apostles of the Lamb.

"And he that talked with me had a golden reed to measure the city, and the gates thereof, and the wall thereof.

"And the city lieth foursquare, and the length is as large as the breadth; and he measured the city with the reed, twelve thousand furlongs. The length and the breadth and the height of it are equal.

"And he measured the wall thereof, an hundred and forty and four cubits, according to the measure of a man, that is, of the angel.

"And the building of the wall of it was of jasper; and the city was pure gold, like unto clear glass.

"And the foundations of the wall of the city were garnished with all manner of precious stones. The first foundation was jasper; the second, sapphire; the third, a chalcedony; the fourth, an emerald;

"The fifth, sardonyx; the sixth, sardius; the seventh, chrysolyte;

the eighth, beryl; the ninth, a topaz; the tenth, a chrysoprasus; the eleventh, a jacinth; the twelfth, an amethyst.

"And the twelve gates were twelve pearls; every several gate was of one pearl; and the street of the city was pure gold, as it were transparent glass.

"And I saw no temple therein; for the Lord God Almighty and the Lamb are the temple of it.

"And the city had no need of the sun, neither of the moon, to shine in it; for the glory of God did lighten it, and the Lamb is the light thereof.

"And the nations of them which are saved shall walk in the light of it, and the kings of the earth do bring their glory and honour into it.

"And the gates of it shall not be shut at all by day; for there shall be no night there.

"And they shall bring the glory and honour of the nations into it.

"And there shall in no wise enter into it any thing that defileth, neither whatsoever worketh abomination, nor maketh a lie; but they which are written in the Lamb's book of life."

Nor is the heavenly Jerusalem to be scripturally understood as the only city to be found in the home of the redeemed, if Christ is to be taken as any authority on the point, since in the parable of the ten pieces of money, Luke records Him as rewarding faithful individual service with rulership over five and even ten cities, and if this is so, how great must the number of cities be to make such a liberal reward possible!

So much for the orthodox objection.

While dealing with criticisms I would here like to notice one advanced, not against myself, but against the whole subject of intercommunion, in the words of a scientist whose studies entitle him to be heard. "The most formidable obstacle to the admission of the spiritualist's hypothesis is in the messages which tend to represent the other world, in which, it appears, matter is not perceived, and space and time are unknown, as being all the same a servile copy of this, or a sketch of it. ...I know of no message in which the communicator has been frank enough to say, 'Of course you may suppose that the form I have here is not the same as I had in your world.' Or again, 'The idea of form differs totally in our world and in yours; I cannot make you understand what that idea is here, so it is of no use to question me.' Unfortunately neither communicators nor controls speak thus; they all say, or allow it to be supposed, that the human form is the same in both worlds." [2]

Now this supposed weighty objection is in reality no more valid than the one offered by my own critics of the religious school. It is based upon erroneous data, and arises altogether from a misconception of the relationship of the two conditions. I am not surprised at this, since the relative position of science on the earth side can never rise higher than that of a moderately advanced class in an elementary school when compared with the knowledge available to similar inquirers on the spirit side. In a remarkably interesting work recently published, New Conceptions in Science, by Carl Snyder, the author having reviewed the scientific achievements of the past, turns his thoughts to what lies before, and says—

"Beyond all that the eye may see, that ear may hear, that hands may feel, outside of taste or smell, outside of any native sense, there lies an unseen, unfelt universe, whose fringe we are just beginning to touch" (pp. 42-43).

Into this unseen the scientists who have put off the flesh have entered, with all their old faculties strengthened and accelerated, and many of them are willing, even anxious, to return and co-operate with fellow-labourers, in leading to yet undreamed-of successes.

[2] "Mrs. Piper and the Society for Psychical Research," by M. Sage. London: R. Brimley Johnson, 1903 (pp. 17-34).

"Then why do they not do it?" cry a hundred voices. "Let them come, and when they identify themselves we will no longer be faithless, but believing."

I will tell you why they do not come; why the intercommunion has hitherto been so very unsatisfactory; why those who are so fully able to astonish the world have not, so far done so. It is for the very same reason that Archimedes and his co-workers of Alexandria did not attain to the successes of modern science—they lacked the necessary instruments. Give to the scientific spirits, who have ascended the region of the physically unseen and unheard, suitable instruments through which to transmit their studies, and the question of intercommunion will soon be universally settled, and earth be richer for the partnership so established. Even with the present unsatisfactory and often doubtful means, much good and useful work has been accomplished, and mighty barriers of opposition have been cleared away. But let earth once truly recognize the possibilities that are rapidly coming forward, then a more glorious era will speedily dawn for a long oppressed and mentally imprisoned humanity.

That the present condition of communication leaves much to be desired I know; but not a little of the difficulty arises from the idea that we on the unseen side are, or ought to be, perfect. This is not only a mistake but an injustice, and the sooner it is recognized the better. Surely the time has come when by common consent a definite attempt should be made to understand the difficulties which exist on both sides, and a deliberate effort be put forth to overcome them by supplying the best possible material available for the purpose. With a little patience, consideration, and a recognition of the possibility that all the brains and intellect are not to be found upon the earth side, a scientifically serviceable communion could readily be established, to the immense advantage of the lower life.

Death does not abrogate the law of sequence, but evolution

proceeds still through the higher human, towards the divine. The soul experiences no disconnecting process, takes no sudden leap, crosses no dividing line; it simply discovers a liberation from certain irksome limitations and takes wing. It loses nothing of value, but assimilates additional powers which supplement, rather than displace, those already possessed. Thus it is not less, but greater than before, having taken another step in the evolutionary ascent. The limitations and annoying barriers in the path of the progress of active minds have, to a large extent, been removed, and every energy is quickened for the conquest of the gloriously attractive future.

No, the old law is not broken; it rather operates with more inexorable justice than otherwise in every higher phase of the soul's advancing condition. The character of the grub still predetermines the nature of the butterfly, and classification proceeds upon well recognized and indisputable lines. Death has no more power to work miracles than the naturalist, and the what-will-be is invariably the sequence of what-has-been. The only duty assigned to death is to receive and disrobe all corners of flesh and blood, then pass the individual otherwise untouched. In its unclothed condition the soul crosses the immortal border, where it affinitively attracts and assumes a garb corresponding to its real degree of spirituality, which clothing bears the colour—verdict of the law of God denoting a righteous judgement upon its holiness or otherwise. Against this decision there is no appeal, and the only murmur one hears at the result is that of surprised wonder that the judgement has taken so many extenuating circumstances into consideration.

But some man will say, "How are the dead raised up? and with what body do they come?"

Since the first declaration of the resurrection as a natural phenomenon, no question has been of such perennial interest as this. It is the very life germ of religion, for if Christ be not risen then is all preaching vain, and faith is also vain. Yet in spite of this all important truth, in no part of its assumed authority has theology so utterly failed to grasp the plain spiritual significance of an event or doctrine as here. 'Of the earth, earthy,' in all its interpretations, the priestly cult has here blindly stumbled into a morass of contradictory entanglements from which all hope of escape appears to be impossible. It has lost sight of the glorious consummation of the work of Christ in the fogs which rise from and hover over the scene of its own confusion, while the hungry multitude it professes to feed receive stones for bread, and wander about in a state of spiritual starvation.

Sad, sad would it be for humanity had not God foreseen this calamity. But it was foreseen. Did not Christ foreshadow it in His parable of the wicked husbandmen? and is not the very mission in which I am now taking part the realization of His forecast?

"What therefore shall the lord of the vineyard do unto them? He shall come and destroy these husbandmen, and shall give the vineyard to others."

Several of my correspondents ask me for information upon the resurrection and the spiritual body. I can here only suggest the line, along which the whole subject will presently be treated, but the argument would require a whole volume to do it justice, and therefore I can only suggestively touch it in this place. Again, I have already freely acknowledged that I am not an expert in biblical controversy, from which side the subject must necessarily commence its treatment, therefore I am quite content to leave its full discussion to abler hands, confining myself more closely to the personal experiences I set out to recount.

First, then, the resurrection is a purely natural and always present phenomenon, not a miracle to be looked for in the future. This I assert on the scriptural authority of Christ (John v, 24-27):

"Verily, verily, I say unto you, He that heareth My word, and believeth on Him that sent Me, hath everlasting life, and shall not come into condemnation; but is passed from death unto life.

Chapter 4 — The Resurrection and its Body

"Verily, verily, I say unto you; The hour is coming, and now is, when the dead shall hear the voice of the Son of God, and they that hear shall live.

"For as the Father hath life in Himself, so hath He given to the Son to have life in Himself;

"And hath given Him authority to execute judgement also, because He is the Son of man."

Christ here bases upon a given condition not only an immediate resurrection, but an absolute escape from death:

"Verily verily, I say unto you, If a man keep My saying, he shall never see death." (John viii, 5 1)

Both these sayings Jesus also confirmed to Martha (John xi, 23-26).

"Jesus saith unto her, Thy brother shall rise again.

"Martha saith unto Him, I know that he shall rise again in the resurrection at the last day.

"Jesus said unto her, I am the resurrection and the life; he that believeth in Me, though he were dead, yet shall he live;

"And whosoever liveth and believeth in Me shall never die.

"Believest thou this?"

I shall add nothing to these quotations, but leave the record to speak for itself as to what the plain teaching of the Christ is as to the time of the resurrection.

The only possible point in dispute here will be as to the interpretation Christ put upon the word 'death.' In the connection in which the word is now used He always preferred to say 'sleep'— 'She is not dead, but sleepeth.' 'Our friend Lazarus sleepeth.'

We pass now to the second question. "With what body do they come?"

I have already paraphrased Paul's idea of being unclothed to be clothed upon, from my own experience, and this describes with eloquent brevity the whole process men call death. 'Flesh and blood cannot inherit the kingdom' across the mythical Jordan, but the physical vestments are cast aside that the robes of the spiritual may be assumed in passing from the lower to the higher classroom. 'It is sown a natural body, it is raised a spiritual body. There is a natural and there is a spiritual body.' Let me repeat what I have said above: in the transition the soul retains every power and faculty save those pertaining to flesh and blood, which have to be cast aside; then as it assumes the spiritual body it also becomes invested with equivalent attributes. It is therefore not less but greater than it was before. How much more it becomes is determined entirely by its likeness or unlikeness to the Christ, Who is the sole standard by which all are judged, while the resurrection body of Jesus is the authorized type and pattern of our own.

This post-mortem body demands and will repay a little careful attention, since it abounds with suggestive lessons for our instruction. Much has been lost and gained since Jesus expired on Calvary and His reappearance at the tomb in Joseph's garden. He no longer says, 'Of Myself I can do nothing,' but rather, 'All power is given unto Me in Heaven and earth.' He is the same man proving His identity by many infallible tests, but it is not the same body. The familiar figure of the days of His ministry has altogether disappeared. 'It was sown in weakness, it is raised in power.' But what power! It is not only a new body— it is a whole series of bodies, never wearing the same aspect on two successive occasions, and playing like a will-o-the-wisp across the borderland of the seen and the unseen. Mary, who knew Him so well, mistook Him for the gardener, until He breathed her name; after this 'He appeared in another form' to two of His disciples on the way to Emmaus; nor did they recognize Him until He brake the bread, then He vanished from sight. Again He stands in the midst of His followers while the doors are shut, but, Thomas being absent and incredulous, the Lord returns later, wearing yet another form, that the doubter may handle him and find the marks his faith demands. He is no phantom spirit, but a substantial spiritual body, able to build a fire on the shore while waiting for the coming boat, and eat the bread and fish of the morning meal, yet it rises into the air at His ascension and is finally lost in the clouds.

Am I unscriptural in this brief résumé? Where? So far as my knowledge and reason can guide me, I have set forth the simple teachings and facts concerning the resurrection of the Son of God, in which, apart from the confirmation of my own experience, I find the fullest warranty for all I have claimed in my own intercourse. 'The works that I do, ye shall do also,' was His assurance to the Twelve, and through them to all who should come after them. Standing on the further side of the tomb, He bade His friends to follow Him, and that this should be done and the fact continually demonstrated is absolutely necessary to witness to the world that all who come to the Christ receive the gift of everlasting life, and death cannot come near to them.

The claim, then, that I make of an open tomb and an uninterrupted intercourse between the true Church, Militant and Triumphant, is simply the declaration of our common Christian heritage, and the gospel we have to expound is that of 'Life—eternal life!'

* * *

CHAPTER 5

THE ANGEL OF DEATH

There is order, sequence and purpose to be found in the afterlife. This I have tried to emphasize in contrariety to the general idea that the regular employment of the soul in Heaven will be found in singing 'Holy, holy, holy' to the accompaniment of golden harps. Do not, however, rush to the other extreme and imagine that I would have you think that life in Heaven means nothing more than work, study and intellectual development. Such an idea would be equally erroneous.

The whole environment of the two conditions is so different that it becomes impossible to conceive what the higher will be while subject to the influences of the lower. If you fail to understand what this difficulty really is, let me ask you to try to form some true conception of a life free from all thought of time, weariness or financial troubles; then go on to abstract the possibility of disappointment, frustrated hope and ruined prospects; and still again freedom from scandal, misrepresentation and jealous intrigue. I might go on further simply with the negative aspects of this life, but these omissions, if you can realize what they mean, will be quite sufficient to indicate a Heaven to be devoutly wished for. But when we consider that beyond these things come the positive features of the rest—the reunions, rewards, enlarged powers and other aspects on which the soul has so long meditated, with the 'evermore' multitude of accessories which lie beyond all our anticipations, one has to give up and exclaim: "It is too high, I cannot attain to it!"

These enjoyments and employments, duties and recreations, ministries and pleasures are beautifully balanced and diversified. Take away every taint of the disagreeable, increase to infinite proportions all that the heart desires, enlarge the noblest, purest love the earth has known so as to include the whole race with the same self-sacrificing devotion hitherto proffered to the individual, and this realization will bring you to the threshold of family life known where the whole family of Heaven and earth are one.

Yes! Drop the book and think, but you cannot understand it. The ocean is larger than a teacup, and the atmosphere far greater than a toy balloon. So do the widest conceptions of earth fail measure the resources of Paradise.

Still the life is love, joy, peace in all their full and God-like perfection.

This life is mine now—will be yours presently. But I would speak of it for your comfort and encouragement by the way.

Among the many pleasures of that cloudless happy land perhaps one of the sweetest is experienced at the announcement that addition is about to be made to the particular group of which one is a member, and this, in common with all other features of our life, loses none of its piquancy or freshness by repetition.

Let me recall one of my earliest experiences of this kind.

Vaone and I had joined a large company in one of the numerous entrancing retreats to be found in our beautiful valley, where we were recounting the past, and tracing its clear connections with present, with ever and anon one of the old familiar hymns, sung by way of illustration, just as I might choose to describe the occasion by those well-known lines:

> *"There on a green and flowery mount*
> *Our weary souls shall sit,*
> *And with transporting joys recount*
> *The labours of our feet."*

That perfect realization of more than I had been able, more than should have dared to anticipate, had I possessed the ability, was a very near ascent to Heaven.

All the toil, the care, the sorrow over, and each soul having recovered from the grinding weariness thereof, it was more than happiness to listen as one and then another travelled the road again, not with complaint and murmuring, but finding in every step the needs-be and divine guidance towards the present goal. It was more than meat and drink to me to hear those testimonies from the lips of men and women who had entered the inheritance from such highways and by-ways of sorrow, and hear the unanimous confession that fell from every lip that "in all their afflictions He was afflicted, and the angel of His presence saved them; in His love and in His pity He redeemed them; and He bare them and carried them all the days of old."

Oh, those afterthoughts, those faithful and true lights of Paradise! How the soul thrills under the revelating beams! How the heart grieves for the blindness and ignorance of the days that are past!

As I listened to all this, my enraptured soul soared aloft near to what I imagined Heaven itself must really be.

Suddenly it seemed as if the temperature had been raised, and with this came a perceptible thrill of added pleasure. It occurred at a moment of silence, and evoked an exclamation of delight from the whole assembly.

I turned to Vaone and asked, "What is it?"

"We are to have an addition to our family," she replied.

"When and whom?" I inquired.

"That we shall know presently." Then she went on to explain that the intimation was received so soon as it was known which group the newly-coming soul would be attached to, and was further explaining matters when Arvez arrived with the information that our new member was a boy known to several of our group.

"And not altogether a stranger to yourself," he said to me by way of conclusion.

"Who may it be?" I asked.

"You remember the little fellow I took from the College?"

"Limpy Jack. Yes."

"Do you also remember his friend, who promised to look after him until his transition?"

"Yes, perfectly."

"It is he. I am now going to the College to bring him here. Will you join me?"

"I shall be delighted."

There was no necessity for further announcement to the community. The general process of such events is thoroughly understood, and as we set out upon our errand, the assembly proceeded to make the necessary preparation for the boy's welcome.

"Well, and have you reached the end of your surprises?" asked Arvez as we went on our way.

"I think that is one of the few impossibilities of this life," I replied.

"You will do well to school yourself to the idea that surprises are part of the natural phenomena of this condition," he answered. "God is necessarily so far beyond all our conception that we must ever be filled with wonder and awe at His continually unfolding manifestations. He is a long way past our finding out, my brother, and therefore must ever be surprising us."

"Even yourself?"

"Ah, Aphraar! Not only me, but I doubt not the angel who stands nearest to Him is also equally surprised with ourselves. I think Myhanene is not far wrong when he says, 'God is evermore past finding out'."

"Then how can we know Him?"

"By growing like Him; and the nearer we draw the more we shall know."

"But if the greater knowledge only reveals how unknowable He is, what then?"

"We shall still be more like Him, and that will have to suffice."

Unable to pursue this inquiry further, I turned to the object of my companion's mission.

"Is the boy you seek coming over at once?" I asked.

"No. I am bringing him on his preparatory visit."

"Is he ill?"

"I think not; but our instructions are never detailed. I shall learn more from the lad himself."

"Is he aware of your coming?"

"No. These visits are never foreknown."

"Do you remember how disappointed he was when you took little Jack away?"

"Yes, and I have seen it repeated on several occasions since then. Poor little fellow, his life has been a singularly sad one, I believe."

"I wish we could bring them all away," I answered as I thought of the coming disappointment of many and the happiness of but one.

"And so do I, if by so doing that particular phase of life could be eliminated, but as the world is constituted at present, the whole colony at 'The College' could be removed and not be missed."

"Does not that thought sometimes dishearten you in your work?"

"No. Why should it? So long as the wrong creating such suffering exists, it is above all things necessary that we should be constant in our ministry to the sufferers. If we were to fail, where would be their hope?"

As we talked, we crossed the boundary between the spiritual and sleep-states, and for the first time I became aware of the demarcation; the light toned away into twilight, and in the lower region, there was a feeling of rawness in the air, not altogether pleasant.

Here we met a fellow-servant of Arvez's acting as guide to a lady who evidently yielded but a reluctant obedience to the command laid upon her. My friend saw this in a moment, and with true brotherly sympathy, stopped to speak to them.

"Life's harvest ripens early for my sister," he remarked cheerily in his greeting.

"Too early—too early by far," she responded tearfully. "For love's sake hear me on behalf of my child! I cannot leave him at his birth. Spare me for his sake, or if not, let him come with me."

"The love of God is greater and more tender even than that of a mother," replied Arvez. "Whatever is best He will certainly ordain. Fear not, He is with thee, and all must be well."

"But God is so far away. Did He not give me my darling? Why, then, should He wish to take me away?"

"Because He sees and understands where we are blind and ignorant. He makes no mistakes, and whatever happens must be well for both of you."

"It will not be well if I am compelled to leave my child. No, no! I cannot come! Please do not ask me!"

"I make no request, my sister," replied her escort, "but they who watch as the eyes of the Lord have foreseen the weakness of the flesh and know that you will be thrust away. It is the body that will discard you; I have been sent to lead you to a place of rest, where you may presently gain strength to return and be even more to your child than if you had remained. You do not know God or you would trust Him, but I will lead you to one who will show you what He is, and ere you part from your child, you will be content to leave him as God determines."

"I was left as you fear your little one will be left," I said, if perhaps my words might comfort her.

"Left without a mother's love and care?" she asked.

"Yes. She died as I was born. I never knew her until I met her here, and all my life was a sorrow for my loss. But it was better so."

"Better to lose her?"

"Yes. Far better. I know it now and both of us thank God for the loss I mourned for forty years."

"Can I see your mother?" she inquired.

"Yes," Arvez replied. "You shall be brought together if you wish it. But where you go you will find a company who have had similar experiences, from whom you will learn how tenderly and wisely God deals with all His children. They will show you how groundless are all your fears of separation, and make known to you the love of God in a hundred ways you little suspect at present."

"And may I go back to my little one again?"

"Yes. You will return several times. So long as the body will receive you, you will be at liberty to go and come. In the meantime, you will get to know the new friends to whom I am about to introduce you," said her companion, "that when you finally come away, it may be without regret or fear."

"Without regret or fear—are you sure of that?" she queried.

"None but the souls of criminals, anxious to escape from the justice of their sins, either regret or fear to enter upon this life," he replied, "and of such, you are not, or I should not be sent to bring you hither."

During this ministry of consolation the rebellious sister was quietly carried across the boundary line into the higher state where the native assurances of God's great and never-failing love were added to the arguments employed to secure her submission to the inevitable. So far, it was the most painful case I had yet encountered of the resentment often shown by professing Christians at the intimation that the time of their departure is at hand. That summons is a genuine test of the soul's true conception of God and Christ, and a very suggestive revelation as to the actual reality of their religion may be gained by watching the effect as the death messenger first declares the purpose of his coming. It is an easy matter under the influence of an emotional discourse on the entrancing glories of the heavenly hope to join tunefully with a thousand voices and sing:

"Filled with delight, my raptured soul
Can here no longer stay;
Though Jordan's waves around me roll
Fearless I'd launch away."

But after the benediction, after the congregation has dispersed, and in the silent watches of the night, the soul stands alone in the presence of the messenger of death; when the emotion is over and grim, reality has taken the place of poetry; when a compliance with profession is demanded; when the earth begins to quake and slip away—ah! then is the time to see the sustaining power of religion; then the true grip of godliness is tested, and a surface faith gives place to a paralysing dread.

The foolish virgins are far more numerous than the wise when the cry goes forth to meet the Bridegroom.

The incident gave me food for reflection, and when the poignancy of the grief was over, I turned away to continue my journey to 'The College', lest my sympathy and concern might interfere with the ministry of Arvez and his friend.

Just a word here as to how we find our way to the friend we seek in Paradise, or to any otherwise unknown destination. The difficulties and annoyances of such an earth expedition no longer exist with us, but granted that the goal is not beyond our spiritual power to reach or we have a legitimate commission to execute, our wish becomes the vehicle of transit, and either by sudden flight or more leisurely passage, we go direct to our destination.

So I passed from the presence of my companions to 'The College,' where I knew Arvez would join me presently. As I did so my mind was busy with the thought of the contrast I should there witness with the scene I had just left—the reluctance of a professing Christian to leave the earth compared with the keen, anxious desire of a city arab to do so. There was no speculation in my forecast of this. I had been present several times on similar occasions and was by now familiar with the scene of eager anxiety I should see consequent upon the appearance of Arvez. Some few of the lads present would quietly retire, because all the fair advantages of earth were at their disposal, but by far the larger number would give him welcome, and eagerly press forward in the hope that the choice of Arvez might fall upon themselves. How I wish the whole earth might witness the joy of those homeless waifs and strays in the presence of—

THE ANGEL OF DEATH

"I stood in the room with the children—
The play-room they use in their sleep,
Where the souls of the fortunate mingle
With less favoured children, who weep.
The sleep-room, the joy-room, the dear Lord has given
Just half-way between this earth and God's heaven.

The children were children—that only
While there all were rich—none poor,
The prince and the outcast were equal
Till an angel stood at the door.
The outcast, man's outcast, cried greeting 'All Hail!'
But the rich ones shrank back all fearsome and pale.

The lads of the street rushed towards him
'Is it I? Is it I?' each cried
But the favoured of earth were more silent,
Contented were they to abide
The angel—God's angel, looked round, sweetly smile—
He wanted an angel—had come for a child.

'Take me, Mister Angel; please take me'
'No no, me!—ain't it my turn now?'
They all crowded round—all were eager to go
With him of the iron-crowned brow.
That angel—God's angel; who is he, I pray?
'Tis the angel of death—the angel of day."

Not a few of the lads knew me, some even connected my

presence with Arvez, and asked me eagerly if he were coming, but since it was not for me to make any announcement, I evaded an answer, and looked around for him in whom I felt a particular interest. I soon had my wish, and patting the little fellow on the head inquired whether his friend Jack had faithfully kept the promise I heard him make to visit 'The College' and speak to them of his new life.

He looked into my face with a quick resentful glance. He was too loyal to his friend to tolerate even the suspicion of a doubt.

"Why, a cors' he did," he answered. "Doan 'e come 'ere a'most ev'ry night?" Then, with an unstudied touch of genuine feeling, he added, "I on 'y wish 'e 'adn't got to come 'ere agen!"

"Why so? Don't you like to see him now?"

"Yes, that's it. I want ter go to 'im—be wi' 'im, live wi' 'im, an' never go back agen. But I doan think as ever that angel-cove means ter come for me."

"But he must come sometime," I replied, more than half inclined to satisfy his longing by telling what I knew. "You must try to be brave while you wait. Perhaps he will not be so long as you imagine."

At that instant the portière was thrown aside, and Arvez entered, to the wild delight of the majority of the lads. The general rush towards him reminded me of nothing so much as the headlong scamper of children at a school-treat to reach the distribution of nuts or prizes.

My little friend took matters more philosophically than usual, and remained quietly by my side. Perhaps the continual disappointment of his hopes was telling upon him, or it may be our conversation had produced the effect. Whatever it was, he watched the others crowd around Arvez as he said:

"I wonder who 'e's goin' to tek now? But there's no such luck as its bein' me."

Arvez was gently making his way through the clamouring crowd, patting one on the head, kissing another, and speaking a kindly word to a third. Think of it. He was an angel with the summons of death, and every lad around him was anxious to accept delivery for himself. Think of it, I say, ye whose lives are clouded with a sense of dread at the thought of death! The children love him, are disappointed when he passes by them, holding out their hands eagerly in the hope that he comes for them. He who is loved by a child cannot be altogether bad. Then there is something good in death.

"'E is comin' ter you!" said my companion, as Arvez continued to make his way towards us.

The remark called for no reply, nor could I trust myself to speak and keep the secret. So I looked away smiling at the scene.

"Well, I'm blowed! Doan 'e want anybody?" queried my friend, who by this time was not a little excited. Then he added somewhat resignedly—"Oh, I know! 'E wants somebody what isn't 'ere."

Arvez had reached us by this time, and we were the centre of the excited children.

"Are you tired of waiting for me, Dandy?" he inquired, gently laying his hand upon the lad's head.

The little haggard face flushed with the sudden hope that flashed upon him.

"But it ain't me yer come for, is it, Angel?"

Arvez answered by lifting the little fellow into his arms and kissing him. There needed no other reply.

"I'm so glad!" said the lad, nestling his weary head on the angel's shoulder. "I only wish yer could take all the others as well."

Dear loving soul, even the first throb of his own great joy was tempered by regret that his less fortunate companions were not able to share it.

"I shall soon come back for them," said Arvez. "It is almost time for many, and the last will not be long."

Then followed the usual congratulations, requests, promises, and assurances I had heard so many times before, after which Arvez folded his charge upon his bosom and we took our leave.

CHAPTER 6

THE BONDAGE OF SIN

Two of my correspondents fear that I have underrated the power and influence of sin in Through the Mists. I would suggest their re-reading the story of "The Harvest of Jealousy", when I feel confident this impression will be removed. I will admit that I refrained from making the volume black and forbidding by the narration of gruesome experiences consequent upon sin, but I was more anxious to fairly represent the after-life as I have found it—and as you, my reader will find it—than colour it in accordance with earth or creedal conceptions. Following the example of Christ, I would rather charm the ear with the story of infinite love than dwell with persistent croaking on the penalties incurred by rebellious children.

With the master-hand of truly divine genius, Christ reduced the whole field of action in the world's redemption and brought it within the scope of His parable of the Prodigal Son. Cause, effect, method, and atonement are there all set forth with due regard to the law of spiritual perspective, and the story is left as a working model for all who came after Him to copy. If I read that lesson aright, it is not so much the suffering brought on by the prodigality of the lad Christ would have me dwell upon— He had perforce to touch it to measure the depth of the prodigal's fall—but He seems to me to hurry away from the sad effects as quickly as possible by bringing the outcast to his right mind, where he remembers the home life and all that has been lost. "Son, remember," appears to me not only as the exquisite touch of agony Christ infuses into the torment of hell, but He also makes it to be the divine incentive to "arise and go to my Father."

Ah! The scourging, arousing power of the recognition of what has been lost! The contrast of what-might-have-been with what-is!

Then—engulfed in that fiercest of all punishments, the hell of self-recrimination—to recall the comparison of a prodigal's disgusting ostracism and the position of the menials who serve at home! Such a picture needs no detail touches; the torture of it is equal to the occasion without enlargement. What blackness could deepen its gloom? What horrors add to its torture? But Christ makes the light of another memory to break through—the Father's love! "The same yesterday, today, and for ever"; "without variableness or shadow of turning"; like a vesper bell ever calling "Come!" and melodious with the promise "Him that cometh...I will in no wise cast out!" Under the influence of such recollections hope revives, delirium vanishes, a right mind is restored, the lad arises and the Father meets him with ring and robe and shoes, while there is joy in the presence of the angels of God.

In whatever experiences it may be my privilege to relate, I do not wish to pose as a pioneer, pushing my way through a hitherto untrodden country, but rather as a follower of One who knew the way and traversed it, treading the thorns and hindrances underfoot that He might leave a clear pathway from the degrading swine-trough and husks direct to the homeland and restoration. He is the Leader—I but follow after. He knows —it is mine only to obey for the present, then I shall know, even as I am known. He understood the full enormity of sin— its strength, its effect, its cure. If, therefore, I deal with it as He directs, if I speak of it as He shall give me utterance, if I declare what He reveals and measure it with the reed which He supplies, surely I shall set it where He would have it stand, and the perspective shall be in harmony with God's eternal truth and purpose.

Following, then, implicitly in the footprints of the Master, and where the trace may be faint always consenting to be guided by the fulfilment of the law, rather than the arbitrary interpretation of men, I am perfectly prepared to examine the question of sin and its results in its relationship both to the present and future.

Let us now make sure we quite understand what it is of which we are about to speak. Sin. What is it? Is it possible there can be any doubt about this? That is the very point I am anxious to determine, and whatever our ultimate decision as to its nature may be, of this I am already most fully persuaded, that sin in theory and practice are by no means regarded as one and the same. To be perfectly plain, I assert that the great majority of men hold a theory of sin which allows themselves to do with impunity that which they would loudly censure in another. Any such standard as this cannot be permitted to exist in the light of God, with whom "there is no respect of persons." In His court, where perfect justice is dispensed, all men stand on an impartial equality, and the rule upon which we shall be judged Christ has laid down in these terms—"With what judgement ye judge, ye shall be judged; and with what measure ye mete, it shall be measured to you again." If this is the law, it would be well to revise the present standard at once, and learn to show that degree of charity to others we hope to have meted out to ourselves, while at the same time exacting from ourselves a consideration for others we have hitherto demanded selfwards from the rest of men.

This suggests that it is possible for opinion to be divided, in practice at least, as to what sin really is, and if so, it is of vital importance for the truth to be known and admitted without delay.

Sin, in its positive aspect, is simply a voluntary and conscious violation of a recognized moral law. "If I had not come and spoken unto them, they had not had sin, but now they have no cloak for their sin." But it also possesses a negative aspect, equally culpable, and necessary to be constantly borne in mind by all those who speciously seek to escape from a clear responsibility. There are thousands who seek a cowardly refuge in what they call 'friendly neutrality', who pursue a course of 'masterly inactivity' for politic reasons, who refuse the support of which a weaker brother stands in worthy need lest they give offence to influence or position. Let all such be wise in time and open their eyes wide to this significant utterance of Christ—"To him that knoweth to do good and doeth it not, to him it is sin!"

Thus defined the responsibility and criminality of sin becomes an automatic and equitable adjustment of every individual in the human family. There can be no classification in nationalities or even families. Like every other of God's laws, it is particular and individual in its action—"That servant which knew his lord's will and prepared not himself, neither did according to his will, shall be beaten with many stripes; but he that knew not and did commit things worthy of stripes shall be beaten with few stripes. For unto whomsoever much is given, of him shall much be required, and to whom men have committed much, of him they will ask the more." This principle Christ does not content Himself with merely laying down, but repeats it again and again with a truly remarkable significance. He whom God has entrusted with ten talents will be held responsible for the use of ten talents; he with five for five; he with one for one, and he who sins without the law will be judged not by the law, but in equity.

When this terribly just responsibility for sin is brought home clearly to our understanding, and one realizes the absolutely personal character of the judgement to be given, he starts with fear and trembling to hear Christ, "upbraid the cities wherein most of His mighty works were done, because they repented not: Woe unto thee, Chorazin! woe unto thee, Bethsaida! for if the mighty works, which were done in you, had been done in Tyre and Sidon, they would have repented long ago in sackcloth and ashes. But I say unto you, It shall be more tolerable for Tyre and Sidon at the day of judgement, than for you. And thou, Capernaum, which art exalted unto heaven, shall be brought down to hell, for if the mighty works, which have been done in thee, had been done in Sodom, it would have remained until this day. But I say unto you, that it shall be more tolerable for the land of Sodom in the day of judgement, than for thee." The declamation would lose none of its force, and it would be quite legitimate to substitute the names of cities of modern civilization for those of Chorazin, Bethsaida and

Capernaum.

It is well the heathen world should know the power of the gospel of Christ unto salvation, but if we possessed the eyes of God and the knowledge of God, one wonders where the most heathen land would be found!

"Judge not, that ye be not judged!"

We must not forget this very timely and necessary caution. Where every man becomes, in a sense, a law to himself, by the selfsame rule he becomes disqualified from acting as the judge of another. We only know in part; justice demands a clear understanding of the whole case. Still, while we may not usurp the judicial seat, we are commanded to watch and use our intellectual faculties in determining the character of a tree by the fruit it bears. "A good tree cannot bring forth evil fruit, neither can a corrupt tree produce good fruit." The insidiousness of sin cannot effectually be hidden. The character of a life is determined by its deliberately chosen environment, as the quality of fruit is governed by the nourishment given to the tree. Like produces like, secret thoughts, habits and motives find natural development in external acts, and even God is morally powerless to change the result. "Whatsoever a man soweth, that shall he also reap." The only difference between the two operations will be in quantity, not in kind. The harvest may not be gathered until "this mortal hath put on immortality," but escape is impossible. At the quarantine port of Death, the soul, subjected to the searching influence of the light of God, will develop the legitimate effect of every precedent cause and the harvest must inevitably be garnered. "Ye cannot serve God and mammon." Know ye not that, to whom ye yield yourselves servants to obey, his servants ye are to whom ye obey; whether of sin unto death or of obedience unto righteousness?" If you have not previously discovered or admitted this, you will be compelled to do so at the quarantine of Death, and find how true was Paul's declaration that there is no escape for those who wilfully neglect so great a salvation.

But the bondage of sin begins to work hand in hand with its practice, and I will illustrate my personal experiences of its effect with a case in point.

I had been visiting the sleep-state in company with Zecartus, who was executing a commission for Myhanene. The duty being discharged, we were leisurely returning and speaking of certain interesting features of our visit, when I was seized with a curious desire to remain. There was no decisive reason for this, so far as I could understand, and in the uncertainty I referred the matter to my friend.

He paused for an instant and listened as one who caught faint sounds from a distance. Then having satisfied himself, replied:

"Someone is trying to find you, but his sympathy is so feeble he is unable to reach you of himself."

"Who is it?" I inquired.

"I cannot say for the instant, but the connection is being established by which I shall be able to find out. Yes. It is your father."

"My father!" I exclaimed. "You are right, Zecartus, there, is such slight sympathy between us that I almost wonder he should remember me."

"It is not a matter of great importance upon which he wishes to see you, or, apart from his estrangement, his wish would have reached you in more definite form. Will you answer it?"

"Certainly I will. Where is he? How shall we reach him?"

"His call and desire are very half-hearted. It is one of those cases frequently to be met with, where the higher nature recognizes an offence which will penalize the soul, and presses on the lower nature the advisability of submission. The man is at war with himself, the earth-side being strong in resentment, but the spiritual struggles for the victory. Here cautious action on our part is necessary, that the higher nature may be encouraged and supported without the lower finding any occasion for vaunting itself."

"I scarcely understand you."

"Perhaps not; your experience of this sleep-state conflict between the two natures is not yet a very large one. It is a condition in which a man is truly divided against himself, and the issue has to be left almost entirely to his own free will. We may extend some slight assistance where the will is definitely in favour of improvement and the weight of character too heavy for the better resolution. Sin, however, is both crafty and cunning, and though it may lose in a present struggle, will find occasion, if possible, to retaliate, and by taunting insinuations afterwards accomplish more than had been lost. it is for this reason that caution is necessary, and until we understand your father better, I should advise that we simply ascertain the locality he visits, then allow him to find us rather than that we go straight to him."

"I will take your counsel. Please act for me as you deem best."

With his greater knowledge and wider resources, my friend quickly grasped the situation, and we were soon as near to my father as Zecartus deemed advisable.

"You may now send an answering thought to his wish to see you," said my counsellor. "It will readily reach him, and by his quick or tardy response we shall be able to ascertain how the struggle goes.

I did as desired, and as the thought envelope sped towards its destination I found in what direction I might look for my visitor's approach.

Someone will wish to ask with what feelings I anticipated the meeting in the light of what has been said concerning the change of relationship. I reply that my use of the paternal appellation is solely for the sake of convenience, and would again call to remembrance that the kinship of souls is one of sympathy—blood is nonexistent in Paradise—and the closeness of the bond is determined by the strength and purity of the affection. In the present instance the wish for an interview came to me in such marked and blurred indecision, that had it not been for the assistance of Zecartus, I should have failed to read it. Under these circumstances I was unable to look forward to our meeting with any great amount of pleasure. I would, had it been otherwise, and my response to the request for an interview was largely in the hope that something might result to his spiritual benefit and uplifting.

"He does not run to meet you," my companion remarked as the reply to my intimation tarried.

"That is one of the last things I should expect," I answered.

"But you must not estimate any man's sleep condition by what you know of his earth life. Experience teaches me that most unexpected combinations are rather the rule than otherwise here. In the body, the full force of the lower passions may have unrestricted control, but in this temporary discarnate state, unsuspected spiritual qualities may rise into operation, and with the assistance of some little outside influence, gain so great an ascendency as to gradually overcome the despotism of the flesh. I always hope to find these latent signs upon which to work, and if I may be so successful in this instance, our visit may possibly be rewarded with most welcome results."

"God grant it may be so," I replied fervently, "and that even beyond your own generous anticipation. But that will soon be known now, for yonder he comes."

My companion had already established a recognition, for I noticed his closely-knit brow, indicative of the exercise of his marvellous power of analysing and dissecting character, the result of which I should have to wait for, he being singularly uncommunicative at such times. For myself, I was assured, by familiar indications that my father was not in his easiest and most affable mood, but that might be due to the presence of two companions who appeared doubtfully welcome, but pressing in their attentions. I moved to meet them, hoping a cheery greeting would dispel the cloud, but Zecartus restrained me.

"Wisdom counsels your patience," he said. "If you would help him, you must not speak first."

I did not understand why this should be so, but as there was no time for explanations, I yielded to his wish.

The three were passing by this time, my father walking between the two, who were intent on keeping his attention. I had perceived no indication of his consciousness of my presence, and concluded that he would pass without speaking, when politely laying one hand apologetically upon the arm of each friend, he coolly stepped back and towards me.

"Frederic," he said with his usual punctilious formality and composure, as if we had parted company only half an hour previously, "I am not sorry to meet you again, since I sometimes think you and I did not altogether understand each other. I may perhaps have been a trifle too exacting—mark me, I don't say I was, but I may, have been—and you were always so unpardonably obdurate. Still, I am willing to try and forget your conduct, as you are dead, and would like to think that you have accepted my apologies if you imagine that any are due."

"Whatever has been doubtful or undesirable between us, sir, think will be far better mutually forgotten and forgiven, than recalled and explained. That is what I desire, and if you will consent, I shall be more than satisfied."

"Certainly,—certainly! Then we will consider everything in the past as amicably settled. But, mind me, I make no admission of culpability on my part; I simply wish to show my generosity towards your stubborn and intolerable defiance of my wishes. I only apologize as an evidence of that generosity should your highty-tightyness carry your conscience so far as to consider I have committed any offence."

"I have made no such accusation, sir, nor have any desire to do so."

"But you insinuate that you could do so."

"Indeed! I have no wish to insinuate anything. I express no opinion whatever as to whether there is anything to be forgiven between us or not, but if you think there may possibly be such, I am as freely willing to forget and forgive as I hope to be forgiven."

"Very well. Let that suffice. I am also willing to forgive all your many shortcomings and offences." Then he added with a very genuine touch of regret, "But it troubles me to think I shall forget all this when I wake up."

Why should this thought trouble him if there was no consciousness of culpability? In the reply to this question lies the weighty lesson of my illustration. I record it as read by the trained eyes of Zecartus; the natural first-fruits of my father's sin.

His life commenced with a fair heritage of natural gifts. To make his way in the world, he had a resolute will, clear foresight, an intuitive sense of an advantage, with energy and promptitude to secure it. Such was his equipment, together with the responsibility for its right or wrong employment.

He rapidly established a reputation for being a cool, shrewd, clearheaded and reliable man of business, with a discreet reserve and a faculty for probing and exploiting others, without allowing himself or his business to be known.

It is only when he became the head of a household that we are able to form any definite idea of the way his character unfolded from the evidence of results produced. At that time he laid it down as an inflexible rule that the obligations of wife and children were comprised in absolute and immediate obedience, and the duties of husband and father were to govern, protect, and educate with a firm hand. His attitude towards the rest of humanity was somewhat similar, tempered, of course, as necessity compelled.

The germ of this was not far to seek. At the outset, he fell into the error I have already mentioned—of condoning in self that which he would reprobate in others. It is the one weakness to which the flesh is more prone, perhaps, than any other—so natural in its inception, but fearfully fatal in its result. It is a trait of character far too frequently admired in the social and commercial world, and not looked upon with the disfavour it merits among professors of

Chapter 6   The Bondage of Sin

religion. If a man is successful, strong, and able to conform to certain elastic requisitions, society and religion are quite willing not to be too inquisitive into details.

But behind all this, when character alone is the accepted standard, and the soul finds its place by the law of spiritual attraction! Here the process of selection is entirely reversed. Superficial appearances are valueless. Inherent qualities now take rank, and fair exteriors are stripped off that the heart of the life may be inspected. It is a searching ordeal, automatic and mechanical. There is no bribery, no favouritism, no mistake, no inadvertence, no possible escape! True character is brought into legitimate and natural prominence, and working back from the result, the whole course of development is laid open until the source from which it springs is plainly visible.

This source in my father's case was but a trivial matter— first wrongs are seldom great—but it placed a preferential and deliberate division between Self and others. The trend of relationship between the two was henceforth oblique rather than vertical, and the estrangement widened as growth went on.

With the first deflection from rectitude, the soul also loses its true sense of uprightness, and the future estimate of morality will be always along the line of its own procedure. Having eyes to see, it fails to see or understand, because the divine standard has been supplanted. It has deliberately chosen the evil and forsaken the good; it is therefore left alone to the consequences.

Am I making too much of a trifling error? How strange, when I was suspected of treating sin too leniently!

The estimate of the soul's value according to Christ is greater than that of the whole world. If this is so, will not the balances of its exchange be made to turn upon a diamond point? The mustard-tree is potential in the mustard-seed, so also is hell potential in the expansion of a single act deliberately performed.

This is what Zecartus saw written legibly upon the soul of my father, and in the expressed regret that the memory of my forgiveness would be lost in his waking, my friend found an opportunity to intervene and perhaps open a way of escape.

"If you will permit me," he volunteered, "I think it possible I might help you to remember."

"And who, sir, may you be, that I should place myself under your unknown control?"

"Zecartus is able to do all he offers, I am convinced," I replied, "and if you are honest in your wish to remember what has passed between us—"

"Honest! What do you mean, sir? It is late in the day, and things are reaching a pretty pass when my own son doubts my honesty."

"I did not doubt you, and regret using the word. I should have said if you desire to remember."

"That is better; but for you to doubt my honesty would be a liberty I could never pardon. Now, sir," turning to Zecartus, "on my son's guarantee I am willing to accept your assistance. How shall we proceed?"

"We will return with you when you awake."

"That will not be for the present," he replied. "I have other matters to attend to first. Where shall I see you?"

"You will find us on the way when you return."

With that understanding he left us, and Zecartus made me acquainted with the facts I have referred to above.

We had left the sleep-state behind and were close to my old home before my father rejoined us.

"Don't you find it somewhat chilly?" he inquired, with more affability than he had yet displayed, and as he spoke he added a sympathetic shiver to the query.

"The earth temperature always strikes me as being so," replied my companion. "I do not notice it to be more so than usual."

"I do—and much more so than usual."

"I am glad to hear you say so. It indicates a degree of spiritual sensitiveness for which I am most sincerely thankful. "

"Now no preaching, young man; no preaching if you are to go

with me. I hate preaching and canting talk as I hate the Devil."

"Your wish shall be respected. I will confine my endeavours to helping you to remember that whatever may have passed between yourself and son has been fully and freely forgiven on both sides."

"That is, if my son considers there is anything on his part to forgive, which—mind you—I don't admit."

"So I understand; though it would be a thousand times better for you if you did admit it. But, here we are. Now, as you retake possession of your body, make a firm resolve to remember all that has passed, and I will do my best to assist you."

By this time the spiritual was gradually being absorbed into the natural body in the process of waking, and Zecartus surrounded both with a sympathetic atmosphere in the effort he had promised. The body turned, stretched, and then my father started up exclaiming:

"Eh! What? Remember what?"

It was easy to see the experiment had failed. He had simply awakened from a troubled dream, the purport of which had been lost. Too closely associated with earth and its material interests, he could not, at will, retain spiritual memories, even with the help at his disposal.

There was also another disturbing and contributing influence to failure present in the person of a hard-featured, malevolent-looking man, seated beside the bed, as if exercising a kind of guardianship over the body.

"Why are you here?" asked Zecartus.

"Because I can't get away," was the nonchalant reply.

"Who are you?"

"Who am I?" he returned, with a malicious sneer. "Are you blind, or don't you want to see that I am bound to this whited sepulchre?"

"But the bond is one of mutual attraction for which both are equally responsible."

"Oh, it's easy to preach, but if you were in my place you would find it quite another thing to do it. It is easier for him to break the bond if he wants to, because he has not lost the power as I have."

"Do you remember how you refused to break away when you were as he is now, and held another as he holds you?"

"Don't preach at a fellow when he's down, but if you have any pity, lend me a hand to get away."

"Do you want to get away? Where would you go if I could help to set you free?"

"God knows! But I would find someone to be with who was not always showing me myself—someone who is not such a horrible monster as this saintly hypocrite! This is unbearable. Why did I not know of it before—when I had time to avoid it?"

"You might have known, but you wilfully shut your eyes and ears, as he is doing now. What he is, you have been, and the punishment of your bondage to him is but a repetition of that you have inflicted on another. He is sowing, but will not hear, just as you have sown and now must reap the penalty."

"But why did I not know?"

"Because you would not. You scoffed, laughed, and would not hear reproof. Sin was sweet to you as he finds it to himself; now You have to pay its bill."

"Then you won't give me a hand to get away. Is that what you mean?"

"I would gladly help you to gain your freedom if you honestly desired it, and your repentance made it possible for me to do so."

"Don't get preaching any tommy-rot about repentance to me. If I can get no help to get away, just wait till this pious hypocrite has finished his prayers"—for by this time my father was engaged in his punctilious devotion—"and I'll warrant me, I will have some fun."

"And what will come afterwards?" asked Zecartus warningly.

"Oh, damn that!"

"In God's name I beseech you to stop your recklessness, and think of the consequences. Have you no fear, no dread? Has not the past supplied enough of torment that you would risk its increase? Have you not pity for yourself even while you complain that I can offer you nothing more?"

The unutterable anguish of the man as he fixed his torturebrimming eyes on Zecartus while he spoke, will never be forgotten by me.

"What am I to do?" he asked, reaching out his hands in a distracted appeal for the help we could not render because he sought freedom from pain only, and not from sin. "Can I endure this in silence? Can I suffer and rejoice in it, even though, as I sometimes hear, it may be necessary for my own good?" Then in a frenzy of sudden rage, he started and added— "No! By God, I won't endure it quietly. If this saintly cesspool makes my life intolerable by his mimicry and damnable reminders of what I was and how I brought this on, I will retaliate and drive him such excesses as shall make him a thousand-fold worse than I am."

"Do you love yourself so little as that, even when you ask to assist in your escape?"

"Don't be ridiculous. I want revenge, and I will have it; hell shall know the reason why."

Zecartus drew me away. To try and persuade a man in that condition was worse than useless, and yet he was the twin-soul with my father, with this slight difference; one was on earth, in the body, able to make reparation if he would; the other had passed the rubicon, and entered upon his reward for deeds done in the flesh.

Even so. Such is our first inquiry into sin; its nature and results. In spite of all the appearances of earth—of men's transgression and seeming escape from penalty—may we now here write:

"Be not deceived, God is not mocked; for whatsoever a man soweth, that shall he also reap. He that soweth to the flesh shall of the flesh reap corruption, but he that soweth to the spirit shall of the spirit reap life everlasting."

Having, however, embarked upon this inquiry into the nature and consequences of sin, let us still further continue our quest till I remove the last trace of doubt from your mind as to my real attitude towards it.

* * *

CHAPTER 7

THE GATE OF HELL

Zecartus is largely engaged with such contentious individuals as this companion of my father's, being possessed of a quick and clear insight, with a remarkable gift for tracing sequences. This man considered himself to be the victim of an injustice, and it was necessary to point out his error, so as to make him understand and acknowledge that his present condition was simply the natural result of his previous career, the penalty for which had to be discharged 'to the utmost farthing' before assistance and freedom could be secured.

I would point out—and have it always remembered—how perfectly the immortal life is provided with competent ministers to deal with every possible necessity that can arise. The law framed and the order established by God are fully able to supply every conceivable need, and carry to complete perfection the great paternal design which will have all men to be saved. The full and just penalty for sin must be paid—the last fragment of its harvest must inevitably be gleaned, but after that, the heart of every son and daughter will turn homeward, and wherever the first repentant thought is born, it must needs find a spiritual nurse waiting to deliver and minister to its well-being.

Well might the Psalmist ask,—Whither shall I flee from Thy presence? . . . If I make my bed in hell, behold Thou art there!"

Thus the rainbow of infinite love sweeps the everlasting span of life—earth, hell, and Heaven—and is everywhere inscribed with the consoling legend, 'God is good!'

My previous visits to earth in company with Cushna now enabled me to make some interesting observations concerning the relationship of the two sides of life, while Zecartus was engaged with my father's spiritual counterpart. The most significant fact I ascertained was that though I was standing in my old home, it was voided of all interest or attraction for me, and the light of it was scarcely more than a softening of darkness. This latter condition denoted the true spiritual barometric reading of the place; God is light, and nearness to or distance from Him is automatically registered in light or shade. Still, though light failed, I cannot say the same of life, for phantomlike forms moved on every side.

"Who are these who make up this apparently aimless and reckless host?" I inquired as we left.

"Earth-bound souls, each seeking to gratify the particular vicious and evil passion by which it is enslaved," he replied. "The study of their painful employments would be helpful to you after what we have just seen if you would care to undertake it."

"I should indeed, if the opportunity affords."

"That can easily be arranged," he replied, "but you must do it under the guidance of someone engaged in the ministry going on here, who will be far better qualified to instruct you than I am."

As he spoke, he dispatched a thought-flash, which was almost instantly answered by the arrival of the leader of one of the bands of workers near at hand.

"My brother, Ladas," said Zecartus, introducing me. "Aphraar desires to know something of your mission; may I commend him to your discretion?"

"I cannot introduce you to the pleasures of Paradise, but it is possible you may see something of its joy," he answered. "Our work lies more in the shadow than the light, but it will show you much of the law and love of God."

"I wish to learn the law; I have already seen something of the pleasure." I replied.

"Ladas is well able to instruct you as you wish," said Zecartus. "I will entrust you for the present to his care, and take my leave."

With this he left us, and in charge of my new cicerone, I was at once so placed in harmony with my present environment as to enable me to approach nearer to those with whom circumstances were about to bring me in contact, and the better establish communication with them, if needed.

"You will already understand the principle regulating all divisions," he began—"every man to his own place, and no barrier or restriction but that erected by character?"

"Yes, I am familiar with that."

"Then you may regard the sphere of our operations as being the earthbound condition, by which I mean the temporary prison-house of those whose vicious passions and depraved natures still hold them in bondage to the earth and lead them to haunt the former resorts of their sin in the false hope of gratifying their evil desires, while every attempt they make recoils with its legitimate degree of punishment."

"Do you wish me to understand that they are still able to exercise an active influence upon men?"

"I do, and such influence—given favourable conditions for operation—is one of the least understood, but most potent agencies for evil, men have to encounter."

"May I ask what these conditions are?"

"They are two, of which the first and essential one is moral weakness or indecision in the individual tempted. In the presence of well-developed and resolute rectitude, these spiritual brigands are utterly powerless. Evil in every form must flee from the man who is bold to resist it, since evil and weakness are synonymous, having no real power in themselves, but possessing a fatal ability to use such as they may succeed in borrowing. The first move downwards is always strategic, then, if an outpost be carried, the captured force is at once utilized in further operations, or in other words, its second condition is to inveigle the tempted one into the charmed circle of its deadly influence."

"I am not quite sure that I understand you."

"I know it, but I require your most careful attention, and secure it by first stating my proposition vaguely. Now that you are doubly eager to follow me, I will make my meaning plain. The association of certain places with particular vocations is too well and universally recognized to need more than mention. The student will work with greater ease and effect in his study, seated in a given chair, occupying an accustomed position. Why? Because the room has become saturated with the spirit of his labours, and that chair occupies the centre of the radiation of past researches. From that point, everything around him has been saturated with his mental creations, and in his accustomed place, the spirit of the past mingles with present effort and produces inspiration. A place set apart soon begins to breathe the atmosphere of its association and the strength increases by use until it is easy to understand, for instance, how complacently one—

> 'may smile at Satan's rage
> And face a frowning world'

when standing in a place which hallowed associations proclaim to be a house of God—a very gate of Heaven. There angels gather round and—

> 'In the secret of His presence, there is rest—sweet rest.'

Now if this principle of sympathetic saturation be applied all the way round, it may be readily conceived how temptations to sin derive peculiar force through the agency of the place in which they are presented."

"This is a new doctrine indeed," I replied.

"It should and would not be if men would consider the plain teaching of the Christ with the same interest they give to commercial matters."

"Why not?"

"Because Christ taught this great and important truth as clearly as any other single point in His ministry, when He spoke of the unclean spirit driven out of a man wandering in search of rest but finding none. You remember how he returned to find his old abode swept and garnished, but secured the assistance of seven more wicked than himself to carry the position, and all dwelt there, making the last end of the man worse than the first."

"How strange that I have never associated that before!"

"It is iniquitous that men should continue to be so wilfully blind, until they come here and the awful truth is practically forced upon them. Then they wonder that no provision is made for their escape from the consequences of their own neglect, and rave at the injustice of sins of omission being treated as equal to those of commission."

"Oh, the terrible responsibility of life!" I rather reflected than expressed, but the effect was the same, for Ladas heard it distinctly.

"The failure to recognize and act upon the spiritual importance of it is perhaps one of the most remarkable and indefensible follies of the human race," he replied. "As a commercial asset, life in its physical phase is one of supreme value; even its adjuncts, accessories, and parts are matters for which armies and navies are brought into existence to defend; in its spiritual aspect the value is practically nil; yet the former is evanescent, the latter abiding; the one vanishing even as we dreamed it away, the other eternal as God Himself. And the men, who thus frolic with the shadow, while they neglect the substance, call themselves wise. We will visit some of them, that you may see what they are after the shadow is lost, and the plea of ignorance has received its just consideration.

"Is the earth-bound condition, then, another name for hell?" I inquired.

"No! It is in a double sense only the gate—the vestibule of hell. In the earthbound conditions are received actively vicious and openly rebellious souls who, having deceived themselves and being bound to earth by reason of their slavery to sin, thirst for and determine to have revenge upon their fellows; hence their cup of iniquity is not yet full, and in the violence of their passion they elect to continue their evil course in seeking to effect the downfall of others."

"And are they allowed to do so?"

"Yes, every individual is free to do as he wills in that respect. We have no barriers of restraint, though all are continually and faithfully reminded of the consequences of their action, and a ceaseless watch is kept for the first sign of weariness in their futile course. Then, when the measure of their sin is known, they pass from hence to the real punishment of hell."

"Then they do not actually endure suffering here?"

"Most mercifully they do, or vague indeed would be the hope of their reclamation! Every soul, as it drops the flesh, finds itself possessed of a spiritual body which is the true essence of the life producing it, and is only adapted to existence in similar conditions to that which called it into being. As in the physical state, fish prefer water and birds the air, so here every soul gravitates to its own place by virtue of adaptation. Here, however, lies the one awful fact we must ever keep in mind or we shall misunderstand everything; each individual soul on entering this life is strung to the same exquisite delicacy of sensation; the brightest saint and the vilest sinner are thus equally sensitive to the pleasure or torment of the position they have deliberately qualified for. In this provision is manifest the perfect justice of God. So long as these rebellious souls remain here and unrepentant, every act of sin brings about its own immediate punishment, until the futility of their course works towards repentance through despair, at the first sign of which we intervene and the prodigal is carried away to commence the discharge of the debt it has incurred in the remedial punishment of hell."

"Then the actual penalty of hell does not begin here?" I gasped in amazement.

"How can it possibly do so?" he replied. "The liabilities incurred cannot be ascertained until the arms of rebellion are laid down, and God exacts strict justice, nothing more. Let me assist you by pointing out the difference between the punishment endured here and that of hell, then you will the better understand what it is I mean. It is possible that the punishment of the present may be equal to that the soul will there experience, but this is simply an effect immediately resulting from an act at the instant of its performance, that cause and effect may be clearly traced, and the mad career stopped. In the true hell, a man is brought face to face with the full account which stands against him, and he is called upon for payment of both principal and interest. Whatsoever he has sown he has there to reap, and the identical sin he is in process of discharging remains visible before his eyes until it is blotted out in his payment of it. That is the difference between this condition and hell."

"But what of all those who come over neither good nor wholly bad, and those who repent in death?"

"They all go to their own place. Let me suggest a crude illustration which will help you to understand this—the legend of Mahomet's coffin. If you will increase the number of coffins indefinitely and consider Heaven and Hell to be the two magnets acting with greater or less force upon each coffin— some for the moment drawn down, others lifted up, according to varying degrees of sympathy, you may conceive what I mean by a man's own place. But you will need to introduce a new feature if the analogy is to hold throughout."

"What is that?"

"Whatever may be the first attractive effects, they cannot remain static, since the law of spiritual evolution demands that the lower force must ever grow less and the higher increase, until all that are in suspense, are drawn into abiding rest around the one Eternal Magnet. But come and see what this condition has to show you."

Thereupon I started upon a tour of revelation, horrible, indescribable, and of such exquisite torture that language has neither strength nor colour to depict it—a veritable chaos of sin seething in a cosmos of overruling law.

Every scene and group I beheld was one of wild, lawless, fiendish passion, a foaming cauldron of iniquity, in which the foulest souls appeared to be tossed uppermost, and maddened vampires fought with frantic energy to reach and drag others into their awful, yet not destroying, agony.

I trembled even for my own safety as I watched the scene, but Ladas assured me of this by pointing out how the influence of every group was circumscribed to the spot which held it spellbound. Beyond these limits outside the struggling, fighting fringe of those who in the riot had been pitched from the centre to the circumference and clamoured to get back—all was order and quiet, where a host of waiting messengers stood ready to answer any genuine cry for assistance.

Nor were my observations limited to where I stood, but through the porch of death I saw the other side as well; saw victim after victim enticed within the fascinating circle over which the different groups exerted unseen and unsuspected, but all the more deadly, influence. Some wavered in doubtful uncertainty before they timorously yielded; some came curiously forward, careless and already half-inclined to try their luck in the speculative uncertainty; others seemed ashamed and anxious not to be seen and recognized; while still more were boldly confident they were able to take the plunge and come back enriched, unharmed. I heard the shout, which from our side, greeted each newcomer; a shout his ears were too heavy to hear, though he elt the force of the tempting influence which went forth with it; also the sting of conscience which smote him as the howl of success told of the punishment of his tempters.

Passion on earth makes men insensible to pain. Not so with us, it makes the agony more acute, but such was the fury of the sin I saw that it grew defiant even as the soul quivered in its supreme fsuffering, and fought to reach even more daring exploits. Hungry, wolfish eyes glared with determination to destroy; greedy, trembling, twitching hands reached riotously out, impatient to drag down the irresolute, though every soul well knew the greater scourge would fall upon himself should he succeed.

No, no! This is no poetic rhapsody, but a true, if imperfect and incoherent, memory of an awful experience which God in His mercy granted to me that I may speak of it and shout its warning to the sons of men. The fire of a Dante's fervid imagination would be as an iceberg compared with what my eyes beheld in living exposition of the truths Ladas had previously expounded, and in confirmation of the neglected assurance, that 'the way of transgressors is hard.'

"Is there no possible way by which amelioration can be brought to such overwrought agony?" I inquired as my conductor led me away from the scene of such excruciating torture.

"None! If any assistance could be of service I could summon a thousand helpers for every suffering soul in want of it. But what could such ministers do? See the number who are already waiting to fulfil the office—hundreds waiting where only units are required, and always at hand before the call for aid goes forth. All that can be provided is as eagerly quivering to rescue as those we wait to assist are impatient to destroy. Fortunately such punishment is too fierce to be protracted except in very rare cases. Pain, like toil, naturally conduces to weariness, and when the fever of revenge and passion has run its course, these spiritual prodigals come to their right minds, learn what has happened to them, accept the inevitable, and cease their useless warfare."

"What do you mean by learning what has happened to them?"

"Ah, that is an explanation I must make before you can truly understand what you have seen. It might have been well had I made it earlier, but it comes quite naturally now, and will make an after-gleam of useful service. What I mean is that most of these unfortunates wake up here without any idea of what has happened."

"Without a consciousness of death?" I queried incredulously.

"Yes! Without the shadow of a suspicion of it."

"Is that possible?"

"Not only possible, but under the circumstances, it almost becomes natural that it should be so."

"Will you explain how?"

"Recall the nebulous confusion and ignorance existing on the other side concerning death; the idea that it is possible for a man to step red-handed from the gallows close to the throne, by accepting a belief; that the moment after death, a newly-born child becomes perfected in all knowledge; that a death-bed conversion transforms the vilest soul into a spotless saint; the doubt as to whether the soul will or will not sleep till the day of judgement, when it will re-enter its physical body and be caught up into the air to be for ever with the Lord. Concerning the wicked equally contradictory and irreconcilable opinions are held; they are at once consigned to the custody of the devil and his angels, who torture them in the fires of hell, from which there is no hope of escape, while, at the final judgement, they are to be brought before the Christ to be judged as to whether they are really guilty or not. Now, when these ideas are accepted, and have the sanction of constituted authority before death, why should it be thought incredible, when, having made the transition, the souls find nothing even remotely associated with any one of the expectations, it fails to understand what has actually occurred?"

"Still one can scarcely believe it possible."

"Why? It is an experience often met with even beyond the earth conditions. Did you at once understand what had happened?"

"No, I did not," I had to confess, for I had fallen into the common error pointed out by Zecartus of judging others by a different rule to the one I used for myself. "But my passage was so sudden—so unexpected; there may be some excuse for the confusion."

"The confusion of the transit is not so dependent upon its suddenness as upon the erroneous ideas as to what it will reveal.

Chapter 7 — The Gate of Hell

Ignorance produces ignorance. Those who prefer to travel in darkness cannot profit by the revelations light affords. The man, who takes his journey by night from England into Wales and sleeps upon the trip, will wake uncertain as to whether the Severn Tunnel has been passed or not, and naturally inquires, 'Where are we?' "

"But I scarcely think the analogy holds."

"Why?"

"In throwing off the body, so many changes have necessarily taken place."

"Had they not also occurred in your own case?"

"Yes, certainly," I was again constrained to admit to my confusion.

"These changes were all related to externals." he went on. "You were, so far as your own judgement went, exactly the same as before, and what had taken place was not so at variance with the past as it differed from what you had anticipated death would reveal. Hence it was much easier for you to conclude that, in the period of unconsciousness between the present and the past, you had rather been the victim of a practical joke than that you had died."

"I must confess that you are right."

"That arises because this continuity of life grows so naturally out of that which has gone before. Changes do, of necessity, take place, but they are only such as doffing a physical garment and assuming a spiritual, which is so much better adapted to the new surroundings, and even this is not new, as in the sleep-state every soul has been accustomed to the daily change."

"But that is not remembered on the other side."

"It might and ought to be so remembered, but to do this would disturb established authority, and the man who advocated the cultivation of such a channel of revelation and inspiration would find himself driven to ascend a social, if not a physical, Calvary. Nature, however, does not adapt her actions to the convenience of ignorance; all her laws are supposed to be intelligently understood. Let us push our inquiry just a little further. The sleep-state, then, makes every being conversant with the truth, whether it is remembered in the waking state or not. The only point we have now to settle is, what is the actual difference between sleep and death—and that is absolutely none. The man who falls asleep dies so far as the process is concerned. All the difference lies in the return or non-return of the soul to the body, not in its liberation. This being so, you need no longer wonder that many of these unfortunates have not yet learned what has happened."

"I thank you for your lucid and patient explanation," I returned."May I now ask for information as to first impulses on recovering consciousness?"

"Yes. Would you prefer to watch such a case for yourself, or shall I tell you of one I have just attended?"

"I am not anxious to see more for the present than you have already shown me," I answered.

"Then I will take my last case as a very fair one to illustrate what you ask. It is that of a man who commenced life as a clerk in a broker's office, where he held a contented and confidential position for some years. Then temptation came, and after many refusals, much dallying, and several corrections of propositions, he at length consented not to betray his employer's trust—he could never do that; Honour forbade it! But for a substantial commission he answered inquiries so equivocally as to serve the same purpose. The commission so gained was then privately used in accordance with the confidential information entrusted to him, and he began to dream dreams of possible wealth along the lines he had chosen, but his duplicity leaked out, and he was discharged. Now he set himself to realize his dreams in other ways, formed an ideal of amassing a fortune of two millions, to which object he, step by step, sacrificed everything, even life, for he was summoned hence when he needed an eighth to reach the height of his ambition.

"Apoplexy was the cause of his transition, and I was in attendance when he regained consciousness. His first surprise was to find he had awakened in a strange place, and he examined his body with considerable suspicion, but remembering he had swooned in the office, accepted the situation, and was anxious to get back without delay, leaving matters to explain themselves as best they might. You must now bear in mind that to all earthbound souls the places and people who occupy the scenes of their bondage are almost as solid and substantial as ever, while they are unsubstantial and invisible in themselves. It is this allimportant but uncomprehended difference which first bares their backs to punishment.

"He returned to his office to discover that his absence had been longer than he imagined, and that many unauthorized and objectionable changes had taken place in the interval; perhaps the most outrageous being the quiet appropriation of his private office by the manager, who appeared to be conducting business without any reference to himself. He peremptorily demanded an explanation, but his subordinate might have been deaf, dumb and blind in his refusal to notice the inquiry. He stormed, raved and appealed to others with precisely the same effect; then in a fury of rage, better imagined than described, he rushed home. Here he fared far worse than in the city, for to his disgust and consternation, he learned that his family considered him to be dead, and he finally came back to us determined to find someone who would come to his assistance by helping him to be revenged.

"You may find this experience more or less perfectly duplicated in half the members of every group you may visit. Nor can we render them the slightest service or assistance until the wildness of their passion produces weariness, and they seek our help."

"And is the earth enveloped with such a delirious crowd of evil?" I inquired, beginning to see, as I never understood before, the dangers of the weak and unprotected in the presence of such maddened tempters to evil.

"No! If such were the case, it would almost be fatal to the ultimate triumph of good over evil. These scenes are the festering pollutions of civilization, and the men and women who comprise them are those who know the right but deliberately choose the wrong in their greed for temporal success— wealth, position and power. They knew their Lord's will, but they did it not, therefore are they beaten with many stripes. Much has been given to them and much required in return, but having wasted their substance and made themselves moral and spiritual bankrupts, that which they have accumulated has to be taken away, and what you have seen is the first part of the stripping process—the commencement of the fire by which their souls must be purified."

"With what terrible emphasis everything insists upon retribution here!" I exclaimed.

"That is because you see law working out its justice—law that is always and invariably inexorable. The fatal mistake of the other side is to regard law as being inflexible in its physical aspect only, but in the spiritual sphere—that is if it should exist here, which is exceedingly doubtful—it is both capricious and easily evaded by repentant promises to do better. No man who understands the nature of dynamite will trifle with it carelessly, and yet dynamite is harmless compared with the spiritual laws men ignore. There is always a possible escape from dynamite, but not from law."

"But your illustration fails if these earth-bound souls are principally the product of civilization, for dynamite will explode equally in the hands of savage or cultured."

"No. My analogy still holds. The explosive is a product of civilization, and is inaccessible as its properties are unknown to the savage. If, therefore, such an explosion occurred, it could only be by the dynamite being imported with some sinister intent, and the responsibility for the disaster would lie with the importer, not the savage. It is precisely the same with these groups of earth-bound iniquity; every individual in all that awful host is entering on the legally and perfectly just reward of the deeds done in the body.

But in further answer to your inquiry, let me point out how every group is bound to a certain place in their aggregate action; drunkards gather around taverns; gamblers on the race-course or other places 'devoted to sport', and so on until you have located every group; but apart from this collective grouping for greater strength, each individual has his own particular bond to the scene of his personal transgression. As I pointed out in the case I have described, much of the torture arises from the fact that the fetters his conduct has forged compel him to witness-bound and helpless—the frustration of the project for which he had forfeited everything; to find that the egg for which he eagerly gave his soul, hatches nothing but a scorpion to increase his own torment."

* * *

CHAPTER 8

ANGELS AND ANGELS

"It is impossible for you during a single and brief visit to gain any adequate conception of the enormous scope and varying details of our work here," said Ladas in preparing to call my attention to other features of his ministry, "but I will select one or two suggestive points likely to be of personal service, and which at the same time will indicate our farreaching operations. Of the vast resources at our disposal to ensure success, I can suggest no estimate, since these are only known to God, though the assurances of the past warrant me in saying they are never failing and equal to any demand that may be made upon them.

"Nor could I speak with systematic lucidity of the knowledge I have gained from my long experience. We do not work by rule or in accordance with any theoretical formula; if we did so, the process might be codified and studied at leisure. But while we recognize the fact that sin proceeds upon certain clear and well defined lines, in ministering to the soul diseased, we study each case with the critical caution of a new development, rather than for purposes of classification. God never aggregates, but always individualizes. It is the one lost sheep we are most interested to find. Though 'God will have all men to be saved', we never forget that the all is comprised of units, which must be reclaimed as speedily and lovingly as possible.

"This is the old gospel of Christ, which He carried to earth from hence—'the old, old story' so unlike the old wives' fables of earthly origin, so like the conception of what a heavenly theme would be, that all men sought for Him that they might listen to its music. It is the Christ-song set to the self-same melody of loving devotion to the needs of the lost we chant in our present ministry—the love-song God composed to fascinate the ears of those who would become bond-slaves of hell, and on the wings of hope and trust bear them higher, higher, higher, until the morning breaks, the discord dies away, sight is restored, and home is reached.

"Earth has broken the sweetest strings in the divine harp and replaced them with unmelodious substitutes spoiling the melody. In the garden of the Lord an enemy has scattered tares, choking the flowers and poisoning the fruit, and the work of Christ has been made of non-effect through false traditions. Thus the true proclamation of the gospel has reverted to us again. The Christianity earth has lost is the native life of immortality which the Father's love outstretched to plant below that men might earlier eat of the fruit of the tree of life. Oh, that love of God! It could not wait to manifest itself in redemption, but ran before to provide salvation from a fall. It foresaw and anticipated the weakness and frailty of the flesh, and yearned to set around the evolving man all possible safeguards from the dangers of the animal nature he was naturally outgrowing. So in the midst of the Eden planted in preparation for the further development, love placed the tree of life beside the river of the water of life, and its welcome shade offered holy rest, the music of the water singing sweet lullabies, with the luscious fruit of immortality hanging overhead, and the angels of the homeland ascending and descending to counsel and advise.

"Such were the provisions of love. But away from the river the garish fruits of sensuous desire were found. The animal instincts prevailed, the habits and tastes of the swine-trough were stronger than the feeble restraint of a newly-born morality; the new man fell under the domination of the old brute, and the spiritual prospect became obscured.

"The teachers of earth have fostered the idea that the tree of life has ceased to exist, as if the eternal love of God had petulantly changed to hatred on account of the frailty of man. How mpossible! The tree of life yet stands in the midst of the Paradise of God, and its leaves are everlastingly for the healing of the nations. The fruit of that tree you will find in every sphere and region of this life, and the ministry and potency of it forms the full employment of all whom you will meet. Nothing has changed. The fruit, the life, the music, the love, the angels, remain from everlasting to everlasting, and the Father so loves that He will still consummate His eternal purpose and nothing can be lost.

"I say the proclamation of the real gospel of Christ has practically been left to us now, and, perceiving that you are anxious to take an active part in this revived ministry, I think I can serve your purpose best by directing attention to a peculiar danger which lies in the way of the re-opening of communication between ourselves and the earth."

"I shall be profoundly grateful for any advice you can give me in that direction," I replied. "Not that I know whether my hope will be realized, but I would like to be well equipped if I should be so honoured."

"The irresistible power of the gospel as preached by Christ lies in its harmony with natural law, which found its full interpretation in the life He lived. God was in and working through Him to reconcile the world to righteousness in the evolution of the spiritual from the natural. The restless activity of life in Jesus reached out towards the Christ, always using its present attainments as a platform from which to reach to still higher possibilities. Modern Christianity has departed from this primitive routine, forsaken the personal demonstration of the Christ-life, and in its stead established a human theory concerning that life, outlined and prescribed by the fathers of the later Christianity in council assembled. This man-invented form of godliness lacks the Christ-power to control the lives of men, and religion has become a dry and withered branch. Still, neither the unfaithfulness of men nor the corrupting influences of sin have frustrated the purpose of God. Angels are now re-ordained to the ministry, who knowing and understanding the working of the law will use it, and thereby bring the world to Christ. But in connection with this ministry, even there is one danger we must watchfully guard against."

"Surely it is not possible for the ministry of angels to fail in its purpose?"

"Quite! It is for this reason I wish to be very careful to make you understand what I desire to show you. There are angels and angels. Freedom to return to earth is open to all alike, and the minds of men are far more in sympathy with those who are in the earth conditions than those who are above them. This constitutes the danger I wish you very clearly to recognize. The souls who feel the first attraction to return and are more generally welcomed, are those who know nothing at all of real spiritual life and government, but they speak and air their ignorance in a confusion of tongues and teachings worse than that of Babel."

"What, then, is to be done?"

"The victory has to be wrested from their grasp. Men are now learning to appeal to reason rather than place a blind trust in authority, and an invasion of the earth is being arranged, as perhaps you are aware, by those who are competent to set forth the whole law of God and make the truth clearly manifest."

Ladas, while thus preparing me for what was to come, had dispatched and received several messages, after which he explained—

"I am making inquiries as to where I can find a better illustration of this difficulty. I would neither exaggerate nor mitigate the matter, but am anxious to show you a fairly representative case and allow you to draw your own conclusions. Such an opportunity is now open; come and watch what I mean for yourself."

As he finished speaking we had arrived within the spacious drawing-room of a prosperous city tradesman, where some dozen persons were assembled to take part in a spiritualistic séance; of the number, two were clergymen; one (Mr. Newman) was somewhat uncertain as to the legality of the proposed proceedings, but the other (Mr. Oldfield) assured him that he would find it more amusing than serious, and free from any objection. Anthony Mairn, as the president of the local Spiritualist

Association, had been invited to meet the clergymen, with the possible hope of securing a new and very desirable convert. The rest of the company comprised Arthur Settle, the host, his wife, daughter, and friends who were all enthusiastically curious to know what would happen. The medium, the half-uncanny centre of hope and uncertainty, was Madame Hansbrac, a popular society clairvoyant, who had found a husband to be somewhat inconvenient, and arranged to make him an allowance in consideration of his not troubling her. There were no children and little difficulty about coming to an arrangement, so Madame left her home for a more fashionable location, and all went well. She had a retaining fee of three guineas a week from Mr. Settle for business consultations, and the present séance was a special engagement for which an additional payment had to be fixed.

These details are necessary to indicate the underlying spirit and motives which gave background to the whole proceedings.

Someone will inquire how I learned these details. It is a pertinent question, and the answer to it throws a flood of light upon what afterwards took place. Every mind in the room was open to our inspection as an elementary class-book. We could read what we would, turning page after page and searching at our discretion into the secret and unguarded archives of the past, where lay any amount of material for the manipulation of the two spiritual attendants already waiting upon Madame Hansbrac.

Just one word here as to whether we have any right to take advantage of knowledge thus placed at our disposal, and I assert that we have every right to read all we wish to read therefrom, since this is our natural source of all genuine information concerning individuals. All judgements on the spirit side of life and all decisions are based upon and determined by records written upon the soul. I would call to mind how frequently I have previously pointed this out. As an instance, in our recent conversation, Ladas referred to my wish to take part in the mission to earth which he had read from my mind, as I have just read what was written upon advantage of knowledge thus placed at our disposal, and I assert that we have every right to read all we wish to read therefrom, since this is our natural source of all genuine information concerning individuals. All judgements on the spirit side of life and all decisions are based upon and determined by records written upon the soul. I would call to mind how frequently I have previously pointed this out. As an instance, in our recent conversation, Ladas referred to my wish to take part in the mission to earth which he had read from my mind, as I have just read what was written upon those around me. What is not right is to make use of the information so gained for purposes of deception, as is too often done by mischievous and unreliable intermediaries.

"Did you ever try planchette, Miss Arbonne?" asked Miss Settle during the fifteen minutes Madame always allowed for her sitters 'to establish the necessary harmonious condition for the séance.'

"No, never."

"Oh, but you should; it is the jolliest fun you can possibly conceive. I have had my planchette properly dedicated—

"What is that, if I may be allowed to inquire?" asked Mr. Newman.

"I scarcely know how to describe it. It is a kind of setting it apart for the use of a particular spirit, to prevent others using it who are not known."

"Is planchette really any good?" asked her lady friend.

"It's just delightful. You can ask all you wish about anyone and it will tell you."

"But can you rely upon its being truthful?"

"W—ell, perhaps not always, but I think it is right more frequently than people admit."

"Do you know," said Mr. Newman to his clerical brother, "my conscience does not quite agree with this intrusion upon the realm of the sacred dead."

"Because it's new ground, my dear sir—new ground and one naturally treads it with diffidence. Wait awhile and you will lose all your doubts in a wonderland Alice never had a chance to enter."

"You will commence with prayers, of course?"

"Oh, dear, no; if there was anything churchy about it I should give it up at once," replied Miss Settle with petulant definiteness.

"But, my dear young lady, do you consider the solemnity of the occasion?"

"No, I do not. Society does not go in for solemnities. I think it time you clergymen consented to confine religion to church, and allowed us to enjoy our amusements without interference. This discussion was not exactly tending towards harmony, so Madame requested Miss Settle to "play something soft and dreamy," after which her clairvoyant descriptions and communications began. I am, however, more interested to record what I saw than what was said just now.

The various spiritual atmospheres had by this time blended, and formed a photosphere enveloping the entire company, on the outside of which we remained undiscovered. The quality of the aura, representing its true spiritual tone, may be described as a compound of curiosity, amusement and doubt. There was no sign of aspiration or spiritual desire from beginning to end of the performance.

Clairvoyance is a somewhat misleading term to apply to the range of phenomena usually covered by this name, since only a small percentage comes within the scope of vision and by far the larger portion are perceived, and the perception is more due to spiritual affinity than any particular sense. It was very definitely so in the readings Madame gave in this instance, all of which, and many more, were easily obtainable from the mental aura by which the group was enveloped, though I should be unjust to the medium to say that she was conscious of the fact. She received impressions from somewhere which were interpreted with startling results to those whose eyes were unable to see the visions open to my observation. This information of men and things, so naturally given from sources clearly outside those considered normal, were accepted as being conveyed by spirit friends present and Madame neither affirmed nor denied the explanation. To her, the gift she exercised was simply a means of gaining a lucrative livelihood, and the satisfaction so generally expressed meant increased business. The sitters were more than satisfied—she had no reason to be otherwise.

But astounding as her revelations were to begin with, there is perhaps no other phase in the whole range of psychic phenomena that so soon grows monotonous. The medium watched keenly for the first indication of this, when with a request for more dreamy music she at once prepared for the second part of the entertainment. Here she was thrown into the hypnotic sleep by the action of one of her familiar attendants, a condition I watched for the first time with much interest. When she slept and the music ceased, I noticed her controlling genius make a suggestion, in reply to which the sleeper started and assumed the character of a little mulatto girl known as 'Frisky.' It was a curious combination of a half-coy, half-precocious child, biting the corner of a handkerchief and shaking herself as she spoke.

"Good evening, all of zou," she began with a playful childish lisp.

"Good evening, Frisky," was the responsive chorus from all who knew the impersonation.

"Well, and what have you to tell us, now you are here?" inquired Mr. Settle.

"Oh, I has to tell zou, zat a lady will call, to zee zou at zee shop tomorrow.

"Do you know her name?"

"Zes, but I must not tell zou.

"Well, what can you tell me about her?"

"She has got a lot of money, and if zou is very, very, very patient wis her, she will buy a lot of nice things."

"Who tells you this?"

"Joey says I must tell zou."

"All right, I'll be careful to be patient with her. Thank Joey for sending me word."

"Oh, I zay! Look! Look!" she exclaimed, pointing to Mr. Newman. "Look at ze long face of Mr. Parson."

"I am very much surprised that you have nothing more than these frivolities to tell us from the other side of death. That is what makes me look so serious," replied that gentleman.

"Is zou?"

"Yes, more surprised than I can make you understand."

"If zou waits till zou comes on our side, zou will be more surprised zan I can make zou understand."

"I can readily believe that, but can you not tell us something about it?"

"No! Frisky never speaks of such things, Mr. Newman, and we don't care for anything creepy-creepy, I can assure you. It will be time enough to think about that when we get there— won't it, Frisky?" intervened Miss Settle.

"Zes, quite. Iz want to make zou happy."

"Then tell me, do you know anything about last Wednesday night when I was in my room?" the same lady inquired.

"When zou went to bed?"

"Yes. Who pulled my hair?"

"I did. So as zou should know I was there."

"Well, it was very good of you. Will you do it again?"

"Zometime; but I mus' go now."

My first lesson regarding the value and effect of spiritual affinities was over, contributing a fund of useful knowledge I was not likely to forget.

"Do you now grasp my meaning as to the danger which lies before us?" asked Ladas as we turned from the chosen scene of the husks when a banquet of angel food had been possible.

"Yes, I think I understand you now. It is the working out of the principle referred to by Christ when he said, 'Every one that asketh, receiveth,' and every man receives just what he asks for—

finds just what he seeks. I see it now as I never saw it before, and shall not forget it. But you also said that the danger may and must be averted."

"It will be so; it is my confidence in this that prompted my pointing it out to you; knowing what it is, you will naturally avoid it in your future intercourse; but at the same time I am equally anxious for you to realize that what has just occurred is not without its value in calling attention to the existence of psychical phenomena worthy of being inquired into. These frivolous and ignorant individuals who represented our side in their proceedings, by their close association with earth, have the power and pleasure of producing effects which appeal to reason and should tend towards inquiry. So far they do a necessary and preparatory work by laying a foundation upon which the whole system of spiritual law may be erected. What has to be done is to mind the inquiry does not stop at this point, and the possibilities be cut short at the stage of amusement, curiosity, or an application to unreliable fortune-telling. Here lies the true danger to which I would direct your attention."

"And how do you propose to avert it?"

"Myhanene would be a far better authority for you to consult on that point, since he is one of the leaders in the new forward movement to that end. I may, however, indicate one direction it must take. You noticed that the emanations— spiritual, mental, and moral—of all present blended to form an attraction for such spirits as were the exact counterpart of the aggregation?"

"Yes, I very carefully noticed that."

"The preponderating influence in all séances is contributed by the person through whom the communications pass. The two who have just been dominating the mind and body of Madame, form a stronger and closer connection with her at every such gathering, unless she releases the bond by spiritual aspiration, and this active, definite influence largely controls and determines the character of the indefinite nebulosity of all others who attend her séances. In the new crusade, therefore, the first essential is to find men and women whose moral and spiritual natures will reach high, and find ministering angels among those who are free from all earth attractions and alike competent and honest to speak of life as it really is and may be. But I must now show you another illustration of a very different kind. You have seen how the frivolous and careless are attracted to each other; you must also see how the malevolent gain their ascendancy."

We entered the combined foyer and bar of a popular variety theatre, where the lounges, chairs—yes, and even the counter—were plentifully occupied with women, who formed an unadvertised but well-known part of the attractions of the house; women wearing model modes of court establishments, who displayed millinery and lingerie with equal and tempting prominence to ensnare the foolish and weak of that class whose purses were sufficiently heavy to warrant their passing the artistically draped and almost closed portiere. It was, on the surface, a picture of dainty and painted wantonness few men would pass without, at least, a second look.

The physical eye, however, is subject to restrictions and able only to see a section of the solar spectrum. Unfortunately, the mental and spiritual vision—not naturally, but from deliberate intent and purpose—is similarly limited. Hence to those of earth but one side of the picture was accessible, but to myself both sides were visible with almost equal clearness. I may even go further and say that I was able to see how the past and present were blended for purposes of destruction and the future already outlined with startling and suggestive horror. The scene was more than a repetition of what I had previously witnessed, since the dead and living meet on equal terms, each tempting and dependent upon the other, where only God Himself could justly draw the line of guilt or—no, not innocence, such virtue would be poisoned in passing the threshold of this temptation. On the one side were the libertine, the roué, the drunken and the wanton, stripped by the action of the

The Life Elysian

tomb of their gilded and masked hypocrisy—not so much men and women of open depravity and sin (only too many of these are victims to the lust and machinations of others)—but those who passed over the stage of earth life socially enamelled and painted to conceal their moral corruption and pollution; such had now found their true level and fought with riotous frenzy to free themselves from the disgusting bondage of tyrannous sensuality or take a wild but useless revenge by immuring others. On the earth side were men who drank, flirted and plotted to accomplish a downfall, or with brainless perfidy, hilariously bearded the tempter in his lair; women who so far had only fallen to the extent of the alluring excitement of the temptation, suggestion, and moral atmosphere the place provided; young men who had been innocently decoyed by intriguers anxious to gain some nefarious ascendancy. But why need I go on still further to enlarge? In a word, it was a place where the leash was slipped from hell, at the daring taunt of earth, to enter the lists of combat for the souls of men and women.

Among the continual entrances and exits connected with this sensuous and gilded attraction, my attention was presently called to two young men, or I had perhaps better say to a man who was still young accompanied by a youth. Neither carpet nor portiére permitted any sound to announce their coming, and I had seen a score pass in and out without attracting attention, but when these two entered, there was a momentary hush in the conversation, and with one impulse all eyes were turned upon them. A chill swept through the heated atmosphere, causing the women to draw their wraps a trifle closer, but the effect was over on the instant, and the laughter and talk went on. The eyes of earth saw not what I beheld. Heaven and hell were both conscious of it, but the veil of sin hung like a pall where sight was needed most.

From the record on the soul of each, I read the antecedents of these two interesting men. The younger had just reached his majority and freedom from his father's condition that he was to give implicit obedience to his mother till such a time, or lose the comfortable heritage bequeathed with a good business still capable of enlarging it. In thus controlling a lad of impulsive spirit the maternal task had been no sinecure, and almost before time had broken the restraint, he was anxious to be away and gratify his desire to know what London really was. He did grudgingly consent to accept a companion of his mother's choice, but it salved her anxiety, since for the father's sake she could confidently trust the lad to the chosen guardian.

This desirable overseer of the lad's well-being was known as a careful and honourable man in his northern home, averse by natural temperament to excess and extravagance of every kind, which was further safeguarded by church connection. He was, as I say, not the lad's choice, but with mental reservation had been accepted to please the mother.

Had she been able to read and see as I had power to do, she might have listened to the lad's first objection, and even let him go alone. Many men are ostensibly virtuous because temptation has not assailed them at the point of least resistance, and it was so with the trusted friend of this commission, who was discreet and abstemious, not so much from choice and principle as penuriousness. When, therefore, all expenses were to be defrayed from another and well-filled purse, the qualities for which he had been selected vanished as a mirage, and the cicerone had tastes, desires and foibles much the same as other men.

Fortunately, the mother's greatest practical trust was not reposed in any arm of flesh—she had found a more impregnable refuge and shelter in time of trouble, and by tearful prayers at the throne of grace had thrown a zone of protection round the boy able to resist even the unfaithfulness of his supposed guardian. True prayer—complete confidence that God can and will do that which is absolutely beyond ourselves if we only faithfully seek it—has a long and powerful arm, and under the canopy it is able to spread all must be well with the lad.

The Life Elysian

Here lay the secret of his disturbing entrance into the foyer. God had heard the prayer and given His angels charge concerning the object of that mother's solicitude. On either side of the youth he was guarded by a messenger from a station higher than that of Omra shining in the glory of their power to turn aside all the tempter's assaults. The mother would save her son against himself, but not being near at hand she had left him with the God she loved and served and God was faithful to perform the mother's righteous wish.

But someone will remind me how often I have pointed out that higher ministers assume a garb of neutral grey when brought into contact with those in lower condition and ask— "Why did these guardians of the youth not obey this law?" I will explain. In all cases I have hitherto referred to where this change has taken place—as in that of Ladas and myself on the present occasion—the visits had been made either to assist or make observations. The two were here present with this lad to protect and preserve him with the temptations of lower agencies, to place him in opposition to and enable him to rise superior to whatever temptation might assail. He must be saved. His mother had left it to God—whose child she was—to see to it that it should be so, and her confidence was strong to carry it to the desired effect. God would see to that.

The two sat down on either side of a small table and the waiter came for orders.

"What will you take?" inquired the elder.

"A small lemonade."

"Won't you have something in it?"

"You know I won't."

"I think I will. Give me just the least dash of brandy in mine."

The waiter retired to execute the order, and at the same moment one of the greedy, thirsty, tempting souls approached, driven to reckless frenzy by his maddening inability to drink from the glasses he had hitherto tried to raise to his lips. He was even quicker than I to read that the guardian had relaxed his usual grip upon himself, and flushed with the possible chance of conquest grew daring in his approach. The defenders of the youth closed around him and invited our co-operation.

"You are not an abstainer when in London, then?" remarked the ward.

"I am never bigoted in my ideas; but to-night I feel a little run down and need a pick-me-up. I should think it is ten years since I tasted anything before."

"Then I should not taste it now."

"I think you would if you felt as I do; in fact, I don't believe a drop would do you any harm now."

"What would my mother think if she heard your advice? Would she believe her ears?"

"Your mother would have every confidence in my discretion, Artie. The journey and hurry to get here, together with all the bustle and excitement, have been almost too much for me. Then again," he added, holding up the just delivered glass, "see what they have given me scarcely colours the lemonade. It is only just enough to do one any good. Here's to a jolly week in town."

As he raised the glass to his lips, that earth-bound soul literally threw himself upon his victim, and while he drank there was a brief but fearful contest for victory. The glass was emptied and set down with an action of contempt at the paltry and childish draught, the cicerone's eyes burned with a strange ferocious light, and calling the waiter he requested him with a peremptory voice to:

"Bring me a large Scotch, neat."

His companion looked at him in speechless consternation.

What had taken place?

He who had been chosen as a worthy guardian of an inexperienced and somewhat passionate youth had fallen under the spell and power of an earth-bound soul—in other words, he had become possessed of a demon who had assailed the man in his weakest point and conquered him. He had deliberately walked into the stronghold of temptation, laid all arms of principle aside, held by a bare reed of character to support him in leaning over the precipice of gratification, and had toppled to ruin.

But the mother's prayer had saved the lad.

There is no more to be said. I had taken my second lesson, and learned from experience the strength lent to sin by association. Had not Christ the fearful consequences of this in mind when in His exemplary prayer He found room for the petition: 'Lead us not into temptation'?

* * *

CHAPTER 9

WHO RULES IN HELL?

"Can you see what the end of this will be?" I asked Ladas. "No! That would require the peculiar gift of Zecartus, which I do not possess, since it would rather hinder than assist my work. There are two courses open to the man which I may point out to you, but cannot offer any opinion as to which he will pursue. The better way would be to admit his error at once, and ascertaining the real cause of his weakness, set himself to correct and retrieve his position, carefully watching against another slip. But the doubtful part about such a proceeding is occasioned by the fact that it requires constant effort, whereas his habit of life has been negligent indifference to the moral weakness contributing so largely to his fall. It was a far easier matter to avoid than it will now be to remedy the effects of his collapse. On the other hand, if he does not exert himself to supply this greater moral demand, every future temptation will lead to another and deeper degradation, because vicious habits combine to destroy."

"Could you not tell him so, and caution him?"

"No. He has made his choice and cut himself adrift from such assistance. Had his religion been more than an empty profession, when the tempter commenced the struggle, you saw he would have cried for help, of which there was more than sufficient at hand to save him. But temptation blew the flimsy cloak of profession aside and exposed the real man ready to take a personal advantage and gratification at the expense of another—the exact affinity of the malevolent fiend who enveloped and readily subdued him. With careless indifference, he had prepared his soul to fall into such an unsuspected trap, and he has to meet with his reward. No! We cannot help him at present. He must first come to himself and discover how he has sinned, then he will find a thousand hands outstretched to lift him up. I have now given you two illustrations of how these spiritual affinities act; I would further point out an instance of the present punishment these unrepentant souls have to bear."

He led me far from the madding crowd of both sides of life, to a little place beside the sea. One of those delightful oases of life, of which Heber sang where, "every prospect pleases, and only man is vile."

A few fishing-boats lay at rest in a miniature harbour. Nature had arranged for the little colony of fishers, who could not afford to build their own protection against the sometimes angry waves, and all around a hundred gems of beauty had been provided in vale, on hill, or pastoral retreat. The homes of the fishermen nestled close to the water's side like constant lovers to the maidens of their choice, but those men who by reason of success, had forsaken their first estate, climbed the hill-side overlooking the bay, and erected more pretentious residences in an anxious desire to obliterate all traces of their extraction.

Ladas conducted me to the largest and most assertive of these houses, built by a man of cunning genius who had climbed from the water side; one who, as a child, was the pride and amusement of the little colony for his artfulness above the lads of his own age, as in after-life he became its anxiety and sorrow by the exercise of the same proclivity. As a youth he learned how to make more money by wits than work—found that the man who could buy fish was better off than he who caught them, and consequently left the boat. Success was assured from the first. It was not a difficult matter for him to climb over the honest simplicity of the men he had left, and he speedily became an influential unit in the community as well as in the church, where he was occasionally to be found in the pulpit. He then began to lend money when times were bad, upon a rate of usury and terms which presently caused half the boats in the harbour to pass from fisher-hands into his own account of arrears of loans or interest, and with the transfer of the boat, the boat's share of every catch also went to increase his fortune and impoverish the village.

His loan department demanded a clerk, and he engaged a girl against whose dead father the English Shylock had been prevented from discharging a debt of revenge. After a period of semi-starvation due to his paltry wage, he planned and carried out her ruin, driving her from church, Sunday school and home, to suicide. The village held its breath, but dared not speak, and the church was blinded by a paltry donation.

Then came the stone-laying of the long-expected 'mansion', in the presence of the President of the Conference and other religious magnates who delighted to do honour to the man whom God had so highly exalted among his fellows. Few men in that countryside had been able to discover what a saint their Shylock was until the President unfurled the banner of his envied success and waved it for the emulation of his hearers, as the reward of large-hearted righteousness; but while strangers from a distance applauded, the men and women of the village groaned inwardly.

It was a glorious, a cloudless day, that of the stone-laying. Perhaps a little too bright—too warm, and just a trifle blatant in its flattery, one or two suggested under their breath; and events proved the opinion to be somewhat well founded, for the roof was not on before the village circuit-steward was peremptorily requested to make up his life's account so far.

"Thou fool! This night shalt thy soul be required of thee; — then!!!"

It was the after of this "then" I beheld when the process had been in operation for a number of years without cessation, moderation or relief. The house, formerly the coveted goal of the man's ambition, was finished, and had become the prisonhouse of his earth-bound soul. I have intimated how every furnishing of the immortal home is the spiritual expression of some act, word or deed of the previous life; it was even so here! Every detail of the place assumed the embodiment of some usurious and unscrupulous exaction, an open robbery of one who could not defend himself, the memorial of a woman's degradation, the food of underfed children, the curse of a ruined family, a lie, an evasion, a theft clothed in words of hypocritical regret, a pitiless revenge, a cool determination to crush success. His life had been a busy one—"A man has to work if he would get on," was his motto—and the harvest of it was also a busy one. A thousand gibbering ghosts kept him well employed with accounts he was compelled to debit himself with. There was no escape. His unrepentant soul would not admit its sin, but though the chances were against him for the present, he would conquer them, and then the world should see what he would do.

Such was his rebellious determination when I saw him. His mask was off, and the rays of his religion had long been lost. He knew he was fighting against God, but would fight till he won.

It was the most fearful scene of retribution I had so far beheld, harrowing in its hopeless struggle to escape, while at the same time, raging with stubborn incontrition. But the keenest pang he suffered was the conviction that his punishment was seen and known alike to all the dead and living who passed by.

Ladas did not speak in explanation, but left me to read the story for myself and draw my own conclusions.

"Are you satisfied?" he asked presently. "If so we will go, that I may show you how we assist such souls when they repentantly seek for help."

We returned to the scene of his general labours, where we found several of his fellow-servants intently watching a wretched woman who had been overthrown in some ignoble conflict. She had fallen, struggling and moaning in her agony, her hands convulsively dragging at her hair and ears, as if she would tear them off in an effort to secure relief if only by a change in the nature of the anguish from which it was impossible to escape. Suddenly she leapt to her feet as if to dash into the fray again, but staggered back as though the vision of another retribution confronted her. She gripped her head between her hands, wavered, and then with a passionate cry burst into tears.

"My God! My God! Will this torment never cease?"

I had scarcely caught an indication of the exclamation before she was surrounded and uplifted by the angels who had been in waiting, among whom there were such tokens of joy as almost to obscure the anguish of the supplicant. In that action I saw and understood the anticipating promptitude which promises, 'before they call I will answer'; I saw for myself how the everlasting arms are continually underneath, needing but a repentant thought to make them spring up and carry the fallen into a citadel of salvation.

"It is ended, my sister; this useless part of your suffering is over now, if you will come away," replied one of the ministering host. "God is always more merciful to us than we are to ourselves. He has already heard your cry, and we were sent in answer to it even before it escaped you. Come, lean on us, and rest for a little while, then we will guide you where no more useless pain can reach you."

"I cannot rest here!" she cried. "Oh, if you have any pity, take me away from this unutterable agony!"

"Come, then, and we will place you in the way that leads to rest. How gladly would we carry you thither if that were possible, but it is only in holiness that perfect rest is found, and the sins of your past have so stained your life that you must needs be cleansed before you can bear the presence of the purity for which you ask. But God, in His unutterable love for you, has made a way by which you may reach it, and with His own hand He will lead you therein. Be not afraid. The worst is over now.

Whatever pain may be your future lot will be in purification and preparation for the rest you seek. God is not angry with you —He pities, loves, and desires to bring you to Himself. Even the punishment you have borne was designed to turn you back from your course of sin to shelter in His love, and what has yet to come will only be necessary to rectify the past. You remember the story

Christ told of the Prodigal Son—you will find that God is just the same in His action to yourself; He will meet you presently with a Father's welcome and a kiss, and will never allow you to go away from home again."

"Go on talking." she pleaded. "I will come anywhere with you if you will speak to me like that. You are kind! You do not hate me! I can trust myself with you. You would make me want to be good— that is, if I could be good! Go on talking, please. Yes, you may talk of God if you like, but do go on. If others had spoken to me as you can speak, I should have listened— should have learned to love God long ago!"

She spoke hysterically with long pauses due to exhaustion between her jerky sentences, but the storm that had so ruthlessly torn her was rapidly dying away, as the rescuing band carried her further and further from the scene of her bondage. It was not only the sympathetic words of the sister-spirit who spoke that contributed to this desirable effect, but the atmosphere of love and confidence by which the band surrounded her acted with continually increasing comfort, as they bore her into the more hopeful condition of her own hell.

"We will not follow them," said Ladas. "Her case would scarcely furnish you at present with a very clear idea of what the regime of hell really is."

Had the choice been left with me, I might have followed to learn more of the woman who had so aroused my interest and sympathy, but my guide was evidently pursuing a definite plan for my instruction, and reminding myself how impossible it is to follow anything to finalities where issues stretch into eternities, I accepted his suggestion and crossed the boundary between the two states in an opposite direction to that taken by the escort of the newly-liberated woman.

Our new route led us into a land of comparative darkness, dangers and pitfalls, noisome and full of fears, in which men and women wandered like frightened shadows anxious to be avoided even while they cried for help and pity.

We had scarcely affected the crossing before I heard a cry which sent a shiver of horror through me.

"Help! Help! I'm blind."

For answer, I heard an echo of laughter.

"What is that?" I inquired.

Ladas called my attention to a woman at a little distance.

"She desires to reach some place where she can feel safe, but that is impossible because she has no confidence even in herself."

"Why so?"

Ladas studied her carefully for an instant before replying.

"She is an example of the hell of moral cowardice. On earth she possessed wealth which was lavishly misused in the vain imagination that she was atoning thereby for neglect of womanly duties. She dreaded anything unpleasant, and having gold, thought she was warranted thereby in escaping from everything having the slightest approach to the disagreeable. For the sake of her donations, she was humoured in her harmless ideas, and assured that it was not necessary for her sensitive feelings to be tormented. God would accept of her service by deputy. Now you see her when the privilege of gold has been lost, in a region where pitfalls of class distinction and noble birth abound on every hand, and moral cowardice has developed into total blindness when the keenest of sight is required to escape a thousand real tortures born of her former ignoble and unworthy fears. We cannot help her. She deliberately designed her own hell, and must now occupy it until, having discharged the last farthing of the debt its erection incurred, she will receive her discharge in the restoration of sight and be able to find her way to the safety she desires."

After this, I beheld an agony I shall make no useless effort to describe. It was the reward meted out to one whose 'inhumanity to man' marks, probably, the low water-line of sin's depravity: Nero, the voluptuous and petulant matricide of Rome. Those who would attempt to gain an insight into this vision must not forget that in hell an inflexible and inexorable justice for every crime committed has to be separately met and discharged; also that the soul of the foulest criminal in the discarnating process is rendered as sensitive to suffering as that of the brightest saint is attuned to the harmony of joy. There is but one standard of feeling in the afterlife, and every soul is strung to its accurate concert pitch. Now, try to estimate the offences to be atoned for in this particular case, and if you can justly do so, make the calculation as to the balance that yet remains after what has hitherto been endured, and the present condition of the soul upon whom the lash of justice is yet falling.

Such, if ascertained, will give a faint idea of hell.

I had no wish to prolong my stay in the presence of such torture; every touch and exaction of which was but the just repayment of what its recipient had inflicted in cool blood and sarcastic ridicule. Nor did I care to push my inquiries further into the adaptation of hell to the variety of penalties it has to claim as the steward of Divine justice. I had seen enough. If only earth could see the vision before me, it would form a plea for righteousness of life and conduct such as mortal ears have never listened to.

"It seems almost incredible," I remarked to Ladas, "that a man can earn such a punishment in the few short years of one life."

"It is a striking declaration of the powers of a man for good or evil," he replied. "It is no part of my mission to disturb or intrude upon this wretched man, or I might have called your attention to the chart always hanging before his eyes whereon he may check and locate every individual pang he endures. He can see what he has already discharged as well as that he has yet to pay. There can be no dispute as to overcharge or injustice in any instance. His memory and conscience sit as assessors in the case, and they can accept no bribe, nor depart from righteousness in any award they may have to make."

"The helplessness of the condition seems to increase the horror of it, but it is some relief to see that he is neither bound nor shut in with prison doors."

"There is no need for these things," replied Ladas. "He is his own guarantee against escape."

"Do they never attempt it?"

"No! Hell is not a place of revolt, but resignation to justice, and every soul within its wide dominion has learned from experience that the love of God is as powerfully present here as in the highest Heaven. This recognition occasions, perhaps, one of the sharpest pangs of hell—remorse that one has so basely sinned against such unchanging affection, which still pities where one would look for well-merited revenge. Here sin is brought clearly home to the sinner as a wilful and deliberate act against what is known to be right, or an equally criminal refusal to protect the right, and the purpose and mission of hell is understood to be the best eternal love and wisdom can devise to effect a complete redemption from sin preparatory to the assumption of Divine sonship. The first stage of life has been woefully misunderstood, misdirected, misapplied; men, in their ignorance, have presumed to interpret eternal laws by the light of so-called human justice, which may be trifled with and is largely influenced by speech, caprice or other weaknesses of earth. Because God does not erect a tribunal in every marketplace and bring each offender forward to immediate and public chastisement, it is imagined that sin is only punished in theory and daring trespassers lift their heads high and race with breathless speed from sin to sin. In all this, men only add to their condemnation. They know and admit that natural laws are not subject to caprice! You cannot bribe a fire not to burn a child, nor hold it responsible for doing so on the ground of the child's ignorance. It is the nature of the fire to burn—it is also the nature of sin to punish. No man can play with either without paying the inseparable penalty. The inference drawn from delay in regard to the punishment of sin is equally fallacious, and in this again men become the most damaging witnesses against themselves. When a criminal is convicted on earth, humanity protests against the infliction of his punishment in public, and mercifully decrees that the same shall be carried out within the precincts of the house of correction. Hell is God's house of correction, modelled to rescue the perishing and lift up the fallen, and so true is it to model, that no soul yet passed its portal but would fully and freely make the admission 'I have sinned'."

"Not one?" I queried.

"No. Such a thing would be impossible. Let me call your attention to a forgotten or neglected gleam of light Christ threw upon this point in His parable of Dives in hell. The rich man was so conscious of the presence of love and sympathy as to believe the boon of cooling water would be granted him, and when he found the condition was beyond the pale of justice, his mind turned instantly to the salvation of his brethren."

"I never saw it in that light before."

"We have all much to see and understand before we fully know the true choral of the gospel Christ proclaimed," replied my companion.

"Is the system of isolation general?" I asked, my inquiry being prompted by the two instances I had seen.

"No. The method of treatment varies as widely as the sin to be atoned for."

"With such a perfect law in undisturbed operation, one almost wonders what remains for the Devil to do."

"What devil do you mean?" he inquired, with the deliberate and musical softness of voice he employed when most seriously emphatic.

"I mean the great arch-enemy of mankind."

"The archangel who fell from Heaven?" he suggested.

"Yes, Lucifer and all his host."

"Have you ever given one moment's thought to what the effect of such a disruption in Heaven would be, if it were true?"

"If it were true?" I gasped. "Why, of course it is true!"

"Why of course?" he asked.

"Because—well—it must be! We know it is."

"Say rather that you have been taught to believe it is. You cannot know, because it is not true! The story is an invention of priests as part of a justification for the existence of their cult. The whole fabric of priest-craft is built up of error and immortality. God's messages to earth are always conveyed through inspired lips of prophets, not symbolically represented by types, ceremonials, and ritualistic vestments. The sacrifices He ordains are passions subdued, selfish advantages forgone in favour of another, the tributes of filial love offered to Him through ministry to suffering. His chosen altar is that of pure devotion set up in humble hearts; His temple is a life consecrated to His service in humanity. Christ was a prophet and was crucified by the influence and hatred of the priests, a fact which ought for ever to have sealed the doom of the usurping cult for which He had no words but condemnation of, and towards which He always maintained an attitude of defiant opposition as being the product of hell—the symbolism of which is (as priest-craft rejoices in symbolism) error, misconception, and need of correction."

"But do you really mean me to understand that there is no Devil?"

"I do. I have never found such a being yet, and if he did exist, I should have met him many times in the course of my mission. But let me ask you to consider for a while what the existence of such an individual means, then you will quickly understand what an impossible, absurd and altogether inconceivable condition of things would be necessary to accommodate him."

"If this is true, all other revelations I have received sink into insignificance beside it."

"Leave that for a time. And going to the very beginning of the fabrication, consider for a moment how such a fall of angels, as he originated in, would destroy the possibility of Heaven."

"How so?"

"If his supposed rebellion ever did take place, Heaven would be more free from the presence of sin than earth. Where would be the perfection and assured holiness of it, since sin had once generated in the mind of one standing next to God? Such a fall would banish rest and confidence for evermore and without these, Heaven could not exist."

"It does seem so."

"Again," he resumed, "the supposition of the existence of such a personality is a blasphemy against God."

"How?"

"Because had such a fall taken place, it was not only foreknown to God, but also foreordained by Him, or He is not omniscient and omnipotent; while if He did ordain it and does possess these attributes, He would neither be holy nor true. Hence it is impossible for a Devil to exist and God remain. Righteousness forbids it; it is a contradiction in terms and irreconcilable."

"But the doubt arises whether the moral difficulty may not be solved at depths the mind of man has not power to fathom at present."

"Some problems are necessarily of such an order, and will require a flight of ages before we can grasp and understand them, but this is not such a one. It is a perfectly safe deduction to make that, what is opposed to reason and truth within the limits of human understanding, can never be reconciled to them on the outside. For instance, nothing will ever make two lines drawn at right angles run parallel, and this is exactly the figure represented in the coexistence of God and a Devil. As I say, the two are a contradiction in terms and impossible of reconciliation in the region of intelligence either now or hereafter. It is vastly different with an inquiry, for instance, into the nature and substance of God— assuming that He does possess substance— in which case we may confidently hope that the future holds such knowledge the present has no power to reveal. But this question of the existence of a Devil starts philosophically at right angles with every moral quality of God, and the further we pursue the inquiry, the more hopelessly does it become involved in contradictions. The only mystery about it is that intelligence can so long look upon the tradition as worthy of consideration."

"Of course, you are now speaking from the higher knowledge afforded by experience here."

"Even though I did speak from such a position, Christ has demonstrated the fact that our knowledge is available for those on the other side, but honest inquiry is all that is required for any man to explode such a proposition for himself. Priest-craft knows this only too well, and for purposes of self-preservation, forbids any inquiry unless accompanied by priestly interpretation. You and I, however, are beyond ecclesiastical jurisdiction, and since I like to root up error beyond all possibility of future trouble, let us look a little further into this question, of which we have as yet scarcely touched the fringe. According to the tradition, the object of Lucifer in stirring up his rebellion in Heaven was to secure more power than he already possessed. Milton says:

"'aspiring
To set himself in glory above his peers,
He trusted to have equalled the Most High,
If He opposed, and with ambitious aim
Against the throne and monarchy of God,
Raised impious war in Heaven, and battle proud
With vain attempt.'

The contradictions of this priestly fable now come fast and furious, and one can scarcely pick the semblance of a logical course through the labyrinth of absurdity. Did Lucifer make a vain attempt? Before his rebellion, he was an archangel wanting power equalling that of God. What did he lose in his failure? His place in Heaven, for which he was never fitted by reason of his inward impurity. What did he gain? A throne—if not the one he aspired to, it was still a throne—with one-third of the host of Heaven to obey his mandate; he gained liberty from service and rose to be Prince of the powers of the air, and God of the world, which by his revolt he wrested from the hand of its Creator. To secure the redemption of this world, God is supposed to consent to the murder of His own innocent Son by which all the previous follies, inconsistencies, immoralities and difficulties are sought to be rectified and put straight, but in what way this is to be accomplished, no one has ever been able to explain. Meanwhile the Devil goes on holding jurisdiction as though no atonement had been made, and by far the larger part of humanity falls to his share, and God is unable to avoid it. Surely I need say no more of such a false and immoral proposition; alike an insult to intelligence and a blasphemy against the love and wisdom of God."

"Then the whole system of theology has to be thrown aside, for without the Devil, it all goes to pieces."

"It is not the aspiration of seeking to know something of God we disclaim, but the worse than fruitless error of forming enslaving dogmas concerning Him upon speculative philosophies, and teaching these to the world as God's revelation concerning Himself, using the name of Christ as an authority for so doing. It is for this reason the ministry of earth has failed, and the declaration of the truth has reverted to ourselves. Neither house nor kingdom divided against itself can possibly stand, and God reigns alone in Heaven, in earth, in hell—always and ever the same all-mighty to save. To us and all through the created universe, there is but one God, and beside Him there is no other."

* * *

CHAPTER 10

NEARER TO THEE

"Come now apart with me and rest awhile!
Rest in my peace—I fain would have it so.
Pillow thy head upon my loving breast
Where none may come but host and favoured guest.
So come that we may love's deep fullness know.

Long have I sought thee, long have loved thee well.
Have known thee, though by thee I was unknown!
Come now apart, that I myself may show—
May speak with thee whom I have loved so
And win thy love, and make thee all my own.

Come, come with me and know divinest love;
Its joy, its bliss and rapture unexpressed;
Its height, length, breadth and depth—its heaven;
Its power o'er death; its peace for tempest-driven;
Its rest eternal! Come with me and rest!"

After my tour in company with Ladas I was very desirous to be alone. So far in my new life I had met with no one who had spoken to me so unreservedly of Christ, and also sought to base all he said upon the simple teaching of that great authority. He seemed to possess a mysterious power—by his manner and method of teaching—of reducing all I had previously seen and heard, into an orderly system in which it stood forth as a consistent scheme I had hitherto failed clearly to comprehend. I had never doubted that such a system did exist, but I had not so far grasped it until, under his guidance, all uncertainty vanished and I stood entranced before the revelation of divine law and order, which silenced and overpowered me with its majestic beauty.

I could now understand the necessity for this surprising silence about the Christ being so long maintained. Ladas did not leave the Master more than any of the others who had done so much for me. It was rather that the fallow ground within myself needed to be broken up and prepared to receive the seed he had sown with such forceful illustrations. All had been workers together to secure the result, each had faithfully performed his part, and the joy and reward of the harvest would be equally shared.

I was not presumptuous enough to imagine that I understood in detail all that Ladas had laid before me, but the perplexing and confusing mists had been so far dissolved as to allow me to trace a definite outline in God's purpose. That outline I now perceived swept and embraced the whole art of creation, and required the three estates, earth, hell, and Heaven, as in the solar spectrum; the three primary colours are blended in the softening gradations of the inter-sphering tones, all of which are necessary to produce the light of day. So that great spiritual spectrum began to blend—or I began to comprehend the blending—into the unity of the eternal day of the greater Fatherland. Both earth and hell were equally necessary to the plan as Heaven and the love of God was manifest alike in each.

The relationship they occupy now stood in legitimate perspective; Earth as an educational establishment in which man is intended to learn obedience to paternal control and receive training in the use and exercise of his divine potentialities; Hell, an equally necessary provision for the chastisement and correction of infraction of discipline and failure to make a suitable preparation to discharge the duties of the future; and Heaven; the Father's house and natural home of the soul, where we shall all gather after the educational course is over.

I have here changed the figure of hell slightly from that in which Ladas used it, but it is equally consistent; or if agreeable it could, with the same force, be considered as a hospital for sinsick souls; in neither case can a claim be set up to detention beyond the purpose for which the place has been established, and since the idea of death has been eliminated, the Father will see to it that the last of the lost ones shall be sought for, if occasion arises, "until He find it."

This is the destiny of the human race, because God is allmighty and will have all men to be saved," for "as in Adam all die, even so in Christ shall all be made alive again." The scope, provision and power of God's redemption is wide enough to rectify the work of sin, and it must do so, since there is none able to stand against Him.

We may not be able to explain the process, by which every tangle in life will be resolved, but God understands, and we may safely leave it there. The best man on earth can only see the fabric weaving from the underside; how can he see and understand the complex minglings in the wonderful design?

> *"God sits in the calm of eternal power*
> *To guide the loom of the life of man;*
> *He sees its warp and weft each hour*
> *Weaving some part of His infinite plan.*
>
> *He knows the use of its countless threads—*
> *Each costly tint in the rich design;*
> *And the shuttles are thrown with matchless skill*
> *For the hand of the Weaver is Divine."*

Don't be afraid; God is working His own design upon His own loom. All must be well!

This readjustment of the attitude of hell, how it sweeps confusion from the Pilgrim's path, allowing the scheme of salvation to stand forth in natural consistence with the eternal love of God, and opens vistas of more than hope to encourage those who are faithfully toiling in the vineyard. The heart grows strong and courageous under the inspiration of the strains of victory now, and we understand where the undeniable emphasis lies as we read anew the promise—"He that goeth forth and weepeth, bearing precious seed, shall doubtless come again with rejoicing, bringing his sheaves with him." How often in the other life did I hear it said—"He that stands alone with God, stands with the majority," but from the earth point of view, I could never see it. The true light had come at length, and the axiom was now as clear as noonday, for God is all in all and patiently works towards the end He saw and appointed from the beginning. Earth, death and hell—if we deliberately elect to journey homeward by the latter route—are each and all stages in the pilgrimage, in which there is but one terminus where the Father awaits us. As long as there is an absent prodigal, the paternal eye will be scanning the distant horizon, ready to go forth to meet the lad who remembers home and comes to ask if but for a servant's position.

That the elder brother may take offence will have no weight with the rejoicing parent. The lad who comes through hell and from the company of devils, if you will, is a son after all, and the tortures he has suffered will both discharge his debts and purify his soul.

As I thought of this the words of my poetess friend came back to me with more striking force than when I first heard them:

"Oh! 'tis not as men would teach us—
Just one step from earth to God;
Passing through the death-vale to Him
In the garb that earth we trod;
Called to praise him while aweary,

Or to sing while yet the voice
With earth's farewell sob is broken—
Could we fitly thus rejoice?
No! We wait to learn the music;
Wait to rest our weary feet;

*Wait to learn to sweep the harp-strings
Ere the Master we may meet.*

*Wait to tune our new-found voices
To the sweet seraphic song;
Wait to learn the time and measure,
But the time will not be long."*

Whichever way the mind turned in contemplation, the horizon lay away in the definite—evermore. Looking backward one could trace the patient, loving, protecting care of the Father in every step of the pilgrimage, not only to the mythical Eden, but away down the avenues of time, too vast for human estimate, until sight failed where it saw Him bending over the Moneron and covering with His omnipotence the helpless nucleus from which in coming aeons He would bring forth a family Divine. Then looking towards the future, even the stronger light lent by growing knowledge failed to bring the goal into sight. Who can measure such a distance? If the mind fails to say how long has been the pilgrimage from the Moneron to the Man, how is it possible to conceive the far greater distance which divides the man from God? And yet we have been seriously taught that when a dying thief came to the dividing line, between the two, he placed his hands thereon and vaulted over like an athlete taking a gate! How different is the truth from the traditions of men! To scale that stupendous precipice of light which rose before me neither hands nor feet would be of least avail, and I knew I had to wait until the uplifting powers of purity and holiness were strongly developed, the rudimentary forms of which were scarcely yet discernible.

*"Eternal Light! Eternal Light!
How pure the soul must be,
When placed within Thy searching sight,
It shrinks not, but with calm delight,
Can live and look on Thee.*

> *O! how shall I, whose native sphere*
> *Is dark—whose mind is dim,*
> *Before the Ineffable appear,*
> *And on my naked spirit bear*
> *That uncreated beam?"*

One stands with unshod feet beside the saintly Binney as he humbly makes this inquiry, and the consolation we receive in reply is, "God knows." That is sufficient. We may rest in that. He is the author and finisher of the course. He planned the whole, marking its times and seasons, according to His perfect knowledge and wisdom. His time is best. It is for us to be careful not to delay. It is for Him to lead us by the way He knows so well. Ages are but as pulse throbs where the day is an eternal one. The infinite cannot change. There can be no late arrivals where time does not exist. The soul that keeps step with the love-march will move forward in the atmosphere of Heaven, its cup of joy overflowing all along the way. What more can it desire? As we grow the joy will increase, but we can never be more than full, and if we are so abundantly supplied by the way, is it not an added happiness to think that the end is yet so distant and unseen?

And then to think that in all creation, past, present and future, there is not one single soul outside the scope and operation of this design. He will "leave the ninety and nine in the wilderness and go after that which is lost, until He find it." Do you grasp this? Ye who could not agree with me when I said earthly relationship did not exist in Paradise, do you not see how much grander, nobler and wider is the law of God? Not only your brother, father, husband, wife, son and daughter are brought in, but every brother, father, husband, wife, son and daughter must come with them that God may be all in all. That is what we shall find Heaven to be when we reach it. Is it not like what a Father-God would do?

How all this contrasts with the man-made idea of Heaven and hell, with the latter holding the larger half of humanity, and the denizens of the former looking over the battlements and deriving an increase of joy from watching the torments of the lost!

But enough of this. The mind turns with loathing and disgust from such a contemplation. No wonder the expounders of such inhumanity find their pews empty and intelligence turning from church to nature's inspiration.

In this reverie, I would let the Master have the last word. 'Take My yoke upon you, and learn of Me; for I am meek and lowly in heart; and ye shall find rest unto your souls.' Rest! Ah, how we all need it! It is found only while yoked together with Christ. A priestly yoke, however gorgeous, will be irksome and wearying. It allows no feeding in green pastures, no refreshment beside still waters, but in the ecclesiastical vehicle to which you are harnessed, is carried the authorized provender supplied by church fathers long centuries ago and supposed to satisfy every demand until all men have crossed the Jordan. But the yoke of Christ is easy and His burden light, because He trusts in God and prays, 'Give us this day our daily bread,' and will do the same to-morrow and every day. 'Sufficient unto the day is the evil thereof' is His rule of life, and the daily need for food keeps Him close to the Father, upon whom he is dependent for supplies. Fresh food for growing souls is His constant care. 'Man does not live by (wheaten) bread alone, but by every word that proceedeth out of the mouth of God,' and Christ would have us eat such food warm with inspiration, not break our spiritual teeth trying to masticate the fossil bread baked by ecumenical councils. Christ was a prophet, not a priest, and the wells of salvation from which He draws the waters of daily refreshment never run dry, but, like God, who sank them, are 'the same yesterday, to-day, and forever.' 'Stoop down and drink and live.'

'Come ye apart with Me and rest awhile.' For God so loved the world—

"So loved! So loved! I can say no more!
Its music-yacht drifted close by me,
I was dream-enwrapped as I stepped aboard
And the 'Peace of God' put out to sea
With the flowing tide in a holy calm
Each wavelet kissing us on and on,
As I leaned my head on the Master's breast
So loved! Enough! He and I were one."

* * *

CHAPTER 11

A LESSON IN CREATION

Let me hope the foregoing experiences with the lessons I have attempted to draw therefrom will show that I have anything but a loose conception of sin and its consequences.

Turning now to other scenes, I would here relate an incident serving to show how Paradise is adapted to undertake, where necessity arises, the whole of the educational work connected with a soul which earth is supposed to perform.

I have more than a passing pleasure in doing this, because I am sure that a glance at the great work of educating children on our side will be of genuine interest to my readers; and second because I would combat an erroneous idea gaining ground in the minds of some that an almost endless series of re-births on earth is demanded to explain 'some of life's most puzzling problems.'

It will be altogether impossible to deal exhaustively with the question of reincarnation at this time, but let me briefly say that it is a subject for which in my earth life, I felt much sympathy and have made wide inquiries concerning it since crossing the boundary, with this result: among the souls who are still subjected to earth conditions—from whom all experiences have to be received with caution, and not acted upon until they are confirmed from more reliable sources—there are many who honestly think reincarnation to be a fact, and teach it to be so; among those who have passed away from these conditions and learned to accept truth for its own sake, who know and study, tracing origins and sequences, many of them through unsuspected ages beyond the rise of history, I have been unable to meet with one holding the theory of rebirth to be true. The origin of the idea is to be found in savage superstition. Without a definite knowledge of immortality and equally certain that there is more in man than simply body, it has always been a problem to the untutored mind as to what happens when the body ceases to breathe and begins to grow offensive from decomposition. The philosophy of ignorance is always expeditious, and the savage solved the problem by allowing a newborn child to inhale the breath of a dying man, and the departing life was thus provided with another body, in which to continue its existence. From this crude beginning, the idea of transmigration of souls has been worked over and over in various ways with much philosophical reasoning and speculation, but it stands still where we found it—a baseless superstition, alike at variance with the law, love and purpose of God.

I am not at all unconscious of the fascination of the subject, and would, for this reason, willingly continue the discussion of it were it reasonably within the scope of my present purpose. But it not being so, I must resist the temptation for the present, with the hope that I may return to it at some future time. I might, however, here call attention to the unstudied side-light which is necessarily thrown upon the question by the record of my general experiences, the which I think will show, with some degree of reasonable clearness, that God has made provision to meet every just requirement that can possibly arise by far more expeditious and less cumbrous means than such a circuitous and hypothetical system.

It must always be borne in mind that all the requirements of God from men are based upon justice. To expect perfection to be produced by imperfect conditions would be to expect the impossible; hence the attainment to Nirvana in the flesh would be a condition as unrealizable as stepping in the mortal body from earth on to the surface of the sun. Let us begin to be reasonable and appreciate the fact that evolution from the human to the Divine must proceed in the future according to the law which has governed the past. We have still to climb from step to step, and as we go, must perforce be continually dropping the lower until by imperceptible gradations we ascend to the goal. In this process

Chapter 11 — A Lesson in Creation

it must needs be that this corruptible must put on in corruption, and this 'mortal must put on immortality' before we reach the zenith and the eye bear the sight of that uncreated beam. From this handicapping limitation of the flesh, the incarnated soul cannot free itself. It is a house of bondage from the influence of which one can only be free by breaking away, and ten thousand births would furnish no increase of advantage, especially where the memory of all that has gone before is not available for guidance.

Like all man-made systems, the speculation of re-birth is a weariness and confusion to the mind, without a place of rest in its ceaseless struggle to escape a spiritual Scylla on the one hand and Charybdis on the other.

God has provided a better way than this, to one phase of which I would now invite your attention.

There was a world of meaning, of promise, of hope, in that command of Christ to His disciples after the five thousand had eaten and were filled from 'five barley loaves and two small fishes.' 'Gather up the fragments that remain, that nothing be lost.' This is the eternal principle working through all creation. Men have now learned, as a scientific fact, that only the form of existence can be changed; nothing can be destroyed. If this is so in the material, which is the instrument, how much more must it be so in the spiritual, which is the operative agent working through the material!

With this principle still working through the life of Paradise, the same watchful care over the fragments is manifested. Nothing must be lost. In the smallest of all particles is hidden divine potentialities. Gather these up, for each must be sent to its own place to be tended, developed and assisted to fulfil its appointed sphere.

It is to one of the nursery-homes of these spiritual fragments I would now conduct you, where we may watch and learn to understand how Paradise deals with the first unfoldment of mind and intellect. I use the term 'spiritual fragments' advisedly in this connection, since we shall meet, not only with souls who passed away in the process of nativity, but others who in the halftime of gestation were able to make no more than one feeble independent movement and then expire. Surely these are fragments of humanity truly, yet they survive, and are carefully assisted forward into a full and strong maturity.

So beautifully and considerably does the sphere of the spiritual overlap the physical that most adequate provision is made to reach and protect all such little ones, of whom earth never takes cognizance. Unknown, with an existence unsuspected, still they live. Nothing must be lost. God's plans are laid for saving even to the uttermost, and the nursery-home over which our now well-known friend Cushna presides is one of the numerous establishments appointed for such work in connection with children.

There is ample accommodation here—and when I say ample I do not mean simply that each child is allowed so many cubic feet of breathing room by measurement, but I refer to the generous overflowing provision so characteristic of all God does—for about two thousand souls ranging from the boundary-stranded infant I have referred to, to those who may have known an earth existence of several months, the limit being determined not so much by age, as other circumstances we need not here discuss. They are drawn from every nationality of earth and brought up together, one of the very first efforts being to prevent any approach to racial differences and establish the unity of the human family. When the preliminary course has furnished ability to proceed, the child goes forward from strength to strength through the advancing and ascending schools of eternity.

Longfellow struck a chord of true spiritual music when he sang of one who had passed into the courts of Paradise:

> *"Not as a child shall we again behold her;*
> *But when, with rapture wild,*

Chapter 11 — A Lesson in Creation

> *We to our hearts again enfold her*
> *She will not be a child."*

Childhood and youth are imperfections, and no more represent true manhood and womanhood than daybreak is synonymous with noon. Heaven, when we reach it, will be found to be a perfect home for a perfect people, and all must attain the qualification to receive admission. Paradise will consummate in this respect what earth has no power to achieve. It is the legitimate function for which God has called it into existence. Childhood has to be carried forward to the full beauty of manhood and womanhood, and age brought back to the strength and vigour it has lost. Cushna, himself, is a striking illustration of this latter effect. I have already spoken of it, but the fascination it exerts seems to increase every time I come in contact with the benevolent Egyptian, upon whose shoulders rests the mystic mantle of evasive age so indescribably and beautifully blending with the exuberant sprightliness of early manhood. The consciousness of this, it will be remembered, was the first impression I received when I met him at the Home of Rest, but the fullness of it was more forcibly brought home to me when I found him so actively engaged in the education of children in this scene of more than fairy enchantment, which I was assured was the better place for learning to know him as he is.

I know not whether the man had produced the home or the home the man, but whichever it may be, the two are certainly related to each other as heat to fire, or light to the sun. The place was unmistakably designed for the encouragement of life's first unfoldments, but in the arrangement of it had not aeons of antiquity been laid under heavy contribution, and their wisdom tempered, softened, mellowed into an adaptability youth had no strength to furnish? Methods of treatment had been skilfully drawn from the best vintages of experience; adaptations had been critically made with a view to naturally meeting every possible requirement. Strength with growth, intrinsic character with interest, sweetness of disposition with progressive determination, humility with competence, love with power, and reverence with success. All these had to be accomplished, and were adequately provided for, together with a systematic but careful extraction of every hereditary proneness to the ignoble and impure. The correction of these latter tendencies is one of the chief features to which special and ever watchful care has to be directed.

The home comprises a surprising number of palatial buildings, each of which is placed at a good distance from its neighbour and located in a retreat perfectly adapted to the particular use of its department. Among them I saw the Nursery where pre-natal children are specially cared for; dormitories—all young children requiring a certain amount of sleep—a gymnasium, museum, theatre, laboratory and other places answering to every possible demand which may arise. But the most striking adaptations were to be found in the open air, where a system of landscape gardening had been adopted, which I can only describe as the interrogative. Everything, everywhere, appeared to be designed to prompt questions, and so effectively was this carried out that I fell into the trap myself, and was asking for information at every turn of my head.

The existence of such institutions in Paradise equipped with every possible educational appliance beyond the powers of an earthly mind to understand, will be regarded by many— especially such as have been taught to think that an instant after death the soul of an infant explosively acquires all knowledge— as miserably materialistic and blasphemously untrue. I should pass such conclusion of superstitious ignorance in the silence it merits, were it not for the obstacle it throws in the path of honest inquirers, who refuse to pass any objection unnoticed.

If we try to grasp intelligently an idea of what it is, we are aspiring to perfection and nearness to God—and the almost infinite distance by which our present imperfections separate us from that goal, then cast our eyes backwards to measure the comparatively short way we have as yet travelled on the journey since the pilgrimage of evolution first began; I think there will be little difficulty in recognizing that these preparatory stages of Paradise are an absolutely necessary provision if we are to succeed. Commercial and diplomatic positions on earth are safeguarded by interim examinations and qualifications tested by service and fidelity. Is it to be thought credible that while men make such exactions in temporal matters God will be less careful in respect to the eternal? The approbation of Christ— "Well done"— is the reward bestowed at the end of loyal, faithful and honourable service, when the tried and trusted steward hands in his audited accounts. For this service, earth under most advantageous circumstances can do no more than pass us through a preliminary examination with honours. The intermediate, advanced and final stages remain for Paradise to prepare us for. If this is found to be so under the most favourable conditions of long life and easy circumstances, how much more will such corrective assistance be needed for the unfortunate, and those whose lives are cut short in infancy, since innocence is not righteousness, nor is non-intelligence holiness. Hence the raison d'être for the homes I am speaking of.

How I regret my inability to paint, either in language or colours, the scene as it first presented itself to my astonished eyes! But if I could find the language, earth would misinterpret the meaning; if I could procure the colours, my critics would say they were unreal, unnatural, and the result a miserable attempt to introduce an impossible novelty into the Arabian Nights' Entertainment. I had better not attempt it, but leave such detail of my experiences until you, my gentle reader, are able for yourself to see it as it is, with eyes adapted to a wider view, and your powers of vision able to clearly trace a longer spectrum.

Still one may legitimately exclaim, "Happy children to be thus cared for and protected! Glorious gospel abounding in such provision! Overflowing compensation for all that has been sacrificed on earth!" Where is the man or woman who would not envy them? But hush; stand still, or we shall trespass here. No man or child liveth or dieth to himself. "Our times are in His hand"; and it is better so. For the present, it may be you see through a glass darkly, but presently you too will understand; then you will find God's leading was right, after all. Great as is the compensation of the child, you may—if you will, by doing your duty nobly—find an even greater reward awaiting yourselves.

> *"Let us be patient; earth's severe afflictions*
> *Not from the ground arise,*
> *But oftentimes celestial benedictions*
> *Assume a dark disguise."*

I have no intention of making a tour of the departments of this institution. The chief features of life and its activities here are not to be found indoors, and Cushna's home is no exception to the general rule.

I would repeat that the first object of every such institution is to foster inquiry in the minds of the children. No instruction is forced upon an unwilling or unready child, but ingenious devices are employed to arrest attention and prompt a question as to the nature or utility of the thousand objects most temptingly located in every part of the fairylike domain. The principle here observed is acted upon in every stage of the life beyond;— When interest is sufficiently aroused to prompt inquiry, the mind is in a favourable condition to receive instruction, and ministers are always at hand to suitably impart it.

Cushna very kindly invited me to join one of the many groups of children who were so pleasantly and enjoyably studying first essons in the school of Paradise, that I might become acquainted with the system of education he has adopted.

A moment later, without attracting more than the slightest attention from the thoughtfully interested children, we had taken our place near a group of some twenty students who were listening to a lady explaining the nature and beauty of a blade of grass, which by its attractive form and colour, had aroused the curiosity of one of the little ones.

From the commencement of her lecture the speaker carried myself, as well as her Lilliputian audience, into a romantic fairyland of botany in her description of the life, habits and antecedents of her subject. Then, by an apparently magical process I was altogether unprepared for, she held within her hands a variety of other grasses from which she drew comparison and contrasts; the coarsest and meanest of which she called attention to as a representative specimen of grasses to be found on earth; the others were from different stages of the higher life. Every inquiry from the children was answered by a simple and forcible parable setting forth the truth she wished to fix upon the memory, and she lingered with almost too leisurely patience that her lesson might be clearly comprehended.

When all this was over, I was further astonished to hear her announce that, if there were no more questions as to that part of the lesson, she would proceed to the practical consideration of it.

Then followed a perfectly entrancing discourse upon the chemistry of that blade of grass and the process by which the constituents of the atmosphere are selected, attracted and utilized to produce the blade in the natural course. Nature was set forth as being a most beautiful, but invisible, machine designed by God to prepare all that was necessary for the protection and sustenance of man, until such time as he should be able to understand how to use the great available forces in producing all the requirements by a much better and quicker process. This led to a beautiful description of the difference between a man and other agencies of creation by setting forth the nature and potentialities of the soul, which possesses latent powers to accomplish all that nature achieves, by a more expeditious process under conditions she set forth and enforced by many illustrations.

It seems almost incredible that such infant minds could be interested in subjects so profound. But God has His own methods by means of which He can reveal unto babes, mysteries He withholds from the wise and prudent, and in the experience before me, I was watching the process by which this seeming impossibility was actually, but gradually, accomplished. In these homes of the children, we are brought very near to the purity of God, accommodated to the minds over which it broods, and passes across thresholds where the shadow of sin has never fallen. Sown in this virgin soil of innocence, how can we, who have been contaminated with pollution of sin, estimate the power and possibilities of omnipotent love?

But to return to the lesson.

After the explanation came the demonstration. The teacher laid the grasses aside and bidding the children watch her empty and extended hand, we saw, with equal interest and surprise, a blade of grass, the exact counterpart of the one upon which her discourse had been based, slowly form before our eyes. When the experiment was complete the original was laid side by side with the created specimen for our careful examination, when the one was found to be equally perfect with the other.

The session was not yet over. It was now the duty of each child to make what effort it could to duplicate that of its tutor, and this, to me, was not the least interesting part of the experience. One by one they were called in turn to the side of their instructor, who encouraged and exclaimed as necessary, then watched the result of those first attempts at creation. Many were total failures, others produced something—enough to astonish and encourage further efforts, and one made a very creditable success as to form, but in colour and detail much was left to be desired.

Congratulations and commendations now followed, causes of failure were pointed out as only to be expected, certainty of speedy success was generously promised, and the teacher went on to explain that perfection is only to be reached by study and the acquisition of knowledge, and the lesson ended by an arrangement to carry the subject farther on the next occasion, at the prospect of which the children were highly delighted, and I almost wished I could continue my studies with them through the whole course which had just opened so happily.

Such is a very meagre glimpse at one of the homes for children in Paradise. Happy homes and happy those who are received therein.

* * *

CHAPTER 12

CUSHNA AT HOME

That school session ended when I would gladly have had it go on. But so it is with all we meet in Paradise. Satiety is unknown. Intellectual banquets come to an end while the appetite is yet vigorous, that digestion may not be overburdened and the ennui consequent upon excess is avoided. Where, however, the dishes are prepared with the adaptive consideration and forethought of that which I had just eaten, no thought of organic disturbance can possibly be anticipated. Where the deep mysteries of chemistry nature and even creation could be so temptingly and digestibly dished up for infant minds, what need to fear for after effects? Such viands so prepared only serve to appetize the mind and make it hunger with more vigorous zest for that which is to come.

But nothing must be lost. Perfect assimilation stands janitor to vigorous health, and here we meet with tutor, nurse and well skilled physician working harmoniously together in one to produce the highest result. From the accommodated tension of the lesson, the children are as thoughtfully released to play some game, relaxing the mind for the present, but by and by, throwing an unexpected revelation upon their study when the teacher is joyously called to explain and interpret. So by study, play and exercise, or whatever for the moment may attract and claim the attention of the mind, each incident and feature in that unfolding life is made to contribute something towards the end to be attained by making the child,

"Beautiful with all the soul's expansion."

Cushna and I passed on; he desirous of showing me more

of the resources and appointments of his marvellous and enchanting home, and I, shut out from participating in the children's game, glad to avail myself of the pleasure of being alone with him once again.

I will make no attempt to hint at the many other features of study to which I was introduced in that memorable visit; it would only be to lay myself open to an inquiry from my critics as to why I do not definitely set forth some one of the scientific acquirements to which earth has not yet attained, and so demonstrate that this record is more than a tour de force of the imagination.

Suppose I did anticipate this request and clearly set forth one of these advance lessons in science with all necessary precision and detail; would it accomplish the end intimated? Not by any means. It might secure the admission that the theory advanced was an interesting one and worthy of following up to see what was really in it, but my critic would change his ground, find some other point of unbelief, and be as far from conviction as ever. Conviction of truth is not reached by such a method. I will therefore content myself with setting out the reasons why I do not make this attempt, as perhaps by a negative explanation, I may be able to accomplish more real good than by taking a fruitlessly opposite direction.

First, then, my present purpose is to recount selections from my own experiences in Paradise, and in doing so, I have already many times had occasion to refer to facts I could not for the moment understand. Just here I recall an incident in the early education of children, where the subject under consideration was, at the time I observed it, as novel to myself as to the youngest child in the company. From such data is it to be expected that I should explain and set forth the whole science of creation? My real point is this—Paradise recognizes that every child it receives possesses divine potentialities—is of divine heritage—and has to be educated suitably to its position. This commences with a preparatory course, and the lesson I had taken part in was the first in its own series. It was principally so with others. Hence I simply record, knowing too well what misconceptions have arisen from earth-conditioned souls speaking of things they so imperfectly understand, for me to court the danger of treading in the same paths. I would far rather refer you to the example of the Christ, which I am quite content to follow. When He blessed and brake and multiplied the barley loaves and fishes, He exercised the same power in the same way as Cushna's assistant in reproducing the blade of grass. Her encouraging promise of success to her pupils was also warranted by Christ's promise to His followers, "He that believeth on Me, the works that I do shall he do also; and greater works than these shall he do, because I go to my Father." Still he never explained, nor instructed His disciples in the process by which His miracles were performed. Why? Let Him reply. "I have yet many things to say unto you, but ye cannot bear them now. Howbeit when He, the Spirit of truth, is come, He will guide you into all truth."

Secondly, though I have been present and witnessed many scientific demonstrations beyond the practice or knowledge of earth—such, for instance, as the results produced by Siamedes as described in "The Magnetic Chorale." and many others in addition to the lesson I have just referred to—I am not sufficiently egotistical to call myself a scientist, nor foolish enough to seat myself in a chair I could not reasonably fill. I am not the spirit promised to lead you into all truth, nor do I wish you to think of me as in any sense approaching the Christ who left so much unsaid; I am simply another forerunner commissioned to cry and announce the approach, yea, even the presence of the Angels of God who have been "sent forth to minister to those who shall be heirs to salvation." I leave the demonstration of science to the host of such ministers who are available and qualified to teach it far better than I can do; philosophy to the philosophers, music to musicians and poetry to poets. For myself I have to cry "Behold!" and offer such encouragement and evidences as may reasonably attract attention.

Thirdly, all channels of communication are limited by purpose and capacity. It might be possible under exceptional circumstances to use the same conduit for water, gas and electricity, but it is by no means advisable to do so. Every surgeon has most confidence in his own instruments. If the music is to be perfect, Kubelik must play upon his own violin, Harper upon his own trumpet, and Paderewski upon his own piano. How much more is it necessary that the instrument of intercommunion between the two worlds shall be set apart and delicately attuned to the special music it will be required to play! The great need of those in the beyond is for instruments worthy and willing to be used in the mission; high, noble, selfsacrificing souls who understand the nature and responsibilities of the work, realize that only purity and holiness within will attract corresponding agencies from without, always bearing in mind that the nearer the angel messenger who uses the instrument stands to God, the greater will be the strain his presence will put upon the organism he employs. It is a high calling to be so used, and the man or woman who enters upon it must do so prepared to become "a living sacrifice well-pleasing unto God." Such instruments are scarce, but when they are found, those into whose care they are entrusted know well their value, and will not allow them to be wrongfully or hurtfully handled. In Myhanene's mission I am allowed the necessary use of his mouthpiece, through which I can do no more than assure my readers that multitudes of souls are waiting to lay the truths and treasures of Paradise at the feet of earth if consistently and honestly sought for, and suitable instruments can be placed at their disposal.

Let me specially emphasize this last thought as to the care shown in the quality of the instrument you offer for our use. Wireless telegraphy has demonstrated the necessity for transmitter and receiver to be fully sympathetic for success. The same law applies between the two worlds, and the reliability of all messages will depend upon the spiritual quality of the receiver.

Chapter 12 — Cushna at Home

There may arise extraordinary occasions when God, for purposes of His own, would speak through the doubtful lips of a Balaam, but if a rule is built up upon such rare emergencies, woe betide those who follow the misleading counsel. Steamships cannot plough through etheric waves from star to star; the microscope can never be substituted for the telescope with advantage, nor can the pen perform the labour of the sculptor's chisel. Each must be qualified for its use and purpose. So must the instrument of truth be constantly clean within and without or God can never effectively use it.

So much by way of answer to the inquiry I have anticipated.

Cushna conducted me from group to group and scene to scene that I might see the general arrangements for impregnating the mind with information. The very atmosphere of the place created an almost insatiable thirst for knowledge; its natural features were musical notes of interrogation, and every response was a pleasure seductively wooing to further inquiry. It was an educational establishment founded in fairyland, with teachers skilled in the use of magic so potent that every effect remained as a reward for the pleasure its performance had created.

All the charm, however, did not lie in the place. I became more and more conscious of this as we moved about. She who told me that I could not know the real Cushna until I knew him at home, spoke truly. To detach the man from the abode was to lose fully half the beauty of either; it was like stripping the sunset of its colour, or music of its harmony. I was highly favoured in knowing him, but infinitely more so in knowing him at home. Here again the limitation of language fails to serve my desire, and I have to leave my crude outline sketch of both with the hope that all who read may come to know the two in combination; then I am assured of their commendation for declining any further attempt to fill in my rough suggestion.

His urbanity inveigles one into the closest confidence, and the soft mischievousness of his eyes captures all who come into his company. He is a great-grandfatherly boy and it is little wonder that everyone loves him.

"Do you know what I think is the prettiest feature of your home?" I inquired of him presently.

"As a son of the land of the Sphinx, I think it is my place to propound the riddle," he replied.

"Allow me to change the order for once, if it is only to test your skill at your own game."

"But you forget that I have power to read your answer by a glance. I will not take advantage of you, however, and play the game as a good Egyptian should, by giving it up."

"Then I don't think anything pleases me so much as to see the children of all nationalities living together so pleasantly."

"How otherwise did you expect to see them?"

"I had never given a thought of it until I saw it was so. It is different in my home."

"Yes. Nationalities are divided in the first three stages above the earth conditions, beyond that they blend, having learned to forget their racial and religious prejudices. Children are brought together at once to prevent any such feelings arising, and from the harmony of colours in nature, we teach the beauty of the diversity in men. Many complexions, but one family; many minds, but one home; many ideas, but one Father."

"O wise and inscrutable Cushna!"

"Not that," he promptly corrected me. "That lesson did not have its origin with me or any other man—it is God's alone."

I read more than one caution in that soft reply.

"I suppose you find a wide difference in the mental capacity of the children?"

"Yes, there is a wide difference, but it is rather individual than racial, especially in the younger ones."

"It must be intensely interesting to watch their development."

"Only those engaged in the work can form the least conception how really interesting it is."

Chapter 12 — Cushna at Home

"I suppose you meet with marked tribal traits of character?"

"With those who have lived longer, it is so to some extent, but in the case of pre-natal children this is very rarely noticed, because our counteractive training eradicates the tendency before it is able to show itself."

"And which of all the nations, according to your experience, shows to best advantage?"

"Are you working round to another riddle?" he inquired with a mischievous smile which indicated more than his words.

"No. I am simply asking for information."

"And suppose I was to reply Egypt, or India, or New Guinea, or Germany, or Turkey; what would you think?"

"I scarcely understand you."

"Did you not wish me to say England?"

"I am not conscious of it."

"Dig down a little, Aphraar. The stream of national prejudice runs deep occasionally, and takes some time after reaching Paradise to dry up effectively. In my home, however, we only receive children of one cosmopolitan family, so we have no opportunity to study national characteristics.

"And they are happy in being cared for by such a wise foster-father."

"Do you think so? But then they are good children; and every one a favourite."

"How long do they remain with you?"

"That entirely depends upon circumstances. In rare instances the taint of heredity demands an early isolation for more strict and guarded treatment. Otherwise they remain until their interest is aroused in some particular form of study, to follow which they are passed forward."

"In to schools of higher grades?" I inquired.

"No, the stimulating and favourable environment, together with our system of education, tends to rapid development of intellect and stature, which are synonymous in children. When, therefore, they leave us, the law of attraction is in full operation, and each goes to its own place, receiving all further necessary assistance in accordance with the one great law."

"Then the interest developed here determines the succeeding path of duty?"

"Always."

"I should like to question you further on that point in reference to myself; but will you first tell me more of those who suffer from hereditary taints—are they punished?"

"Certainly not! Justice does not punish one for the sin of another. The taint has been transmitted from the diseased soul of an ancestor, and in such a case, the child is a victim to be compensated, rather than punished, for the injustice it has sustained. Do you not remember that 'the sins of the fathers may be visited upon the children (even) to the third and fourth generation,' but they remain the sins of the father still, and he will have to requite justice for the consequences of them. The child is isolated for greater care and to prevent contagion."

"Now I wish to put a question relating to a belief which is supposed to have originated in Egypt."

"You mean that of the transmigration of the soul."

"Yes, it naturally arises out of this question of heredity."

"I will hear your question, but before doing so, I must protest against the error that such a doctrine had its origin or any formal sanction in orthodox Egyptian religion. A few men may, and no doubt did, hold the opinion in a limited form, but as it was afterwards known and taught in India and Greece, our priests did not know it, our religion was opposed to it, our ritual did not contain its teaching, and it is as erroneous to say the empire recognized it as to assert that England offers human sacrifices because such practices were common to the Druids."

"Then you do not regard these hereditary taints in your children as the result of previous existences?"

"How can they be so when there has been no previous

personal existence? The method of creation is not one of trying and repeating experiments until God attains success; He is perfect, and His first effort envelops the potentiality of success. The seed of a tree contains the germs of a thousand generations in the image of itself, if the necessary conditions of nature are obeyed to unfold and bring them forth. So with the man, the soul-germ of an equally long succession is climbing up the slopes of evolution towards personality, to follow after the generations who have crossed into Paradise before them. All that has been, is, and will be was thus carefully planned, designed, and divinely concealed within the primal germ God sent forth to execute His will when He commanded, 'Let cosmos be!' He speaks and it is done. He never speculates or experiments."

"I thank you for the simple but pregnant illustration. I am anxious to reach the truth, and could not resist the opportunity to learn your opinion. Now shall we return to the thought that interest in a subject here determines action?"

"Yes, if I can help you by doing so."

"You already know how interested I am in the idea of returning to earth?"

"Yes, and in that I long ago read your commission to take part in Myhanene's mission, as soon as you are prepared for it."

"But why did you not tell me?" I inquired.

"It was not time to do so then, but I did the best thing to help it forward by showing you how easy it is to accomplish such an object when desirable links are formed."

"And in doing so you greatly strengthened my desire. But I never hoped my wish would be granted until Ladas hinted at it when visiting the scenes of his labours. May I really take a share in that work, Cushna?"

"Certainly you may, but be careful to be well equipped before you begin. That ministry has more responsibilities attaching to it than you may conceive."

"Ladas has done much to make me acquainted with many of

them. I have been with him to earth and seen what is done by earth-conditioned souls in their communication. I have, under his guidance, watched most, if not all, the points you have previously spoken of, and then travelled with him to see the punishments of those to whom he ministers."

"All this will be most helpful and instructive, but let me seriously advise you to take every advantage to increase your stock of information. Whenever opportunity affords, cross the mists with one or other of Myhanene's band, and make good acquaintance with him who has been chosen as our mouthpiece. But let me adjure you not to attempt to speak without permission, and when this is given, do not attempt to say all you know, but mind that you do know all you say. The floods of error are already deep enough on the other side, and you had far better keep silence than add to them, for the old law still maintains, 'Whatsoever a man soweth that shall he reap.'"

"Do you wish to dissuade me from my purpose, Cushna?"

"No. My object is to caution and protect you. You have chosen well; if you are careful to rise to your opportunities, your reward must be a great one. But see, a message awaits you," and he pointed to a thoughtflash hovering over my head.

"Vaone is calling me," I answered, and with a goodwill we parted.

* * *

CHAPTER 13

"CAN THIS BE DEATH?"

Those telepathic bells of Paradise are not only a useful, but also a very necessary institution. The absorbing interests of the life are so numerous and fascinating, opening from one to the other in ever increasing succession, that once launched on an inquiry, it is doubtful when one would return—whether he would ever return—without some summons reminding him that loved ones are awaiting his coming.

How little Stennett knew of the blessedness of the life when he sang:

> *"O the transporting, rapturous scene*
> *That rises to my sight!*
> *Sweet fields arrayed in living green*
> *And rivers of delight.*
> *All o'er those wide extended plains*
> *Shines one eternal day;*
> *There God, the Sun, for ever reigns*
> *And scatters night away."*

I wonder what kind of hymns Watts and Wesley would have written for the church to sing if they had seen what my eyes have beheld and their ears had heard what I have heard before they commenced their labours.

I almost think I shall ask Eilele sometime to write one or two new ones, and either transmit them herself or allow me to do so, when I begin to speak to earth.

But I did not begin this chapter to anticipate what I should do in my new sphere of labours. I was talking of the bells of Paradise recalling us from protracted excursions, or should I rather say enabling us to remain in constant touch with home wherever our interests and studies may carry us.

The record of one such recall will bring me back to an incident from which I have necessarily wandered in my desire rather to follow consecutiveness of thought than action.

"Did you hear me call?" asked Vaone as she greeted my return.

"Yes, I heard, and think it is well you did so. If you do not look after me I shall surely be tempted into leaving you altogether."

"Wherein lies the danger?" she inquired with smiling confidence as she clasped her arms around my neck, laid her head upon my bosom, and turned her love-lit eyes full upon me.

"You may smile, but I tell you the danger is real—far more so than you appear to imagine."

She gently shook her head and pressed it a little closer before replying—

"You have already forgotten something, my Aphraar. At least, I think you have."

"What is it, dear?"

"That dangers are impossible here. But what or who is it that tempts you away?"

"The ever-increasing and engrossing interests I am everywhere discovering."

"I know what you mean," she answered reflectively. "It exerts a similar fascination over everyone. The comparison is crude and ridiculous, I know, but it constantly recalls to my mind the attraction of Regent Street in the height of the season, where carriages, people, costumes, shop windows—everything, holds one as by an irresistible spell. But you must follow my example and avoid temptation by remaining at home. Why go away when there is so much to enjoy and study here?"

Why, indeed! And yet, while I saw the force and reasonableness of her suggestion, I was equally conscious of a strong resentment to my acceptance of it. This may have been due to the comparison she instituted, which while being a perfectly

Chapter 13   "Can This be Death?"

natural one to the feminine mind, was far from impressing me as a happy one. Or perhaps I had misunderstood her. At least I would give her the opportunity to explain.

"What a curious simile to use!" I remarked.

"Do you think so? I thought it was an inspiration. But then you are not a woman."

"No! Perhaps that explains it. But may I ask why you sent for me?"

Again she turned her dear face upwards—in its nestling it had fallen easily upon my breast—until her laughing eyes looked full into my own.

"Suppose I was to say it was simply because I missed you?" she replied.

"I should be glad to hear it."

"Would you? Then allow me to say I had a very different reason for what I did."

"Then you had two reasons, for I am sure the one was part of it, whatever the other may be. Now, confess; am I not right?"

"If you prefer to think so, do. But I have a mission to perform in which I thought you would like to keep me company."

"I shall be delighted. Though I am ignorant of its nature, I am confident of its interest. It would be impossible to find a mission here divorced from pleasure and instruction. What is its nature?"

"I am going to earth to assist in the passing of the little friend Arvez recently brought to us."

"Little Dandy?" I exclaimed. It was the only name the boy knew—an appellation of the gutter we had to retain until we received his new name. "That will be a pleasure in more ways than one. When do you go?"

"Myhanene is sending Azal to receive him. I go to assist, but I am sure he will be glad to have your company. I await his coming now."

"Does Dandy know?"

"No! Azal will tell him when he arrives."

"Is the lad here, then?"

"Yes! He is to be detained a little while. I think his accident —as men would call it—depends on his over-sleeping himself."

"Then he is to come suddenly?"

"So I understand. It is far more merciful for such as he. But here comes Azal, and we shall soon know the details."

He joined us almost before Vaone had finished speaking, and readily assented to my addition to his escort.

"It will be a new and interesting experience for you," he added. "But we must find the boy, or events will be in advance of us."

This was a quest ending with its commencement. Dandy was with Jack and several other friends who had spent most of their time with the little probationer since Arvez had introduced him to our valley home. They were busy revising some scheme of operations to be carried out when Dandy's coming and going should be at an end.

"I wish I'd wakened up for the last time," I heard the little fellow remark as we approached.

"What makes you wish that?" inquired Azal, introducing himself.

"You don't know much abart what I has ter put up wi', if yer don't know that," he replied, eyeing his strange visitor with a curious and doubtful interest. Then recognizing myself he came and took my hand.

"Who is he?" he asked. "I know you, but I doan know 'im."

"You know Arvez—the angel who brought you here from 'The College'?"

"This ain't 'im."

"No, but he is a friend of his."

"An' wot's 'e want?"

"I have come," Azal answered for himself, "to do just what I heard you wish for when we arrived."

"Wot's that?"

"Why, did you not wish that you had wakened for the last time?"

"So I do." Then he added with a touch of pathetic weariness,

Chapter 13 "Can This be Death?"

"But it's such a while comin' I'm tired o' waitin' for it."

"Poor child! Come with me. You will not wait much longer now."

"Yer ain't a goin' ter tek me away from Jack, are yer?"

"No. Jack can come with us if he wishes."

"But wheer are we goin'?"

"Back to earth for a little while."

"I doan want ter go back; why can't I stop 'ere?"

"Because your body must waken and pull you back. It is going to waken perhaps for the last time, as you wished, then you will be able to stop here altogether."

It was a strange and indescribable look that rose from the depths of his consciousness through his eyes and covered his wondering face as the meaning of Azal's words was divined. It was something of impatient gratitude and a wild desire to grasp a fortune that might vanish, prompting him to dart from myself and hold the speaker as a hostage to success.

"I know wot cher mean!" he gasped. "Yer goin' to kill me. I ain't afrightened at it. I shall like it. Will yer do it soon?"

Hear, O heavens, and give ear, O earth, to the eloquent decision of a child in a choice between life and death!

Azal smiled and affectionately patted the dear little head.

"No, I am not going to kill you," he replied. "But when you fall asleep we shall just break the cord by which the body pulls you back again. Then you will have your wish, and stop here."

"It won't 'urt, will it?"

"No. You will not feel it."

"An' shall I be dead then?"

"Your body will."

"Well, ain't that killin' me? But I doan care. This is a lot better 'n livin'. Come on, I'm ready."

"Then we will go," said Azal.

"Ere! 'Old a minit! Theer's frepence ap'ny in my pocket. Let me see Bully Peg, an' gi' 'im the money, before yer do it, will yer? 'E 'as a awful time, 'e does, an' frepence ap'ny'll set 'im up in matches."

Even Azal did not hurry to reply to that appeal. It was a prayer for time and opportunity to do a Christian service, powerful enough to stay the hand of death; it was a declaration of faith, an act of worship, a Christ-like atonement sufficient to wash out the stain of not a trifling sin, which called for and received the recognition of a holy silence, and we each bowed our heads in the presence of it.

"Yes, you shall do as you wish," said Azal as soon as he could speak.

"Then I don't care for nuffin'. Come on."

I am afraid if our passage earthwards had been witnessed by mortal eyes it would have occasioned comment by the violation of orthodox ideas respecting the nature of our mission. But I think the infringement came more from the one most closely concerned than either of his companions. Never was schoolboy more elated at the prospect of vacation than this almost friendless guttersnipe at the one thought which filled his mind.

A few moments ago I took from my Recorder's bookshelves a volume written by a clergyman and read: 'The truth is no one, except under very exceptional circumstances, can restrain a shudder at the thought of dying. ...Why is this? ...Is it because death is unilluminated by hope, and there is no expectation of a Resurrection and a Heaven? No, both truths may be implicitly believed, but they are future facts—how future is not known—and meanwhile, what? Nothing definite. No intense conviction of the unbroken continuity of life. No certainty that the moment after death we shall be the same living, thinking and feeling personalities that we have been the moment before." [3] This is after two thousand years of preaching, and it represents not the author's individual opinion, but the results arrived at by ecclesiastical and theological Christianity.

---

[3] "Our Life after Death," by Rev. Arthur Chambers. London: Charles Taylor, 1894 pp. 68-69.

Chapter 13 "Can This be Death?"

I say our passage would have shocked the orthodoxy of such a profession. But Dandy had been made acquainted with what the church might and ought to know, and instead of crying, in the language of another:

"But timorous mortals start and shrink
To cross this narrow sea;
Stand lingering, shivering on the brink
And fear to launch away,"

he was at one with David longing for the wings of a dove that he might fly away and be at rest. Why should we be sad and mournful?

But we are at our destination.

The morning had broken, and the busy wheels of London life were already at work. Our little friend had certainly overslept himself. He sought shelter last night among the packingcases piled up under the archway of a wholesale warehouse. It was a favourite spot, warm, snug and out of the way of police interference. The friendly carter had given permission, and Limpy Jack had formerly shared the quarters with Dandy, but since the former's decease, Bully Peg had taken the vacant place.

"Theer I am," cried the lad, pointing to where his sleeping body lay; but, ikey! ain't I late! Why Bully's gone, an' I want ter gi' 'im my frepence ap'ny!"

"Never mind, I think I can manage to bring him back," said Azal.

He could not leave the lad even for an instant at such a juncture, but there was abundance of help at hand, so that Bully Peg was speedily brought back again.

How was it done?

That is easily explained, and it will not be amiss to linger carefully as we watch this incident through.

Dandy had constituted himself guardian over the child, the two being brought into a very close and real fellowship by kinship of misfortune. Between them existed a mutual sympathy and anxiety for success, upon which they leaned first to one side, then to the other, for the only meal the day most frequently provided. Thus a double connection had been established— business and family. To this foundation, based on genuine affection, it was not a difficult operation for the ministering angel to telepathically attach Dandy's wish and thus transmit to his friend a thought of anxious concern respecting his oversleeping protector.

Bully was engaged with two companions when the recalling thought struck him, but he turned on the instant, and without either apology or explanation, started back on his errand.

It was all accomplished in less time than it requires to write it, for the distance to be covered was only a short one, and Bully Peg stopped suddenly at the threshold of the gateway where Dandy was still sleeping.

Two men were at work turning over and clearing away the packing-cases, and the little fellow was too frightened to speak of the danger in which his friend was placed.

He hoped the noise would wake the lad. Why did it not do so? Then he feared one of the cases had already fallen and killed him. This fear so terrorized him that when he presently gained the necessary courage to speak, it had robbed him of the thought to do so.

But why did not that clattering, deafening noise wake the lad? Under other circumstances the silent presence of the constable would have caused him to start and creep further into the darkness.

The explanation all lies in the difference of circumstances. In the present instance they were of God's more immediate care and design, of which Azal held the plan and had to superintend the working. Dandy's earthly course was run, but glad as he really was at the prospect of it, in his excitement and shrinking from the process of passing, he would have frustrated it had not a strong restraining pressure been put upon him.

Chapter 13   "Can This be Death?"

"Let me go and wake myself," he cried at one time, trying to secure his liberty to effect the purpose.

"Wake yourself and live?" Azal inquired.

"But I doan want ter be 'urt."

"It will not hurt so much as you think. We will mind that, and the little pain will be the price of freedom."

"Will yer mind me, then?"

"Yes—but go back!" and like a lightning flash he was thrust into his body as a great case toppled over and fell.

There was a piercing shriek of agony, enough to make one's blood run cold. The two men started and leaped from the cases, dragged the fatal one aside, and there lay the crushed and unconscious form of our little friend, with a stream of blood running from his convulsively twitching mouth.

While the two terrified men were securing help and arranging to carry the lad to the neighbouring hospital, I was busy watching the work of Azal. Though the shriek was painful, I was glad to know that Dandy himself had scarcely felt anything before he swooned. From this he revived, just as they laid him on the improvised stretcher when, in an interval in the operation due to a policeman's inquiry, little Bully Peg darted forward and stammered through his tears:

"All right, Dandy, I'm 'ere," as if such assurance would be a comfort to the sufferer.

The head turned somewhat towards the speaker, the eyes half-opened for an instant, and beneath the canvas that covered him, a finger moved as if to beckon the lad nearer.

I knew what he wished to say. His mind was on his friend and the coppers he wished him to receive. Even the pain of the working of death was not strong enough to turn him from that one desire.

Five minutes later he was unconsciously lying upon the hospital table, where the rags of clothing were expeditiously but tenderly removed in preparation for the house-surgeon's examination.

The Life Elysian

I wonder whether those kindly nurses or doctors ever think how often the angels of God are witnesses of their humane labours. How often such as we wait to supplement their efforts to relieve?

It may be that they did so on this occasion, since they dealt very tenderly and gently with the little arab. That one limb was fractured was at once ascertained, but the kindly surgeon administered restoratives to revive the lad in the desire to ascertain the extent of his internal injuries.

Presently Dandy breathed a heavy sigh and opened his dull, wondering eyes.

"That's right," the doctor exclaimed encouragingly. "We shall soon be better now."

The trembling lips moved in an effort to speak. The doctor dropped his ear to catch the words.

"Money? Yes, I hear," he said. "Bully Peg? Give your money to Bully Peg? Is that what you mean?"

The lips parted in an attempt to assent, but he could do no more.

"See if he has any money in his pockets."

"Two or three coppers," replied one of the students after examination.

"All right. Bully Peg shall have it," the doctor assured him.

Again the lad feebly smiled in signification that he understood.

By this time it was certain that severe internal injuries had taken place, and the surgeon indicated the fatal nature of the case. The injured limb was speedily splintered and made as comfortable as possible, after which the patient was removed to one of the wards to await the end. Here exhaustion triumphed over pain, and little Dandy rejoined us while his body slept heavily.

The change that had taken place in this temporarily liberated soul in the short space of time was almost incredible. He was no longer the happy, light-hearted lad we had accompanied back to earth. The sacrament of dissolution was pressing heavily upon him, and I saw the beautiful adaptation of the ministry of angels to such occasions. It was the twilight hour of life. The day was beginning to break. The soul, weary with the sufferings of the night, was longing for the morning from which it hoped for strength, and the blackness was softening into a hopeful yet almost doubtful grey. The night-watch was nearly over; only a few more oscillations of the pendulum, and the hour of relief would strike. Earth had done its last service; Heaven, with its more efficient ministry, was lovingly insinuating itself into consciousness and the overpowered soul lay helplessly floating out on the ebbing tide.

Azal caught the lad in his arms, and gave him the support he sadly needed.

"Have courage, dear; it is almost over now."

"Eh! What!" he exclaimed, waking as if from a dream under the invigorating influence of the strength his host of friends were affording him. "Oh, yes! I remember all about it now. Am I dead yet?"

"Not yet; you are sleeping at present, but not soundly enough for us to liberate you. God will send one of His bright angels shortly; then you will soon be free."

"Have I got to go back again?" he inquired piteously.

"Not for long."

"Oh, I wish I hadn't! I can't remember you there, and it's, oh, so painful."

"You will not forget us again, and we can so assist you now that you will feel no more pain."

"Shan't I?" and he brightened wonderfully as he accepted the assurance.

"Let me go back, then, an' get it over quick."

"Wait a little longer; we are not quite ready at present."

"All right; you are werry kind to me." Then he started under the sudden impulse of a thought. "Ere, did Bully Peg get my frepence ap'ny?"

"Not yet; but the doctor has promised that he shall have it."

"But the doctor don't know 'im. Can't yer find 'im an' let 'im 'ave it?"

"We will try." Then pointing Dandy to where his little friend lingered at the door of the hospital he said, "That is him, I think, waiting on the steps."

We had not left the precincts of the hospital.

"Yes, that's 'im. Can't yer tell 'im ter go in an' arsk the doctor for it?"

"No; he would not hear me speak. But I think we can find a way to manage it somehow."

Azal looked around. Then I saw him concentrate his will upon the young student who had searched and found the coppers in our friend's pocket. For a little time the effort produced no effect, then it began to work, and I watched the contest between a strong impulse to go to the front entrance of the institution and continuing to read a medical article upon which he was engaged. It was an interesting experience to watch the gathering force of that strange and unaccountable effect upon the man, which presently became altogether irresistible, and throwing the paper aside, he yielded to the impulse simply to get rid of it.

Standing at the top of the four or five steps leading to the door, with his hands in his pockets, he looked to the right and left, but finding nothing to attract his attention gave a satisfactory laugh at his own foolishness, and was about to return when he caught sight of the cringing little outcast who had tried to squeeze himself between the wall and pillar supporting the semblance of a porch.

"Hello, Tommy! What are you after?" he inquired.

The timid trespasser pushed one finger into his mouth, looked at his toes, and tried to squeeze further behind the pillar, but said nothing until the student dragged him out and repeated the inquiry.

"I on'y wants ter know 'ow Dandy is?" he stammered.

"Who's Dandy?"

"A box tumbled on 'im an' they brought 'im 'ere," was the best answer he could frame.

"Yes, I know. Is he your brother?"

"No, but 'e looks arter me."
"What is your name?"
"Bully Peg!"
"Bully Peg! He was talking about you, and wants you to have his money. Here is sixpence for you."

The lad looked from the coin to the doctor, then back at the coin again, but utterly failed to understand his good fortune.

"Is it a good 'un?" he asked incredulously.

The doctor laughed.

"Why, of course it is. Do you think Dandy would send you a bad one?"

"No, but 'e 'adn't got this much."

"How do you know?"

"Becos I seed 'im count it."

"Perhaps it has grown, but he told me to give it to you if you called."

"Is he better?"

The young fellow thought for an instant before replying.

Medical students are not always the most sensitively balanced individuals, but he seemed to feel there was something in this instance he could not lightly trifle with.

"He will be better presently," he answered.

"Can I see 'im? 'E would like it."

"Not now. I think he's asleep. Come again on Sunday."

"I shall want ter know ter-night 'ow 'e is."

"Very well. If you come up, we will tell you."

This satisfied the lad so far as it was possible to do without a sight of his friend, and he took his reluctant departure until night.

The result was a very welcome diversion for our little invalid, who was more than delighted at Bully Peg's good fortune.

There is little more of a preliminary nature to be said. The preparatory sleep was drawing to a close, the certainty of which was made known to me by Myhanene's arrival.

"Is you the angel as kills 'em?" Dandy asked as soon as he saw him.

"No. We only save from death."

The lad turned towards Azal with a look of disappointment as he murmured:

"I wish 'e would come. I doan want ter stop now Bully's got the money."

"Neither shall you stop. Come, we must wake you for a few minutes."

"Will it hurt me?"

"No, you will not feel any more pain now."

"An' yer won't go away, will yer?"

"No, we will not leave you. You will see us all the time till you fall asleep."

The body moved feebly, and the soul was at once drawn back.

The watchful nurse was at his side before his eyes were opened.

"Are you better, dear?" she asked kindly.

Dandy looked confused for an instant, then almost inaudibly said:

"I'm so tired."

"I know you are," she answered. "Will you try to go to sleep again?"

"Yes, I want—to—sleep."

It was all over. The quivering life-cord snapped, and Myhanene sped with the sleeping soul to the home of Siamedes.

* * *

CHAPTER 14

THE MANY MANSIONS

It will perhaps appear strange, even contradictory to most of my readers, that the soul, which never for an instant during its connection with the body, loses consciousness, should upon its final release experience such an effect for a longer or shorter period as determined by necessity. This, however, is the case in the great majority of instances, especially where the dissolution is occasioned by what is called an accident as just described.

I need not here re-discuss the immense loss earth sustains by failing to educate the memory to retain the experiences men and women pass through in the hours of sleep, and thus lose the benefit of the lessons learned in the most valuable half of life. All this I have dealt with in Through the Mists, but I may with advantage pause to consider the reasons for the unconscious interval succeeding the final separation of soul and body.

This decree, absolute in the great divorce, only differs in one respect from the nightly repetition of falling asleep. In the diurnal experience, the soul leaves the body for a longer or shorter period; its return being assured by means of the life-line connecting the two; in the sleep of death this line is permanently broken after the slumber has commenced, and return is thus prevented. Hence death is nothing more than a final sleep in which the soul is no longer recalled from the associations it has been forming during the years of its pilgrimage, which associations have been negligently forgotten or treated as superstitions in the effort for worldly success.

In view of making this statement, I have conducted an extended inquiry as to personal experiences in the passing, with the result that only a very small percentage of my friends would describe the process of death as other than falling asleep, and these exceptions one and all speak of the effect as analogous to swooning or fainting. In no single instance have I met with an experience where the separation was accompanied by any peculiarity of a more alarming nature.

If I had been even indifferently successful in indicating the governing principles of life in Paradise in what I have said above, I think it will be clearly recognized that, while the transition fails to effect any change in the character of the man, it cannot often be said to deal so leniently with the position he holds. The throwing off of the body marks the rubicon between the apparent and the real, the profession and possession, the false and the true. Henceforth every man has to be himself, not what he wishes to appear. The true character is no longer concealed by a cloak, but it furnishes the only dress he is permitted to wear; and the station he fills, the employment he follows, as well as the company he keeps, are all determined by the spiritual fitness thus declared. This, in not a few cases, amounts to a complete reversal of the previous order. The wheels of success—oftentimes of misfortune—have to be brought to a stand before they are made to revolve in the contrary, which is the true direction. It is this stationary moment we are now dealing with in the history of the soul; the moment of inactivity when the false is at an end and the real is coming into action. There is an interval of calm and restful silence that the vibrations of wrong may die away and the true career be started free from any disturbing results. In the region of mechanics this would inevitably be so; so in the higher realm of spirit 'God giveth His beloved sleep' for such necessary period as to allow the readjustment consequent upon the crossing from the temporal into the eternal condition.

In the hush of this pause Dandy slept.

Azal's mission at an end, he was relieved, and over the sleeper's couch Vaone's watch was shared by one who had previously known and occasionally befriended the little outcast.

All these changes and arrangements were superintended by

Chapter 14 — The Many Mansions

Myhanene, and when they were over, he turned, placed his arm across my shoulders, and led me towards the terrace.

"Come," he said. "This duty being accomplished, I am glad of the opportunity of speaking with you again. I need not ask if all goes well."

"More than well," I answered; then, catching sight of a sleeper lying upon a couch we were passing, I added, "Pardon me, but surely I know that face."

"Whence comes our sister?" Myhanene inquired of one of the watchers.

"From childbirth."

Then I remembered who she was, and my companion, as if divining my thought, asked again:

"And the little one?"

"Is also with us."

"That is well."

I wish, with the transcription of these simple words, I had power to convey a suggestion of the music of his voice. So far, in all the records of my intercourse I have tried to represent those I have met as being natural men and women. Perhaps in this I have succeeded too well for many of my readers, who expected to find in everyone in this life an archangel with wings of opalescent splendour and language such as earth ears could not possibly listen to and live. Had I been romancing, I might have tried some useless flight in this direction; but this is not my object. I am no poet, not even possessing a desire to aspire to such a claim, therefore I have not turned into paths where I might borrow from the wealth of Milton, Dante, or Homer. Their eagle flights of brilliant imagination would rather confuse than serve my purpose. I only wish to speak of the things I myself have seen, and indicate the nature and mission of those messengers of God with whom I have been privileged to commune. In every instance I have found them to be more like the angel who was revelator to John (fellow-servants and colabourers) than those sketched by Dante or Milton, and as such I desire to present them.

In higher heights than I have reached there may be—must be more glorious beings than I have known, but so far I have not met them, therefore decline to speculate upon their nature and characteristics. Every stage of existence between myself and the Absolute, I have reason to believe, is peopled by beings acclimatized thereto, of which I find the suggestive assurance in Myhanene himself. Did I but know Omra better, I am confident he would reveal more in this direction, but I must be content to remain uninformed on this point for the present, and confine my argument to what deduction can be made from my knowledge of Omra's messenger.

Here, however, we are brought into contact with a personality through which the supra-natural begins to insinuate itself upon our attention, and we find strange combinations and seeming contradictions, occasioning first doubt, then study, before we reach a settled confidence in the new presentment of manhood.

Let me illustrate what I mean from this last rejoinder of his which has led to the present explanation. Few would use such a phrase in the connection it is here employed—it is not the happiest or most relevant to be found, but it is a habitual one on the lips of Myhanene. The soft, musical, almost nonchalant "It is well" is the termination of everything with him with the regularity of an "Amen" to a prayer. But more than this, to those who hear it for the first time, coupled with the sparkling airiness of his bearing and the almost, flippant tone in which it is spoken, it comes with something of a surprise, and one turns to ascertain if the speaker is not void of natural sympathy. To affirm such a thought, however, would be a mistake speedily to be repented of, for before the music of his voice has died away, the airy touch of his butterfly's wing will stir depths within the soul with a power that overawes, and but for the tender firmness of the hand around the shoulder, one would draw away from him in reverent obeisance.

"It is well!" The music rolls from the deep undisturbed

confidence he has in God. He may not altogether understand, but he knows enough of God to be assured it must be so, and hence he speaks.

In the case before us, however, it was doubly well, for my reader will not have failed to identify the sleeper. Her prayer had been answered. The child was saved from earth.

We had reached the terrace before my companion spoke again.

"Now that you have a longer and better acquaintance with this life," he began, "I want to know whether it loses any of its charms, wonder, or surprises?"

"It loses nothing," I replied. "Everything increases rather than otherwise."

"So it is always and with everyone," he affirmed, gently nodding his head in the reverie absorbing the other part of him I could not understand. "So it will ever continue to be—always more to follow. As God manifest in the Christ was so much more than earth could comprehend, so the God in Heaven will always be so much more than the redeemed can know or understand."

"I like to hear you speak of God and Christ and love."

"Do you? Why?"

"I seem to comprehend more of its sweetness and fullness when you are speaking. Sometimes in the lower life, I reached out in an endeavour to find it, but as a reality it always evaded me until—"

"Until when, my brother?"

Again his arm crept tenderly across my shoulders, and he drew me closer with the gentle caress of one who would woo life's sweetest confession; drew me nearer and nearer, but did not speak or otherwise disturb the eloquent silence he so frequently employs more effectively than speech. The answer would come; he knew it better even than myself, and in the meantime nothing was lost. In such interludes, hearts knit and affection tightens its embrace till the soul becomes too full and the lips must speak.

"When I met you," I replied, and something bowed my head upon his shoulder as if the confession had been one of love.

The pressure of his arm was slightly accentuated.

"But if the poor unworthy reflection of His love from myself has been so much to you, what will the fullness of the rapture be when you are able to see Him as He is?"

"I know not. I am only grateful the revelation is withheld until I shall be strong enough to bear it."

"But you would not delay the fullness of your joy, would you?"

"No! I would neither delay nor hurry it. I simply wish to do my present duty and leave all the rest to Him."

"That is well, but tell me what you are now doing towards it?"

"At present I am waiting—or rather have been waiting, but first Ladas and then Cushna have pointed me to very congenial work."

"All employment here is congenial."

"So they have assured me, but I doubted whether my own choice could be the right one."

"Such is the law of our lives."

"And am I really free to join in your ministry to earth?"

"Yes, if you desire it, and I shall be glad to accept your service. But you must first learn something of the nature and scope of the good news we have to declare before you will be able to preach it. The earth ideas of this life are as yet bound in swaddling-bands which only constrain and fetter the soul. We have to proclaim liberty, but it is always a liberty granted and secured by law. This law you must study and understand in such of its bearings as will be most required."

"Where shall I begin?"

"With the pulling down of the error that this life possesses only two classes of divisions of souls—the saved and the lost; and in its place, building up the knowledge that, no matter who or what a man may be on arrival here, he will go to his own place—the place for which he has spiritually prepared himself by his actions and motives, without any other testimony or witness than the evidence

Chapter 14 — The Many Mansions

written upon his spiritual body."

"This I have in a measure already studied and learned to understand, but there is at least one subject arising from what you have just said upon which I sadly need to be informed."

"State the point, and I will try to answer it."

"Granted that every man must go to his own place, when we consider the almost infinite number of conditions into which humanity must necessarily be divided, where can all the places be found to satisfy the demand?"

"It is a question earth will often ask, and one you must also be prepared to answer. To one whose mind is free from parochial limitations, a short and suggestive reply will be sufficient; that however large the demand may be, it cannot exceed the finite, and therefore can be easily provided for in the economy of an infinite God. Few men, however, make any effort to reach a wider circle of thought than the ideas they inherit, in which they understand infinity as unlimited mercy and indulgence towards themselves and an equally unmeasured extent of wrath upon all who differ religiously from them. Justice, righteousness and truth in their essential purity are too high for them to attain to, hence, any attempt in that direction is considered to be useless."

"Earth ideas are a secondary consideration to me for the moment; I am first anxious to know the truth for myself alone. Not that I doubt, but I would also understand."

"And I will gladly do my best to enable you to do so, though I am fully conscious how little that best will be in comparison even with that I know from experience, and I myself have scarcely yet begun to comprehend what the whole truth may be."

Here he paused as if for the purpose of shaping his further reply. I did not speak; having enough to think of for the time in making sure I understood what had already been said. Presently he resumed:

"I shall find no better introduction to what I have to draw your attention to than the words of the Master to His disciples: 'In My

Father's house are many mansions; if it were not so I would have told you. I go to prepare a place for you.' It is in those many mansions where the provision we seek is made. Have you ever tried to think what and where these mansions are, and made an effort to estimate the number of them?"

The question came so unexpectedly, and put the hitherto nebulous idea in such a substantial and tangible form that I could only stupidly reply:

"No. I had not thought of it in this way."

Myhanene smiled. He loves to lay these unsuspected traps, and knows well how to use them to emphasize his teachings.

"I suppose not," he answered. "There are not many who give much intelligent free consideration to these matters until they arrive here. Now let us proceed gently in our inquiry as to number in the first place. Paul said he at one time ascended into the third Heaven; he also once assured the Ephesians that Christ 'hath ascended far above all Heavens'; and of God we are told that 'the Heaven of Heavens cannot contain Him.' We are thus scripturally warranted in using the plural number in speaking of the Heavens, just as Christ spoke of the many mansions. Now, the foundations of part of these mansions, or Heavens, are not so invisible to our friends on earth as is generally believed. I think they estimate the number of stars discernible at about one hundred millions, but of all this number with the added darker bodies remaining invisible, so far as I have learned, those that serve the purpose of preliminary existence, as earth, do not exceed the number of your fingers."

"Myhanene!" I exclaimed.

"The rest are nuclei for varied grades of spiritual ascent. You have already seen how one class of soul is held bound to the earth, the influence of which attenuates until one is able to break away and seek other conditions?"

"Yes."

"So from the material body of every star does there radiate an attenuated substance from which a seried ascent of spiritual conditions is built up, forming the divinely majestic staircase linking Heaven with Heaven, until the Heaven of Heavens is reached."

"Such knowledge is too wonderful for me; I cannot attain to it," I replied, lost in the magnitude of the conception, "but with such an explanation, I can no longer wonder as to the provision for every need."

"Of course the demand is great, but God is greater; we have always that confidence, though we may not be able to measure and comprehend the details of the requirements."

"Am I right then, in surmising that in the intercourse of this life passage from star to star is possible?"

"Not only possible, but absolutely necessary, and is as easily accomplished as that of passing from house to house on earth, to all who are qualified or able to do so. When I return from hence home, I shall take such a course, but you would not be able to follow me, because not yet conditioned to the passage. When you saw my home you did so by means of the power I loaned you for the purpose. I mention this in order to point out how safe the higher planes of life are from lower invasion."

"Is there such a—may I call it a bridgeless void—between here and earth?"

"Call it an inter-stellar barrier. Yes, you pass across one when returning to earth."

"Why have I not noticed it?"

"Because the transit is too rapid generally for such an observation. It is accomplished on the flash of a thought to be there, and sight can take no cognizance of the operation."

"And does the universe exist for the maintenance of ten, twenty, or even fifty such worlds as earth?"

"The universe as you conceive it," he replied.

"It seems scarcely credible."

"That is because of man's unworthy ideas concerning God. Now let us turn the conception round and look at it from Christ's

The Life Elysian

standpoint for a moment. Here, a single soul becomes of much greater intrinsic value than the whole world, and at such a price one marvels at the incomprehensible wealth of God as represented in the produce of earth alone."

Still I could not escape from the overawing thought, and inquired:

"Is this the measure of God's 'so loved' that all creation should exist for comparatively so few?"

"I did not say all creation, but rather the universe as man conceives it," he answered.

"But wherein lies the difference?"

He smiled and drew me closer to him, with a pressure of indulgent sympathy.

"If I have already astonished you by what I have said, how shall you be able to understand the truths I am now engaged in studying?"

"Could you not indicate what they are?"

"I will try to do so by illustration. Will you suppose an orange divided into sixteen or more parts?"

"Yes."

"For the purpose of my parable I will ask you to consider that all the stellar universe, as known to earth, is comprised in one of those sections which we will name the White Group, and each of the other divisions is appropriated to Pink, Green, Blue and other Groups, until all the parts of the orange are employed; even then the whole of the systems within the universe, as known to friends in the higher stages we are able to reach, will not be included."

I did not speak, but lifted my head to gaze at him with unutterable amazement.

"When we have grasped the meaning of this," he went on, "we shall only be crossing the threshold of the infinite, for beyond this hypothetical orange are numbers of others forming constellations in a grand august system we cannot conceive, in the centre of which, it may be, the throne of the Ineffable will be found."

"Well might the old patriarch inquire, 'Who by searching can find out God?'" I exclaimed.

"We shall all find Him," he answered confidently. "The most necessary and serviceable question for us to decide is whether we are making the best possible effort to accomplish the purpose."

"Pardon me if I am wrong," I humbly ventured, "but does not that sound like predestination?"

"Not the predestination of theology—saving a few and condemning the many; but it is the predestination of God 'who will have all men to be saved.' Man can no more escape from that determination than from the omnipresence of God. In the finality God must be all in all, for beside Him there is none other, but within the bounds of the finality there is ample room for the exercise of free-will, also for the punishment of sin and restoration from its effects. Let me illustrate. I imagine a branch line of railway running from a central station to a suburb. A train leaving the terminus has no alternative but to reach the central depot. The only doubt is as to the time the journey will occupy, which has to be largely determined by the officials in charge, who have power to hasten or delay."

"Suppose there should be an accident?"

"That is impossible upon God's line of life."

This was said in one of his soft unanswerable affirmations to which there is no reply.

"But, Myhanene, do you consider how inaccessibly remote you thus place God"

"I have done no more, my brother, than lend you what assistance I am able for helping you to understand the position God has always occupied. The error was manufactured on earth; I have only done something towards correcting it."

"But when will the best of us be able to reach Him?"

"That is to be the great employment of eternity, and we shall find that provision is long enough for even the last laggard child to reach his destination. Let us, however, be up and doing, never forgetting the responsibility we are under in relation to delays."

"The importance of that caution applies to the earth-life; you do not suggest that the danger of delay exists here, do you?"

"Wherever progress is attainable, side by side, with it exists the possibility of delay. Never forget that. Of course, the higher we ascend and the more we are transformed into the image of God, the greater will our energy be increased, and the less liable shall we be to tarry by the way. But for the present, let me ask you to study life as you will find it in your present home, where the last feeble influence of the earth has but recently snapped, and every soul rejoices in the newly-acquired perfect freedom. You will there find a decided tendency to rest, a wish not to be disturbed, a satisfaction already attained, a pronounced feeling of contentment, and the idea of having reached a Heaven that has no need of improvement. It is this I wish you to guard against, and for which I am glad to have had the opportunity of pointing out the length of the journey lying before us."

His words threw a lurid light upon that obscure remark of Vaone's I have already noted. Was he aware of it? I do not know. Myhanene is not so easily understood in all his movements as one might be led to think from first appearances.

"I thank you for that intimation," I replied, "and will promise to profit by your caution. But, tell me, in speaking of my present residence as being just over the boundary of the earth conditions, do you wish me to understand that it is but the next stage in progress from that through which Ladas has recently conducted me?"

"No. There are many degrees between the two. Ladas and his friends are working for the deliverance of earth-bound souls, who's every faculty and power is given to and held in slavish bondage by the desire still to achieve earthly success or take some cruel revenge. Ladas works to convince all such of the futility of their efforts, to point out the inevitable penalties they incur, and, whenever successful, to conduct the repentant ones —with such assurances of God's unchanging love as he may be able to give to the place where their purification begins."

"This is not altogether contrary to the Catholic idea of purgatory."

"There is a slight resemblance, but a great difference," he explained.

"The error lies in the claim of priestly power to liberate the soul by the instrumentality of the mass, or in other words, for a monetary or other consideration, which it is not now necessary to tell you, is one of the false traditions by which men have been blinded. Still, even that claim is not more Goddishonouring than the rival assumption of consigning all unpardoned sinners to an eternal torment."

"May I ask for information respecting the other stages in the earth conditions?"

"The whole region is occupied by the vast army of souls who on earth lacked aim, purpose or moral energy. They neither helped nor resisted anything, but simply breathed, ate, slept, and existed. Social, moral, spiritual driftage which were equally objectionable and despised by good and bad from lack of character. Like all other classes, they remain the same here, lying helpless and stagnant between the two active streams of life, and presenting the most difficult problem of regeneration we are called upon to solve. Ignorance and wrongly directed energy are simple cases of spiritual treatment, but in these palsied souls we have first to recover the use of shrunken, withered, and dried-up natural channels before the slightest sign of improvement is visible. It is a work almost like the effort to reanimate an Egyptian mummy, and were failure in any department of our work possible, this is the field where it would be found. This, however, is out of the question, and though results are achieved so slowly, the real danger the condition presents to earth inspires the efforts of all engaged in this part of our ministry."

"Wherein lies the special danger?" I inquired.

"Stagnation is always a menace to health, and for this reason alone it could not be allowed to remain. But the most serious aspect of such existence is found in the dangerous sympathy such souls form with any to whom they can cling. They are drawn to such as are drifting towards their own conditions like needles to a magnet, and it is in this connection you will experience more trouble than you imagine when your mission to earth commences."

"Kindly explain to me what you mean."

"The real danger of opening intercourse between ourselves and earth lies in the almost entire absence of the true Christ spirit in the majority of men. This, as you will well know by this time, establishes a close association with kindred souls from this side, and the active hypocrisies of men make natural draft upon those most like themselves. Our invasion of the mortal sphere with the evidence of immortality has most largely attracted men and women with greater development of curiosity, or desire for loaves and fishes, than spiritual knowledge and life. This inquiry is naturally answered by souls who are themselves 'of the earth, earthy,' who in turn prey upon this characterless multitude for such information as may assist to establish a false identity, and thus deceive the inquirers who seek gratification and marvels rather than holiness and God."

"But cannot this deception be prevented?"

"No! When God opens a door, it is opened for all without respect of persons. Whatsoever earth asks for, it receives, and if it does not receive the best, it is because it asks amiss. In the nature of the case, ignorance and deception lie nearest to the earth, and may be reached with greater ease; the higher life needs effort, energy, and sacrifice to attain to, hence few there be who reach it. Still there are a few, and we have to make the best use of these for the present, in the full confidence that righteousness and truth must conquer, and such conquest means the gradual extinction of this lifeless existence lying in what is known as the earth condition. All this will work out more clearly for your understanding by experience. For the present, let us make a brief visit to earth, where I will introduce you to him through whom we speak, and give my permission for you to use him under our direction."

* * *

CHAPTER 15

I BREAK DEATH'S SILENCE

It seems absolutely incredible, regarded from the earth point of view, that one in Myhanene's position should so leisurely place himself at my disposal as to suggest his accompanying me on a visit to earth for the purpose mentioned. Why did he not call one of the multitudes of messengers who wait to serve him, and bid him attend and introduce me to his psychic?

In that 'Why' lies all the voluminous difference between the two estates.

How frequently has earth been known to say, 'Who would have thought such a trivial event would turn out to be so important?' Paradise is ever conscious of the potentialities of the mustard-seed, and orders its action in accordance with safety. Simplest duties have an instant and imperative claim. In a condition of life where it is no derogation for God to say, 'Let there be light!' rather than depute the office to an underling, there can be no service too menial for the highest of His angels to perform.

How harmonious is this with the teaching of the Christ— 'He that is the greatest among you shall be your servant!' It is one of the operating spiritual laws the Church on earth has mislaid and forgotten; that is why Myhanene's action appears to be strange and incredible.

I had just been accepted for service in the band of workers my companion had organized to return through the tomb from Paradise and re-proclaim the gospel of Christ to earth. For this work, so far as the agents and methods he employed were concerned, he accepted the responsibility, and being a mission rooted and grounded in his love to God working through mankind, his fidelity was such that the service must needs be love's perfect offering. It was in this determination to render to God a worthy

The Life Elysian

service where the raison d'être of his action lay more than in a desire to render a personal service to myself. His sanction and permission were needed before I could be permitted to break the silence of death through the lips or instrumentality of the prophet he had chosen as his own agent on the earth side. In the realm of law, there are no accidents—only ignorance and neglect—producing disappointment, and Myhanene is not the man to run risks of which the responsibility would rest with himself or others through him. Against the possibility of inadvertence, he took all precautions, and on the earth side, drew his agent close to himself by bands of confidence and protection of the strongest kind. The security thus established furnishes a repetition of that Satan discovered to be so inviolable in the case of Job, "Hast thou not made a hedge about him, and about his house, and about all that he hath on every side?" It was permission to pass this hedge I now required, for which no personal authority, but that of my companion, would be accepted.

The visit also afforded a splendid opportunity for demonstrating the subject we had been recently discussing. In our flight Myhanene suddenly arrested my progress that I might appreciate the dividing space between world and world! It was an awe-inspiring lesson! We two were poised in awful solitude in space! We might have been alone in the primeval silence! Far away like a pencil-point of light, he showed me from whence we had come; then turning, at a seeming equal distance laid the end of our journey, and in between, to me, there seemed to be nothing but a void!

I shuddered! The appalling majesty of the etheric ocean; the august and terrible silence; the over-powering feeling of isolation, except for the certainty that God was there in a nearer sense with nothing to come between—than ever I had considered possible, was too much for me to bear. I was afraid at the sacred holiness!

"Let us go," I prayed.

"Come," he replied, "it is seldom we make the pause, but I was desirous for you to know and understand what these invisible barriers are that lie between the stages of our ascent—these spaces between the steps of Jacob's ladder."

"You are kind to draw my mind to that thought of it," I replied with some relief. "The idea it inspires is more of the great gulf fixed between the two."

"Either thought is equally appropriate. You will not forget them, and the experience will lend an added force to your use of either when you may refer to them. The school of God is full of grandly majestic lessons."

I would like to ask you respecting the divisions of nationalities and tribes, if I may."

"That is only a temporary arrangement applying to the plane bordering on the earth conditions," he answered. "Souls crossing that boundary are subject to survivals of vibration from earth influences for a time. I have already spoken of the easy content you will notice among many of those who have reached your present condition. They rest and are willing to continue to do so. National and religious prejudice lingers for a time, as does the sense of weariness, until the soul grows acclimatized to its new surroundings. For this reason, isolation is desirable to avoid friction in the first stage past the boundary, but in the second, only very feeble remnants are found to survive, and in the third, you reach the general assembly of races and religions, never more to be divided since all have learned there is good in each, which good it is designed they shall each and all discover."

"Love again," I commented.

"Yes, always, everywhere, love."

We were now at our destination, but Cushna had preceded us and was engaged with his psychic in an operation that excited my interest and curiosity, quite as much as it demands careful explanation before being in any measure understood.

At the first glance, the relationship of each to the other was analogous to that I had previously witnessed in the variety theatre where that malicious soul threw himself upon the hypocritical guardian of the youth. The two were blended in a confused combination. Then order took shape, and I saw that Cushna was simply over-clothing his sensitive in order that he might the better perform the office upon which he was engaged. This condition was secured by first inducing a hypnotic sleep, liberating the tenant soul of his medium for the time, while Cushna over-clothed the body, and through it, performed the benevolent duty of manipulating the withered limb of a girl which he presently restored to a normal state.

"Demoniacal possession," some of my nervous doubtful readers will exclaim. "Not so!" I answer, "but prophetic inspiration!" Both are equally scriptural, and similar in operation, but they differ widely in the nature of the controlling power.

Men are quite familiar with and convinced of the reality of the former; about the latter they are not nearly so assured nor inclined to be, even though it were equally demonstrated. But it is high time men consented to be honest towards God though it may be at some expense to their ignorance and prejudice. There are still many more things in Heaven and earth than are yet imagined, and why should not God be equally generous to His friends as to His enemies? If He gives permission for demons to control the bodies of unfortunates-and nothing takes place outside the realm of law-is it incredible that He should also have provided for angels to employ the same agency for benevolent purposes? What means this assurance of Samuel to Saul when he had just been anointed King over Israel, "The spirit of the Lord shall come upon thee, and thou shalt prophesy...and shalt be turned into another man; and let it be when these signs are come unto thee, that thou do as occasion serve thee; for God is with thee"? (1 Sam. x, 6-7) Can there possibly exist one side of anything without the other-wrong without right, evil without good? Does not the one always presuppose the existence of the other? I ask for honest reply and seek no favour.

Chapter 15   I Break Death's Silence

For myself, step by step with slow and measured progress, the gulf of separation between the two stages of life was being effectually and permanently closed up. I had learned how completely personal influence was exerted from side to side, by many instances both happy and joyous; I had listened and proved how clearly the voices of friends could travel the distance, and every inflection of love be distinctly heard; now I was brought face to face with the fact that we could touch each other, and the vital flow of health from Paradise was available for the conquest of disease and infirmity on earth.

"How much farther can these revelations go?" I asked myself, and from the mystic depths within me spake a still small voice saying, "Hope thou in God, for with Him all things are possible."

How literally true this is, beyond the wildest dreams of anticipation was about to be made known to me, as will appear.

Cushna's treatment at an end, he withdrew from his medium, who again woke to a normal condition. At the same moment Myhanene bade me watch closely what was about to take place, since he proposed to speak with our Recorder by another and more preferable method.

For this purpose he withdrew to a little distance, where by a process I could not then understand, but which I have since learned to employ with ease; he gradually assumed a grosser and physically tangible form in which he stepped forward and greeted his agent.

"Has Cushna left you very tired?" he inquired.
"Not if I can do anything for you," James replied cheerfully, turning to greet his new visitor with a smile of welcome.

"I have a friend I wish to introduce. He is about to join our mission, but for the present is unable to assume the visible form."
"I feel a strange presence-and yet, if I mistake not, he has already been here."

"You are right. He did once visit you with Cushna, but now he comes as an addition to my band if you will allow it."

"Is it your wish that it should be so?"

"With your consent to his using you in the presence of some second member of our mission until such time as I give other permission."

"By what name shall I know him?"

"Aphraar."

"For the truth's sake and your own I bid him welcome."

"I knew you would. But now, while we establish his connection with you, let me give you a communication you may send to one of your journals if you will, with the hope it may be like a drop of oil on troubled waters."

While James was making ready to incite the message, I may say that it was given when a very heated discussion was proceeding on what was called "The Downgrade Movement". I propose to copy the communication in extenso as taken down at the time, because of the liberality of thought it breathes, which illustrates very beautifully the true spirit of Paradise.

"I am ready," my Recorder presently announced.

"I will give it to you in verse form; and you may head it:

"THE BATTLE OF BELIEFS"

"Brethren, cease the wild contention,
Words are only seeds of strife;
Let us drop the killing letter—
Grasp the spirit; this is life.
Why should we raise heated cavil?
Has Christ made us judge of creed?
Have we all of revelation?
Know we only how to read?

Are there not twelve gates to heaven?
North and south and east and west?
May not they of every doctrine,

| Chapter 15 | I Break Death's Silence |

Enter that eternal rest?
Every kindred, clime and colour,
Every creed and tenet too—
Shall they not be represented?
With the dogma taught by you?

When the Master counts His jewels,
What a blending will be there!
Whosoever's beauteous diamond
Flashing light beyond compare.
Set amid the Calvin sapphire,
Roman ruby, High Church beryl,
And the Independent opal
Purified in times of peril.

Amethyst of Wesleyan beauty,
Pearl of Presbyterian hue,
Topaz washed in Baptist waters,
Emerald of the Pagan too;
Coral from Pacific Islands,
Chrysoprase from Africa's plain,
Chrysolyte from China ransomed,
Gems from Greenland's icy chain.

Gems of lustre most exquisite
From Mohammed's darkened mine;
Stones we never knew the name of
Taken from the Buddhist shrine;
Vishnu pouring out his treasures,
Greece and Egypt adding store;
Crystal tear-drops shed to idols,
Rendered precious evermore.

Shall not these form the galaxy?

Of that wondrous diadem?
Up then, brother, cease thy cavil,
Go, for Christ, in search of them.
Hear him crying—'Who will gather
In the harvest field to-day?'
See, thy sun is fast declining!
Art thou Christian; haste, away!

Time will not allow disputings—
Men are calling for thine aid;
Preach the gospel Christ has given thee;
Preach! No need to be afraid.
Christ is Judge. We are but striving
In the race where others run,
Let us each by faithful service,
Gain a prize and glad 'Well done!"

I would say before leaving this message that the voracious jaws of the editorial basket made short work of it, and Myhanene's verses have so far not been published. But to myself they have been full of suggestive thought, and I record them here in the hope that even now they may serve something of their intended purpose.

It was now my turn to take control of that most marvellous of all telephones and try to make my voice heard for the first time across the supposed unbroken silence of death. My several experiences had fully assured me how illusory and full of ignorant superstition was the earth idea of death's sealed silence; nevertheless I must confess to a feeling of something akin to uncanniness as Myhanene intimated his desire for me to proceed.

"Can you hear me?" I asked, but my voice sounded strange and hollow even to myself.

"Yes, perfectly."

I can convey no idea of the effect this question and reply made upon me. That must be left, my gentle reader, until you probably experience the sensation for yourself. When Myhanene was speaking, I watched the whole operation with a renewal of the wondering surprise I had experienced when first I heard Cushna speak across that supposed unbroken silence, but when I took my position at the mysterious telephone, the sound of my own voice startled, almost terrified me, and I shrank back from the clear response with the indescribable feeling of one who, for the first time, looks upon a ghost.

Myhanene was highly amused at my perturbation, and my Recorder, though he could not see me, evidently grasped the situation, and also appreciated my discomfiture.

"Did my voice startle you?" he asked.

"I can scarcely say that it did," I replied. "I suppose I did not really understand what all this meant until I heard you speak for and to myself."

"I can perhaps understand that better than Myhanene is able to do," he answered. "However completely one may recognize the existence of natural forces at our disposition, the explosion which, at one blast, razes the foundations of death and leaves an unobstructed passage does shake and surprise one, to say the least."

"I have had the same experience," said Myhanene, "but I thought it much better to let you feel the full force of it, than attempt to prepare you for what I knew would occur."

"Never mind," responded James, "it is all over now; the last enemy has been destroyed for you, and henceforth we shall be able to meet and commune upon perfectly easy terms. Now, may I hear your name again, and I will make a note of it?"

"Aphraar," I answered.

My Recorder smiled, then opened a small book and added the name to an already lengthy list.

"Why do you smile?" I inquired.

"At the satisfactory evidence the name affords of your

connection with Myhanene," he replied.

"In what way?"

"All his friends hide their identity for a time in a nom de plume, but I generally manage to learn the real name in the long run."

"I have no wish to keep you in any doubt as to my own, if you will do me a great favour."

"I will if I can," he answered readily.

"Would it not be better to know what I wish to ask before you make a definite promise?"

"Not if your request is a legitimate one. If it is at all doubtful I should refer it to Myhanene, and be guided by his decision. He is here now, so you had better speak, and unless he objects, I shall be pleased to serve you in any way I can."

"Since I have learned that it is possible for me to speak with the earth again," I answered, "I have had a most consuming desire to send a message to my father, in an attempt to rectify two mistakes."

"Where can I find him?"

"He resides in South Kensington."

"Do you wish me to see him, or would you prefer that I should write the message?"

"Would you see him?"

"Yes, if you desire it, and Myhanene consents."

"I have no objection," our chief replied.

"I am afraid you will not receive a very cordial welcome," I was constrained to add, for I knew my father's attitude towards anything savouring of the superstitious.

"That is a matter of small consideration to me," said James, "providing your message contains satisfactory evidence of its origin. Will you give me the name and address?"

"The name is Stephen Winterleigh," the which, together with the address, my Recorder made a careful note of.

"And now for the message," he went on, prepared to make what notes were necessary.

Chapter 15 — I Break Death's Silence

Years have passed since the interview I am recounting, but I feel all that bewildering wonder come back to me, and again I almost ask myself whether the possibility of such an intercourse is really true after all!

Oh, the unfathomed depths of the infinite love of God!

"Tell him how deeply I regret the annoyance I have occasioned, by lending the volume of Lodge's Portraits to my friend and neighbour in chambers, Mr. Ralph Unacliff. Say I only granted the loan two days before my-I suppose I must say death to be understood-and if he will kindly see Mr. Unacliff, the volume may be at once restored. Further-and this will be the unpleasant part of your message-will you also tell him that the claim of my man, Acres, for twenty pounds on my estate, is perfectly valid. He entrusted me with that amount to invest, but I had not the opportunity of doing so on account of my accident, and I should be glad if he would repay it."

"Is that all?"

"If you can get those two matters attended to, I shall be satisfied."

"I will try to see your father to-morrow and do my best to secure your wish."

So ended my first attempt to break the silence of death, which I record because it is a personal experience, showing how easily it may be accomplished where the connection is suitably and carefully made and safeguarded. It is only a grander telephone constructed upon the lines of spiritual, rather than physical law.

* * *

CHAPTER 16

"THEY WILL HEAR HIM"

It was quite natural for me to take more than a passing interest in the delivery of a message forwarded under such extraordinary circumstances-a message destined to put to the test the unselfish plea urged by Dives that his brothers would hear one who returned from the dead. My father was not a reed to be shaken by the wind, but a man strong of convictions, and courageous to a fault in his defence of them, rather than given to being inclined to the superstitious. Hence the outlook for such success as I wished was by no means so hopeful as I could desire, unless my message might revive in his memory some vibration of our recent interview in his sleep, and so contribute to results I could neither foresee nor estimate.

Alas! I had not then learned what I know by many experiences now-how much more conscientious the soul is, even in its temporary discarnation, than when it walks abroad clothed in its mantle of flesh and blood. If men only knew how the mask of flesh disguises their true identity even for themselves, they would stand aghast at the revelation. There was pity as well as philosophy in the advice of the Grecian sage when he said, "Man, know thyself."

The study of psychology is already revealing the fact that the idea of multiple personality is not altogether a fiction. It will not be long before it goes even further and recognizes that Robert Louis Stevenson wrote with an inspired pen and drew a characteristic picture of the race in the supposed creation of Dr. Jekyll and Mr. Hyde. The portrait is only that of man asleep and man awake.

"O wad some power the giftie gie us
To see oursels as (angels) see us!
It wad fra monie a blunder free us,
And foolish notion."

But what unnumbered errors we stumble into because such a priceless boon never rises beyond a poetic expression rather than an honest desire, and man goes on content to remain a stranger to his own true self equally as to his fellow.

That I was somewhat too sanguine in my hopes the sequel will show, but the lesson it taught me was a useful and necessary one. In my hope and expectation I had failed entirely to consider the earth influences in balancing the probabilities. Myhanene knew this, as I afterwards discovered, but he did not interfere, because these neglected forces tell like weights of lead in their opposition to our efforts, and it was better that I should discover it in practice rather than learn it as a theory.

My error lay in estimating probabilities according to the standard of my own condition, where everything is seen as it really is and may be accepted at its face value. Acting upon the change I found in my father in the sleep interview, I was led to apply this estimate to him in relation to his dealings with the message I had just transmitted. I hoped the evidence it would afford would impress him, and probably lead to a nobler future by inquiry and recognition of the indisputable evidence of available facts.

"How bright some visions break upon us!" said Myhanene presently, arousing me from my thoughts by one of his enigmatical utterances.

"I scarcely understand you," I replied.

His smile revealed more than his words.

"I think this last experience has confused me somewhat," I said.

"I have almost forgotten everything in wondering what effect the message will have upon my father."

"You must not hope for too much. But would you like to watch its effect for yourself?"

"I should indeed, if such a thing is possible."

"It can easily be arranged," replied my friend.

Chapter 16   "They Will Hear Him"

Then speaking to our Recorder, he inquired:

"Will you let me know when you are about to deliver the message?"

Listen, all ye who are accustomed to think of death as the last dread enemy of mankind! Myhanene was speaking to one on either side of the tomb. He was equally heard by each, yet his voice was not louder than a musical whisper. He was making a request that, when his fellow-servant on earth proceeded to execute a commission on the morrow, a telegraphic message should be sent to him in Paradise to acquaint him of the fact.

"Yes, certainly," was the ready response.

"Then Eusimos shall call Aphraar, and they shall go with you to learn the result."

With such arrangements possible, how far away from earth are we removed?

Eusimos kept the appointment, and when James and my father met, we were present, though unseen.

The reception was such as the host generally accorded to strangers, especially those who were regarded as socially inferior to himself; proud, cold, and quizzically suspicious.

"You wish to see me?" he inquired without offering a seat.

"Yes, but my reason for doing so requires some little explanation."

"Make that as brief as possible. I am a busy man, with no disposition to waste time."

"Nor can I afford to do so, but being asked to deliver a message, I ..."

"Excuse me; from whom do you bear the communication?"

"Your son, Mr. Frederic Winterleigh."

"It is false! My son is dead, and there our interview must end."

He turned to open the door.

"Very well, if you so elect," replied James, "but I think your son, whether dead or not, would like to know you had recovered your lost volume of Lodge's Portraits."

He turned sharply, without opening the door, to inquire warmly: "What do you know about the book? Let me caution you sir, that I am not a man to be trifled with. If you have lost the volume in your possession, produce it without trying to levy blackmail upon me by any spiritualistic nonsense, or you will find yourself in a serious corner."

My messenger's cheeks flushed with indignation at the unfounded suggestion.

"If you think any financial consideration brought me here, you make a great mistake. I would scorn to touch your money though you proffered it, so you may dismiss any thought of blackmail from your mind."

"But why do you not tell me where the book is?"

"Because I have lacked the opportunity of doing so."

"Then you have it now."

"I have two messages to deliver from Mr. Frederic..."

"I tell you my son is dead, sir!"

"Did I deny it? Will you excuse me, Mr. Winterleigh, but this interview is quite as unpleasant to me as yourself; if therefore you will allow me to say what I came to say and take my leave, I shall feel obliged. What course you choose to take upon the information I have to give can be determined afterwards. I am asked to say that the claim of the valet, Acres, for twenty pounds is rightly made."

"Oh, that is your purpose, is it? You are a confederate of his, are you?"

"No. I know nothing of the man, and have never seen him."

"Then how do you know about this money?"

"I decline to discuss that under the circumstances, but will you kindly allow me to finish the message and go? My time is equally valuable as your own."

"What is it you have to say?"

"That two days before your son's accident, Acres gave him twenty pounds to invest, an investment which your son had not time to carry out, and he wishes you to return it from his estate."

"That will be for me to make inquiries about; but what about the book?"

"On the same day Acres entrusted him with this money, your son lent the missing volume to his friend and neighbour in chambers, Mr. Ralph Unacliff."

The quiet and unassuming tone in which this information was conveyed, as if it was an ordinary and everyday communication between friend and friend, was too much for my father's self-assurance and assumption of superiority. The human nature in every man is reachable, given tact and occasion, and this startling message had for the moment shaken, if not completely penetrated, my father's vulnerable spot.

"Do you recognize the stupendous significance of what you say, should it prove to be true?" he inquired.

"Perfectly; and it is also true. But I am too familiar with such communications to share your astonishment."

"You must explain yourself. Won't you sit down?"

"No, thank you; I have executed my commission and we are both busy men."

It was the visitor who was calm and reticent now, and my father was visibly disconcerted.

"But if this you tell me should prove to be true, it is the most astounding thing I have ever heard."

"Then I would advise you to put it to the test, and afterwards, take what further steps the result demands."

"But won't you offer some explanation?"

"It would be useless until you have verified the message. After that, I shall be pleased to render you any assistance in my power. You have my card, and I am at home on Wednesdays after seven to help inquirers. Have you any reply?"

"What reply can I make in the first moment of such an unprecedented communication? If you could spare me half an hour, I might be able to say something intelligible. I could telephone to Unacliff and prove the whole thing at once."

"Speak to James," I appealed to Eusimos, "and suggest that he accede to the request."

"No, it would not be well," he answered.

"Not to finish breaking down my father's prejudice?" I inquired.

"It is for that I am carefully working," replied my friend. "James is not left to himself in this matter, but is giving expression to answers I am furnishing. If your father is honest in his desire to know more of this subject, let him accept the invitation for Wednesday, and in the meantime, assure himself that the communication is true. But he will not do that."

"Are you sure?"

"His attitude is one of piqued curiosity. The two will never meet again, or it might cost the inquirer twenty pounds, and that will be more to him than truth as soon as his first astonishment is over. Further knowledge might demand other restitutions, and your father is not the man to court such risks."

I am afraid he read him aright, therefore I said no more.

"It is impossible for me to spare more time than I have already given, and if you have no reply to make, I must wish you good morning."

It was no use for him to press further; I could see from what had been said that Eusimos had James well in hand. What my father asked for was easily obtainable if he was sufficiently honest in his desire to seize the opportunity opened out to him. Whether he would do so or not after testing the communication was to be the proof of his sincerity. That is the law under which we work. We reciprocate, first furnishing a proof, then making a demand. We do not come to earth as so many seem to think, as criminals to a bar for trial, and anxious to secure a hearing upon any terms, but, rather knowing what is needed and able to render assistance, we volunteer our services, meeting confidence with confidence until such time as better acquaintance establishes a firm and solid friendship.

Chapter 16   "They Will Hear Him"

My father did not consent to this arrangement. He recovered the volume, but did not discharge the debt. There the result of my message was reached. He is with us now, knowing the truth, and were I to visit him and ask the question, he would gladly give all the gold the world contains, did he possess it, for the opportunity and its possibilities he then so lightly threw aside.

Still it is doubtful whether his moral standard was below the average on the whole. But when we stand in the light of eternal verities, it seems almost incredible that men of sound business instincts can allow themselves to be so completely blinded by false dogmatic assurances in the matter of their spiritual interests. No man will complacently regard himself as safe in the commercial world when he knows his cheque at the bank will be dishonoured, and yet the same individuals go through life smilingly confident in their condition of spiritual bankruptcy, convinced that when the hour of need arrives, they may draw heavy cheques on the bank of faith where their names are unknown, which cheques will be honoured at sight and every spiritual claim find payment through a dying prayer. 'Be not deceived!' if you have been able to mock your fellow successfully, you will meet with a rude awakening when you try the same on God. He will never become the accomplice of a dying thief seeking to evade justice. No compositions are accepted in the Court of Death, but every debt must be fully discharged with legal interest. Mercy is left behind as you cross that threshold, and Justice is the only judge occupying the bench. Not that God has changed, but the sinner has been arrested and brought to trial. Mercy defers the arrest, but Justice follows it.

With all the prayerful solicitude of a soul who has passed along the way and knows what lies before, I would place myself as far as possible on the earth side of the brow of the hill from whence the descent into the valley begins and shout, "Be cautious how you proceed, for the hill is dangerous." When once the descent begins, there is no escape. If you have not made your preparations in advance, woe betide you. The promise secured by the appalled soul of the dying thief was nothing more than a promise to be heard and justly dealt with on his arrival in Paradise. He was not forgiven. He could not be forgiven in the face of the law which enacts that, 'Whatsoever a man soweth that shall he also reap.'

Mercy has opened the gate of Paradise, and Christ has lovingly rolled away the stone from the door of the sepulchre, that the voices of those who have passed into the beyond may be heard on earth testifying to what they have discovered for your instruction. But ignorance blinds your eyes and stops your ears, and you are lulled into a false security by vain traditions, moving towards your fate with a sharper sword than that of Damocles trembling overhead till its hair is snapped, and you wake to find yourselves in the presence of an inexorable law from the consequences of which your trusted dogmatism had assured you a full discharge had been granted.

* * *

CHAPTER 17

THE HALLELUJAH STRAND

From the surroundings in which I move, I am so conscious of the value of character built upon accurate information, that a strong desire prompts me to linger over every detail of my narrative, lest I miss some apparent triviality upon which a mighty issue should afterwards be found to hang. But my difficulty lies in the certain fact that upon every point I am constrained to mention, almost infinite possibilities are centred. The germ life in a single grain of wheat is inestimable. Life knows no such differentiation as greater and lesser; these distinctions apply only to its powers of selection and assimilation controlling growth and production. One grain draws the sustenance upon which it feeds and thrives from one source, another from another; and where all have to be equally provided for duty, demands that all shall be considered.

This is the terribly startling truth we can never lose sight of. It is this that makes me so frequently reiterate, that with us there is nothing small or great, or perhaps I should rather say, everything is great and nothing small. Every suggestion I use is weighted with inestimable significance, because I speak of truth, and would gladly tarry to open every seed I scatter and show the potential value of its contents. But my duty is to sow and leave the increase to the future and to God. Still I wish I could sow my thoughts with a pen of living fire that they might burn and bury themselves deep in the lives of all to whom I speak.

Under the most favourable conditions, the law of growth is a wearily slow process, and when we look back to ascertain honestly how much we have already accomplished of our pilgrimage towards God, we tremble to speculate as to how long it will take us to reach perfection.

The powers of God repose in the nature of God, but we find

little of them in ourselves at present. It is the continual recurrence of this fact as I look back from my higher vantage ground that would make me pause, but duty calls me forward, and I must needs obey.

As an illustration that it is simply an environment and not the soul that is changed in the process of discarnation, I may very usefully here introduce the awakening of our little 'Dandy.' It is a case of peculiarly marked characteristics, well exhibiting many of the definite points of interest respecting which earth is somewhat anxiously doubtful. It was also the first occasion upon which I had watched the process from both sides, and I was therefore specially desirous to trace how much was remembered and how much forgotten before the little fellow touched the point of recollection where all would become perfectly clear to his memory.

Vaone notified me of the impending event, and when I arrived, I found Eilele (the poetess, whose acquaintance we have already made), who was present with Jack, as the nearest friend to offer the first congratulations.

Dandy was still sleeping peacefully, but what an astonishing change had taken place in his appearance since we last saw him! The pinched and haggard look had passed away, and in its place we saw the rounded healthy face of a well-developed lad. There was the suspicion of a smile playing around his mouth, and a kind of nervous tremor as if his naturally vivacious precocity was impatient to exercise itself in new and more favourable surroundings. In the days of the past the preternatural humour of the lad had been mercifully granted as an offset to hardship and suffering, and in his sleep he already seemed to understand or anticipate that he was about to wake and find the shadow had passed away, leaving the sunshine with a brighter sparkle than he had known before.

I looked from the sleeper to Jack, who was actively impatient for his friend to open his eyes and learn that his one great wish had been actually granted. In Jack I saw the first-fruits of Eilele's devoted training. His still mobile character had yielded splendidly to the moulding of her Christ-like mind, and the lad in every way represented the possible transformation Paradise can effect by its system of adaptive culture. It was only a crude block of individuality Arvez carried to her home when I first met her, but Eilele had worked upon it with skill and genius until the outline of the angel form could already be fairly well discerned. Ah! this divine study of soul sculpture is glorious work indeed!

From Jack my eyes wandered to his instructress, whose face shone with the soft glow of one of her far-away contemplations, but at the moment she raised her head, and our eyes met.

"Is it not beautiful," she inquired, "to watch the unfolding of such treasures in the garden of the Lord?"

"I wish it were possible clearly to understand the whole of the beauty," I replied. "As it is we lose so much because we can appreciate so little."

"I have given up the idea of ever being able to understand the all. My cup runneth over; and I try to be satisfied if I can add to the sweetness of my life's contents some new, if only faint, idea of the music contributed by each new experience."

"Can you be satisfied?" I asked.

"No, no! I think mine must be a very restless, daring, aspiring soul."

Then, with one of her meditative outstretches of reverence, she added:

"And yet it is not that so much as God's great love, drawing me ever nearer to Him at a rate that refuses to allow my slowly expanding soul to keep pace with His wonderful developments. Oh, Aphraar, who is able to understand this incomprehensible life into which you and I are but just unfolding?"

"I wish you would grant me an opportunity of speaking to you on these things," I ventured to ask, encouraged by her inquiry.

"In your earth-life you were so active in the cause of the Master, whereas I scarcely gave a disinterested thought to Him. I see my error now, and when I hunger to know so much of Him, I know of no one, save perhaps Myhanene, who could help me as you might do."

"Come home with me, when our little friend awakes," she answered, "and we will help each other to understand more of the Father's love than we know at present."

"Yes, I will gladly come, and thus gratify another of my long deferred desires."

"Is that really so?" and a softly indeterminate smile lighted her face as she spoke. "The pleasures of His service are more than passing sweet, especially where the ministry is so personally remunerative."

"Then Shakespeare spoke by inspiration when he said that Mercy—

> *"'is twice blest;*
> *It blesses him that gives and him that takes.'"*

"It must needs be so with all the gifts of God," she replied. "They exhale a blessing on every receptive soul they pass."

As she spoke, Myhanene with a company of attendants arrived to give the lad a welcome from the hardships he had so patiently and unselfishly borne. No longer was the benign young ruler dressed in the neutral robe he wore when last I saw him, but in the resplendent raiment with which he came to kiss those sleepers in the Magnetic Chorale back to life. He had again the self-same office to perform, and with more than a royal welcome, awakened a soul whose body earth had already hurried unnoticed and unwept into a pauper's grave.

> *"Carry him hence, at the public cost,*
> *Bury, dissect him, or do as you may;*
> *Nobody knows him; no one will miss him,*
> *Homeless and friendless, take him away.*

Chapter 17 — The Hallelujah Strand

Back of the death-veil, hidden by shadows
Angels were waiting in regions of light,
Anxiously waiting to bid him 'good-morning'
Who passed from the earth without a 'good night'."

Such was actually the difference in the conditions of the lad—between ignorance and knowledge, humanity and divinity. Values at sight are not always faultlessly accurate. Tell a connoisseur the name and subject of an old master and he will fairly estimate its real value in hundreds or thousands, but the ignorant boor win turn disdainfully from the dirty canvas for which he would not give five shillings.

Just so in the merchandise of souls; the highly-coloured St. Dives is hung on the line, in most favourable light, even in a church exhibition, while Lazarus is left to the care of the dogs. Poor Dives! Happy Lazarus! Mistaken ecclesiastics! Ignorant humanity!
What an absolute necessity exists that a court of justice should be established where righteousness reigns.

Myhanene took Jack by the hand and led him to that side of the couch towards which the face of the sleeper was turned, then bending over, he gently kissed the lips that had been already twitching as if impatient to give utterance to the lad's surprise.

The body stretched to its full length, the head half-turned, a faint "Oh dear" escaped the lips, then the eyes opened, and the bewildered lad jumped into a sitting posture.

"Wheer am I? 'Ello, Jack! Why! Wheer 'as I got to?"

"You are at home now," said Myhanene.

"Yes, Dandy, you are dead now and have come to be where I am," cried the delighted Jack.

"Dead, Jack? Get out! I look like a dead un, don't I?" In his astonishment his eyes roamed round the place and the company surrounding him; then he asked, "Ere, what are they bin doin' to the 'orspickle?"

"Don't you remember me?" asked Myhanene.

The lad looked at him doubtfully for an instant.

"Yes. Worn't you the doctor?"

"No. Think again."

"Oh, yis! I remember now. Yer said yer wouldn't leave me, didn't yer?"

"Yes. Then you went to sleep, and I brought you here."

"Is this another 'orspickle then?"

"Yes, this is one of God's hospitals, where everyone gets well."

"You are better now, Dandy, ain't you?" asked his little friend.

"Yes, I'm better. But Jack, am I dead, straight?"

"Why, don't you feel dead?"

"No, I'm better. Slep' mysel' better, I s'pose, an' I didn't want ter."

"Well, you know I am dead, don't you?"

"Yes, you're dead enough, but what about me-I ain't."

"Then how can you see me? Do you think you are asleep?"

"No, I ain't asleep"-and he looked bewilderedly around as if searching for some explanation, "becos somebody wakened me."

Then he turned appealingly to Myhanene. "Say, you know. Tell me what's the matter?"

"Yes, I will tell you all about it. You remember the hospital?"

"Yis, an' I was so bad!"

"Do you remember asking me if I was the angel who was going to kill you?"

"I think I does, but I was so bad, yer knows."

"You remember Bully Peg?"

"Yis. Did 'e get my money?"

This enabled him to touch the first point of recollection, and a portion of his memory became clear, so that without Myhanene reminding him of more, he went on:

"Oh, I know all about it now. 'E 'ad a tanner from the doctor, didn't 'e? An' then yer said I'd got ter go back, an' it wouldn't 'urt me, but miss said I was to go to sleep, didn't she?"

"Yes."

"Well, then, wheer am I now? 'Ave I got to go back agen?"

"No, it is all over now."

"But I ain't dead yet."

"Are you not? Why the nurse and doctors say you are."

"But I ain't, am I?"

"Of course you are, Dandy; all the dead there is for you," said Jack.

"Am I tho'?" he doubtfully appealed to Myhanene.

"Yes, I think you may take your little friend's word for it. You know all of death you ever will know."

"But I doan know anythin' about it. It didn't 'urt a bit."

"I told you it would not."

"An' can I get up?"

"Yes, we want you to go home now. Jack is going with you for a little while."

"An' when you go to th' College, yer'll take me wi' yer, won't yer, Jack?"

"Yes, I will take you everywhere I can."

"An' we must see Bully Peg, becos I want ter know 'ow 'e's goin, on."

How long the enumeration of his first desires would have taken, it is difficult to say, but Jack told him they would arrange everything presently, then, Myhanene led the little fellow on to the terrace, where a host of new friends gave him a welcome that I am afraid was mostly lost upon him in the delight of the thousand beauties that surrounded him. Especially was this noticeable when Myhanene, having finished his part in the proceedings, took his departure, accompanied by his companions from his higher home. Their course through the air rendered Dandy absolutely speechless with astonishment, and he looked from one to the other of us as if begging for some explanation of the uncanny phenomenon.

It would be interesting, did space and necessity permit, to

follow the course of these two boys for a while, and trace the ministry of the one who had so wonderfully improved under the instruction of Eilele, in his effort to enlighten his newly-arrived friend in regard to the initial features of this new and surprising existence. Jack already knew enough to be of valuable service at the outset, and Dandy would accept his assurances with far more unquestioning faith than those of a stranger, while the information imparted would always be within the knowledge of others near at hand to correct or explain if necessary. Thus we see how the law of Heaven condescends to accept even the most feeble service as competent to take part in the work of a soul's salvation. For the present the little initiate would have to be led gently forward until his bewildered mind was able to touch the final point of recollection and he could intelligently connect the present with the clearly recalled memories of the past, which I have already referred to in my own experience. Jack was quite competent to do this even better than an older teacher, and therefore his choice for the work, which we must content ourselves to imagine, rather than follow in detail.

In recording this incident, I have kept my attention fixed on the three central figures, simply because all the interest for myself was confined to that little group, and the surrounding accessories were not consciously in existence for the time. Myhanene's presence was official, and his duty to wake and welcome the little pilgrim to the new sphere of existence. This accomplished, he returned, and Eilele at once assumed control by reason of her more advanced condition.

The lad's eyes were still riveted on the ascending company who had just left us, when she knelt beside him and gently laid her head beside his.

"I say!" he asked, scarcely daring to turn his eyes for an instant lest he should lose the vision; "is they really hangels?"

"Yes, God sent them to bid you welcome home."

"Well, wheer's their wings, then?"

"They have none."

"Then they ain't real hangels."

"Yes, they are God's real angels."

"Then they ought to ha' wings. I never seed a hangel wi'out 'em before."

"You have only seen pictures of angels before and in pictures they give them wings so that we might know them from men."

"That's why I didn't know 'em. But I don't think they're reg'lar real hangels now."

"Why not?"

"Becos they didn't sing a welcome 'ome to me as we allus sung about at th' mission."

"But they kissed you and bade you welcome."

"That ain't it. I wanted 'em to—

"'stand at th' 'allelujah in the Strand
an' sing me a welcome 'ome.'

I likes singin' better'n kissin'."

Dandy had seized on an orthodox idea of Heaven for himself, and unless the programme was strictly carried out according to preconceived plans, he was somewhat dubious about its genuineness. It was the ignorance and suspicion of an unlettered lad, but since his time I have watched the arrival of scores of educated adults, who have raised the same ignorant objection and even insisted that they were not suitably received.

Such souls, however, were mostly of those who arrived empty-handed; the weary ones from the harvest fields were seeking rest and found it.

* * *

CHAPTER 18

LIFE'S MOSAICS

Poor Dandy's mind was in the state of doubtful spiritual confusion frequently experienced by many who have been far better circumstanced than himself in the earth-life. He had, like others, permitted his fanciful ignorance to mould and fashion the superstitious speculations of his dogmatic masters and pastors concerning an after-life into a nebulous uncertainty, and when he entered upon it, was surprised to find a condition of law and order, where he had anticipated an indescribable unnaturalness coupled with intangible eccentricities.

In this lies the root of the confusion experienced by almost every new arrival. The life Elysian is too real, too much a continuance of our old selves with only new surroundings adaptively arranged in harmony with the nature we have cultivated; it is too much the effect of causes we vainly imagined our mask of religion had concealed even from the suspicion of existence; it binds the two states too closely in one where we have comfortably deceived ourselves that death would end the whole and begin a new life, where spiritual ancestry could not be inconveniently traced.

Be not deceived, death is only an incident in life, not an end. Whatsoever is sown in the springtime of earth must be reaped in the autumn of Paradise.

Happy are they who can resume existence in the hereafter with no greater confusion than that of Dandy; we can listen to the expression of his bewilderment-even smile at it, but I have known many instances where the revelation appalled with its agony.

"Yer sure I is dead, Jack?" he asked his friend after again looking carefully around him and comparing his present with his past environment.

"Of course you are. Why? Don't you want to be now it's too late to alter it?"

"Yis! I'm glad er that. But I wish them mission coves wouldn't tell such lies, an' stuff kiddies as they do. Wot are they got ter say that the angels'd meet us for, when we die, at the 'allelujah in the Strand, an' sing us a welcome 'ome? They know it ain't true."

"No, they don't, Dandy."

"Well, I do, then. The 'allelujahs ain't got a place in th' Strand. There's the Tiv'li an' the 'Delphi an' the Gaiety, an' the Law Courts, but I've looked many a time for a 'allelujah place, but I never seed one yet."

Eilele smiled and drew the mistaken lad closer to herself as she discovered his false impression and prepared to remove it.

"Now I understand the cause of your disappointment," she said, "and will explain the mistake for you. You thought the angels would meet you at a Salvation Army meeting in the Strand."

"Ain't they the 'allelujah people?" he inquired.

"Yes, sometimes they are called so. But the meaning of the hymn is that the angels would meet you on the shores of the gloryland.

"O-oh! I didn't know that."

"No. That is how you made the mistake. Now, Myhanene and his friends met you just before you died, and did welcome you home."

"But 'e didn't sing it?"

Poor little fellow; he wanted the letter verified. Like many who are older, better circumstanced and of greater intellectual capacity, the spiritual truth was lost to him in a verbal inaccuracy. But Jack, and several friends who had known Dandy at the College, carried him off and would speedily satisfy his most exacting demands, not perhaps in the manner he desired at the moment, but they would satisfy him none the less.

"Is this the first awakening at which you have been present?" Eilele asked when we were alone.

"It is."

"Then you will scarcely understand the confusion of it, until you recall your own experience. Everything is so very different to anticipation, especially the discovery that death is nothing more than an ordinary sleep during which an unexpected transformation has been worked in everything but ourselves, and that alone, which we expected death would change, remains untouched. Was it not so with you?"

"Partly. I was sorely perplexed as to where I was and what had occasioned the change in my location. But, had someone been present from whom I could have received an explanation, I do not think my surprise would have been so great."

"Then you were allowed to wake upon the slopes, and in your previous life had not troubled yourself much as to the nature of this existence?"

"No, I took very little interest in what always appeared to be useless speculations. My idea of religion was to do the best I could with the duty of the moment, and leave the future to look after itself. I hope my candid admission will not disturb you."

"Not now," she replied, with a somewhat amused smile. "It would have done so at one time, but I have learned to take a broader view, and understand more of the truth than I knew on earth. Much of what I once regarded as essential I now see to be more of a hindrance than assistance, and much that I despised would have helped me wonderfully. I lived more in the future than the present, and sketched my plan of Heaven with even more of detail than I myself imagined until I opened my eyes upon this life and realized the error. Perhaps that enables me to sympathize more with the disappointment of poor little Dandy than you can understand."

"Kinship of experience would give you that advantage," I replied.

"But such experiences are not to be coveted. He had only one confused idea of what Heaven would be-that of angels meeting him on some sort of Salvation Army platform he had located in the Strand, and singing him a welcome home. I can almost see the picture which had gradually taken shape in his mind; the crowded hall, and the platform filled with white-robed angels wearing golden crowns and opalescent wings, and he, the hero of the occasion, being led forward while the welcome home was sung. When I think of it I can sympathize with his disappointment, and do not wonder he refused to believe. The whole of his Heaven had disappeared; it was not quite so serious with myself. After my first recoil of surprise I found, if the accessories were absent, I had entered upon the rest; though the architecture was different, I recognized the Father's house; though the wedding garment was not ready, I was conscious of having come nearer to the Bridegroom, and when I realized this, I was content."

"Only content-not satisfied?"

"The soul can never be satisfied until it awakes to find itself bearing His full likeness," she replied gravely. "While we remain unlike, we shall also be absent from Him. The light of His holiness must radiate from ourselves before our sight will be pure enough to enable us to see Him. Then, and not till then, shall we be satisfied."

"Did the discovery disappoint you?"

"In a measure, yes. But only for an instant, then I was glad. Everything was so different to all my expectations that I was compelled to revise every conception I had framed. But in doing this I was able to begin with the consciousness that everything immeasurably surpassed all that my former visions had pictured. With these great advantages available in my new arrangement, I no longer regretted my fictitious loss, but gloried in the gain. For instance, it was no hardship to drop the limitations of ecclesiasticism that I might have my hands empty to grasp this life."

"But you do not renounce Christianity?"

"To that I must reply both Yes and No, but in doing so I want you clearly to understand what it is I renounce and what I retain. Looking back from this life I see religion to be a very different thing to even my own earth conception of it. As the light in passing through a prism becomes separated and forms a rainbow-tinted spectrum, so God's truth in passing through humanity breaks up into many forms of religion, each emphasizing some particular ray. In God's bow of promise there is room for every combination of colour. Justice and truth demand this recognition. Each is known and takes rank according to the fruit it bears. 'All ye are brethren-love one another,' is the Father's law. Now, I try to apply this standard equally all the way round, and of my own church I ask, 'Is its history one of making wars to cease? Does it systematically protect the weak against the strong? Is the policy of invasion of other countries always governed by a Good Samaritan motive? Has it always been characterized by freedom and good-will? Do the Christian nations always act with brotherly unison in the matter of carrying their gospel forward 'in honour preferring one another'? Which so-called Christian church, by reason of its humility, is to be accounted greatest? Is the Eastern Church of Russia, or the Western Rome, or England, protesting against both alike, the ideal leader of the forward movement? Where is the spirit of the Christ for which we naturally look in the forefront of the policy of a nation calling itself by His most holy name?' Yet, not one of the so-called Christian nations moves its army or its navy for action, but from every pulpit in its land God is called upon to bless the slaughter for which they go forth and to crush the nation against whom they move. These are the broadly defined lines of systematized Christianity as it appears from where we stand, and such I now renounce as being anti-Christian-a wolf in sheep's clothing. The Christ of God gave Himself for every man; the Christianity as exhibited to the world gives nothing unless it can take more from any or every man. On the other hand, I retain and hold that which Christian theology has forgotten and lost-the true Christ-life, which all who truly follow Him enter into and enjoy, between which and the theology usurping His name, there is a gulf fixed across which no man is able to step and keep one foot on either side."

"But you do not deny that there are good men within the church?"

"There are always men who are better than their creed, who remain within, but not of, their system-the heretics of to-day who will become the saints of to-morrow. Christ and modern Christian theology are irreconcilable. The teaching of the One is, 'Let all your striving be to make your own calling and election sure until the Christ-power, generated from your own life, shall compel others to come in.' The other practically allows, 'Having been justified by His death without any effort or commendation of our own, without consideration of character, morality or fitness, we are commissioned to go into all the world and compel men to be better than we are on pain of everlasting torment.' These are the simple laws governing a life and a system so much at variance as to be irreconcilable, the latter of which I am compelled to renounce that I may consecrate myself to the former."

"I am no apologist for the churches," I replied, "but when I hear you speak in such a strain, I can scarcely believe it."

"Your personal interest in the life and work of the Master has not yet led you to study these things in the light of the present," she answered, "or you would not wonder at the expressions I use. I have no doubt but few of those who have read my writings would think me capable of speaking as strongly as I am now speaking, just as I myself once failed to understand how the meek and lowly Christ could scourge the priests and teachers of His day with the awful flagellation recorded in Matthew twenty-third. I can understand and cease to wonder at it now since He saw and understood what is here so plainly visible. But I must repeat what I have already said, there are good and holy men, saintly and self-sacrificing, whom the officialdom of theology has been powerless to touch; salt of the earth still preserving its savour in spite of the corruption; standard-bearers of the Master who keep the torch of truth burning in their holy lives as a protest to the Judas legion by which their Lord is betrayed. God has never left His people without this leaven, and it is in connection with this you will be able to work when you commence your ministry."

"May I ask how you know what work I am about to engage in?"

"There is no secret in that," she replied, "but you are not yet accustomed to think how easily we are known and read of all men in all things which pertain to the kingdom. It is my consciousness of this that led me to speak to you as I have done, because I am desirous that you should have my testimony as to the uselessness of many of the things our friends on earth most prize. Don't forget in all your communion that Jew or Gentile, bond or free, church or chapel, Protestant or Romanist, Christian or Buddhist, profiteth nothing, but the one essential necessity is a new creature from whose life all the old things are passed away."

"I am glad that you have been led to speak of my coming labours. It was in connection with this I most wished to speak with you and ask your counsel and assistance. I have but recently learned that my hope in this direction will be realized, and already the weight of the responsibility it entails seems to be too much for me."

"I can well understand that, my brother. Of all the vocations to which a soul is liable to be summoned here, I can conceive of none more important than that in which you will be engaged. It arises not so much from the difficulty in declaring what is true-that is comparatively simple when the teaching of the Master is taken to be the rule of what is declared, and you confine yourself to the things you know-but the complications and difficulties will arise in attacking those errors which have for generations been taught as truths, blinding the eyes of men and hardening their hearts until they have eyes that see not, ears that hear not, and but little true understanding is to be found in them. This will double your responsibility, try your patience, tax all your resources and test your powers. Still you need not fear if you take Christ's yoke upon you; linked with Him your yoke will be easy and the burden light, for He is able to subdue all things to Himself, and with Him you cannot go astray."

"I wish I had your knowledge and experience to begin with."

"My knowledge and experience alone would be of little service to you in such a work."

"Do you think so?"

"I am sure of it. If they really were the preparation for such a work as you imagine, I should no doubt be called to it myself. But in that I am not so called I know that I am not qualified for it. At present, it may be wisely hidden from you wherein your own aptitude may lie, but you will see it, and then you will understand how my experience would have rather disqualified you than otherwise. If Myhanene has accepted you for service, you may rest assured that God has so ordained it, and you have no need to be afraid."

"Will you allow me to wish that I had your faith?"

"Yes, if that will help you, but when you know the Master as I know Him, I hope you will have a stronger faith than mine. You do not know Him-have not seen Him yet, have you?"

"No! Have you?"

"Y-es! I-have-seen-Him! And the rapture of it is unspeakable! It was a vision and a revelation, changing, explaining, correcting, and illuminating everything! At the sight of Him I understood what John affirmed-'In Him was life, and the life was the light of men.' Yes, life and light; eternal and shadowless! Full, overpowering, abounding! Away, away into the everlasting evermore!"

I was silent. Her soul had taken wing and soared upward into heights I had no power to scale. In her sacred memory she had caught an echoing reflection of the vision of the King in His beauty, and worshipped in a holy consecration too exalted for me to reach. "It was in the light of the radiance of that sight I spoke just now when you could scarcely understand the strength of my language," she continued as she awoke from her reverie, "by which I also assure you that 'what thou knowest not now thou shalt know hereafter.' Have only one fear-to know Christ and speak the truth as it is in Him. Then all must be well!"

"Your experience also confirms that?"

"It does! It must! 'He is the Alpha and Omega; the beginning and the end; therefore, what begins must of necessity end in Him and be well. As He, in your ministry, has to be your theme, let Him also be your model. Speak simply, that all may understand you; kindly, that all may be drawn to you; patiently, that all may feel they have a friend in you, and naturally, that all may find in nature an exposition of your gospel. As far as in you lies, avoid all mysteries, but as the reaping is always governed by the sowing, so let it be known that the counterpart and consequence of all actions must eventually be found. Shall I read you another of my songs on this subject, the thoughts of which may prove helpful and suggestive to you?"

"Do, please! I shall never forget the assistance I received from the other."

We had by this time reached her home high up on those delectable mountains from which one seemed able to look down the vale of an entrancing futurity into the eternal rest that remaineth. On either side the glory-crowned hills rose like janitors of peace, and the music of hidden cascades sang love-songs to the flowers. I sat me down where one of the fairest prospects gave invitation, and an instant later Eilele sat beside me, with her book lying on the table before her, from which she, without a word of introduction, read:

LIFE MOSAICS

"Life Mosaics. Who can answer?
How, or what, or when, or why?
To the thousand mystic problems
That perplex us constantly?

The Life Elysian

Every heart is full of murmurs;
Every head is racked with pain;
Useless are all disputations,
Still the mysteries remain.
Life seems naught but showers and sunshine,
Mountain-tops or valleys deep;
Burning summers, freezing winters,
Toil and dream-distracted sleep.

Here are days of sombre blackness,
Now a few of pallid white,
Mingled with the grey and murky.
Still continue;-all is right!
Now the golden tints are needed,
Emerald or sapphire tones,
Jasper, ruby or carbuncle,
Pearls and other precious stones.
Here a groan and there a tear-drop,
Now a sigh that rends the heart;
Then a shout of exultation,
Life Mosaics, these are part.

Now come days of preparation
And of working-as He will,—
Fashioning as He designeth
With His wondrous matchless skill;
Sudden sweeps and sharper angles
We can never comprehend;
But He knows the why and wherefore,
How and when the task will end;
Knows the number of each colour,
Counts all tears and every sigh;
Finds the counterpart of sorrow
In some long-forgotten joy.

Chapter 18 — Life's Mosaics

Other builders toil and labour
Bringing marble, wood and stone,
Other hands will come and finish
That which we must leave undone.
He who blasts the stone in quarry
Cannot carve the angel face,
In the rough hewn block of marble,
Full of tenderness and grace.
He who digs the ore can never
Fashion-chase the cup of gold;
Nor can he the robes embroider
Who attends the sheep in fold.

Weary toiler, think a moment,
God has given but a share
Of mosaics for thy portion;
Thou couldst never all prepare.
Other hands are working with thee;
Neither can they comprehend
Whither all these constant failings
And catastrophes may tend;
But the Architect well knoweth
All the plans which He has made,
Therefore do His bidding simply,
And thy penny shall be paid.

Learn-the discord in the music,
May but serve to change the key,
And become a fitting prelude
To some sweeter harmony.
So the groans which thou art breathing,
And thy fellow's deep-drawn sigh,
May produce a touching trio
Blended with another's joy.

In life's agonizing piercings
Precious jewels may be set;
But the stones God is providing
Are uncut, unpolished yet.

When all quantities are ready
God will show the rich design;
And His own unerring fingers
Will the chosen tints combine,
Dovetailing the joys and sorrows,
Happiness with days of doubt,
Seasons of long disappointment
With the short triumphant shout.
Every shade and every pattern,
So-called flaws, will find their place,
Forming parts of decoration
Of surpassing matchless grace.

Thus all lives are spent in labour,
Often bitter, sometimes sweet;
Every action seems disjointed,
Every fragment incomplete,
But the Father wisely orders
Every consecrated life,
And will bring the sweetest music
Out of this apparent strife.
Trust Him-leave Him to resolve it
In His own appointed way,
Knowing we shall share the triumphs
Of the coming crowning day."

She closed the book as she finished reading, gently pushed it from her, rested one elbow on the table and her head upon her hand while she looked dreamily away down the valley.

"Perhaps the thought will seem vague, mixed and uncertain," she said, "in its abrupt transitions from one side of life to the other, from doubt to confidence, from incertitude to clearness of vision, but I penned the lines just as the inspiration came, and they seemed to be governed by an easy adaptation to the subject of which they speak. I could not have written such verses in the lower life; I should not have felt the natural intertwining, but everything is so different when looking back; the guiding hand reaches out from the mysterious draperies, the shadows light up so beautifully, and the presence-the hitherto undiscovered presence-of the Master is so visibly near, perhaps closer in the seeming failures sometimes than we realize in the successes, that one needs must look them up and set them side by side. Ah, me! If we could only read the present in the light of the future, as we can read the past in the golden halo of the present, how much more faithful would our service be." Then turning her soft, moist, poetic eyes with keen inquiry full upon me, she asked, "Do you understand what I mean?"

"Partly." I could not trust myself to say more lest I should disturb her.

"I suppose that is as much as may be for the present. We are only able to know in part; how, then, can we hope to understand in full, especially when the ocean of Providence is so broad, so long, so deep? Who has been able to trace its confines? What mariner has discovered its ten thousand isles of beauty and holy romance? What compass is able to guide to its poleless haven? The ocean and the secret hiding-place of God; how can we reach it? Must we ever drift upon the tide of Providence, upon the unknown, until some morning we awaken as our keel grates on the strand to find ourselves, 'For ever with the Lord'? It may be so. He knows, and I am constrained to be content with that. I can only look back and see clearly before us lays the unknown for which we all must trust Him."

CHAPTER 19

THE GOD OF MEN

Looking back from the heights and after-light of Paradise, all the earth-scenes and connections are viewed and read in the light of a new interpretation, especially when one like Eilele undertakes to direct the vision. Her loyal soul had patiently learned how to trace the sequences in the confidence that springs from close communion with Him whom she had loved so well and long. I knew Him at present only by the hearing of the ear; she had been with and learned by Him, had caught something of His spirit, tasted of His tenderness, leaned upon His bosom, and could speak as she had heard Him speak. From such a vantage-ground all the past was seen to be flooded with a divine light, a divine compassion, a paternal consideration for and estimate of our weaknesses, and from this was reflected confidence and assurance for the future.

There had been moments in my recent experiences when the thought of the responsibilities of my chosen service made me pause and almost wish I had made some other choice, but with Eilele I viewed my mission with a confidence I had never felt before. Under the influence of her inspiration I ceased to think of the long period of probation I must necessarily serve to equip me for my duty, and recalled Cushna's early assurance that time did not exist in Paradise. I no longer dwelt upon the desirability of going apart to reflect upon all I had seen and heard lest I should lose the lesson each incident was designed to teach, but discovered that every detail had been indelibly written upon my memory and stored away for use whenever an appropriate occasion should arise. Then the searchlight of recollection swept for an instant across the mass of information I had already garnered, and as I beheld, I was astonished at the unsuspected resources available for my use.

Still, however much knowledge I had acquired, the one great subject of religion had never been definitely discussed with anyone with the fullness it deserved and needed before I could confidently enter upon my new work. Who was there in all the hosts of Paradise to whom I could appeal for assistance in this matter, as to my present companion? When we were yet unknown to each other, and I was sitting in the darkness and desolation of the lower life, her poems came to me with a strange inspiration of consolation. She seemed to speak to me as no other could or did speak; she understood me even better than I understood myself; comforted me with songs no other voice could sing. Was she conscious of her power to stir my soul to depths no other influence had ever reached? It might be so, since on both occasions of our meeting she had voluntarily touched upon that one great subject I so desired to hear her explain. If she would but reach out her hand and lead me in the paths wherein she delighted to wander, allow me to follow where she could lead, assist me to climb to the heights of her own exaltation, what truths might I behold, what visions might I not see?

I was thus dreamily, hopefully meditating in the wake of what had already passed between us, but she, as usual, had taken flight into those regions I could not gain without assistance. I may have reached the outer portal of the shrine I fain would enter, but she had passed within and was worshipping in the inner presence where God was. I looked into her eyes, as she sat beside me, bright with the glory of the sight upon which she gazed; I saw her ears which I knew were ravished with the exquisite music of holy voices, but I could not see, I could not hear; my eyes and ears were not attuned to such vibrations. Yet it was good to be with her.

Presently her eyes lost their fixity; the lids drooped; she drew her hand automatically across her face and breathed a soft sigh like a half-expressed and reverent 'Amen,' then smiled as if in apology for her forgetfulness.

Chapter 19 — The God of Men

"I have been away," she said, "travelling in distant but surpassingly lovely scenes."

"More beautiful than these?" I inquired, looking about me on the enchanting surroundings of her house.

"As this transcends the earth," she replied, "so also does it fail to suggest what I have seen. Ah, Aphraar, we can never know in looking forward or around, it is only in the looking back that we are able to understand. Life, love and God can only be known in the light of the afterglow, the soul will never be strong enough in the present to comprehend the overflow of that which surrounds us. God ever drops over us the half-obscuring veil of love when He is near; it hides Him from our sight while we inspire strength to move to heights of comprehension on which we turn to find that He has passed, then only can we see and understand."

"You speak of heights I have not climbed; but I long to reach them if you will point out to me the way by which I may do so."

"Yes, I will speak-will go with you, and together we will climb this sacred hill of the Lord."

"Tell me of Him, for I know so little, though I desire so much. If I do not know, how can I speak of Him to earth?"

"I understand," she answered softly, thoughtfully. "You wish to be fed that you may be able to return and feed others. I was only thinking of yourself. I can speak with you, but I cannot speak through you to others."

"Wherein lies the difference?"

"I cannot explain, but the difference certainly exists. Did I not tell you my experience would not qualify you for your work? The request you now make brings me practically face to face with my own incompetence. I can speak to you as soul to soul, but to speak to others through you is quite another matter. Still, there are many friends who are able and ready to do so, and Omra will be pleased to send someone for the purpose."

I saw a thought-flash take flight as she spoke, but as yet I was not accustomed to think that a decision and action thereon are synonymous, until we were joined by a stranger Omra had already deputed to instruct me as desired.

Rhamya is another of those youthful ancients upon whose shoulders the mystery of ages seems to rest as an invisible mantle of wisdom. Tall, calm and majestic in appearance, the first impression he made upon me was that of a magnificent mountain rising in stately grandeur from the bosom of a troubled sea. But a second glance speedily declared that in addition to granite walls and scrapings, here was to be found assistance, refuge, shelter, and brotherly compassion.

Before he spoke I understood the wisdom of Eilele's action. Our new friend was undeniably a teacher, my companion but a pupil in the school wherein I was desirous of studying for a time.

"Aphraar is joining Myhanene's mission, Rhamya, and asks for such help as you can give far better than I am able."

"So Omra tells me, and I am glad to be of service. Let us speak together in the light of God."

"You are more than kind," I replied, "and I can only hope that my future work will show how deeply I appreciate your effort."

"Let us say pleasure and profit rather than effort," he returned, "since in what we are about to do, we shall be constrained to work under that fundamental law laid down by Christ-'Give and it shall be given unto you.' This at once changes the venue of obligation, and rather makes me to be the debtor for the privilege you have afforded me."

"Experience teaches me the futility of discussion," I answered, "therefore I will at once concede the point, though I shall insist on adding my own gratitude as a personal acknowledgement."

Being thus placed upon the most affable terms, Rhamya immediately addressed himself to the purpose of his visit.

"Now let this be my first word of counsel to you in relation to your forthcoming mission; whenever you are consulted as to any thought, action or opinion, be careful before replying to place yourself as far as possible on the same ground in relation to the question as Christ Himself occupied, and where you have no clear statement of His to guide you, be sure your interpretation of the general law He has laid down is natural, consistent and reasonably clear. There are other teachers, but none of such authority as He who was 'God'-i.e., as much of God as it is possible to be-'manifest in the flesh.' Whatever adds to or takes from the fundamental basis of His teaching, no matter under what circumstances or by what authority, is not of truth. Do you understand what I mean?"

"Perfectly!"

"We have then to discover what was the true position of Jesus Christ towards authority, for this one question will be the one pivot upon which the strength of your own position will rest. Fortunately He has left no possible doubt upon this point. His command is to 'render unto Caesar the things that are Caesar's, and unto God the things that are God's.' There can be no two opinions as to His meaning here-in all things temporal, submit to temporal authority; in all things spiritual to God alone. This law of Christ is far more drastic, when fully applied, than appears at first sight. It allows no shred of divine authority to any purely human foundation-no ecclesiastical or religious corporation exists as a Christian institution. This Paul understood when he declared to Timothy, 'There is one God, and one mediator between God and men, the man Christ Jesus'; there is no room for any human foundation here and this teaching is quite harmonious with that of the Master to the woman at Sychar-'Ye shall neither in this mountain, nor yet at Jerusalem, worship the Father...God is a spirit, and they that worship Him must worship Him in spirit and in truth.' Hence the true church of Christ is a spiritual communion, not a visible assembly governed by a human authority. Still the attitude of Christ towards the existing systems of His day was rather one of tolerance than denunciation. If He offered no sacrifice at the Temple-which as a prophet he could not do, as we shall see presently-He did not rail against its services, but occasionally was to be found within its precincts. He was always glad to recognize any tendency towards the betterment of men, and, as shown in His parable of the Tares, never in undue haste to destroy the evil lest He might also bring the good associated with it to naught. At the same time, His opposition to the unspiritual leaders of the Temple was never for a moment in doubt. Such is the Christ attitude towards ecclesiastical institutions of every kind, and such of necessity must be that of His church."

"Can you assign any definite reason for this necessity?"

"There is a very cogent and all-important reason for it, which I shall be glad to set before you. Unassisted humanity in its best, noblest and highest aspect is always imperfect, limited and absolutely unable to conceive a condition of being beyond the cognizance of the five senses. Its highest conception of God is bounded by these limitations, and never rises beyond the magnified proportions of a man with a moral nature leaving much to be desired. For this reason, if for no other, it would be impossible for God to submit Himself to the authority of any foundation of men. The religious faculty is the divinest endowment of the soul, and is it credible that when physical science is already marching with conquering strides across the plains of the invisible, that while intrepid pioneers are scaling the heights of the intangible, God should commit the welfare of the soul to the hands of men who would clip its wings and hold it imprisoned in the grip of so-called Fathers, who forged its fetters long, long centuries ago? All this God and Christ foreknew and wisely ordained the non-authority of any human institution in spiritual matters."

"Do you forget the existence of inspiration?"

"No. On the contrary, I am ever willing to admit that the origin of most religious systems is to be found in inspiration of a certain kind, but the admission does not affect the conclusion. Inspiration is not a vision granted to Moses, Isaiah, Paul or even Jesus with an infallible authority binding upon all who come after the revelation. Christ was very definite upon this point, 'I have many things to say unto you, but ye cannot bear them now. Howbeit, when He, the Spirit of truth is come, He will guide you into all truth.' Inspiration, then, is rather a river following humanity, an evolution with a succession of revelation after revelation, a heritage to be entered into as humanity is able to bear them. Hence by another inference, no inspiration is perfect in itself, but each, if rightly apprehended, leads on to something better until the last, whenever that may be attained, shall lead us into the presence of Him who alone is perfect-our Father God. Let me make myself clearly understood here in saying that no perfect inspiration has ever reached earth through man, nor can it possibly do so, since man himself is imperfect. I make no exception in this respect. Christ acknowledged this when He said there were things which were known, 'not to the angels which are in Heaven, neither the Son, but the Father' only, and where He makes such an admission as to His own limitations, we may well content ourselves not to claim more for less favoured individuals or institutions. I point this out that you may see how I keep Christ first."

"I am carefully following all you say," I replied, anxious not to disturb or turn him aside from the argument I could well see he had not yet concluded.

"This question now leads me to another fatal objection against the authority of ecclesiastical religion. God has, from the first, chosen that this stream of inspiration, ever flowing in broadening, deepening and increasing capacity of service to humanity, shall be His channel of communication with the evolving soul of man, but the recognition of this arrangement would be destructive of any hierarchal pretensions, and for that reason there has always been a deadly feud waged against the prophets by the priests, a thought which brings me back to my statement that Jesus, as a prophet, could not join in the sacrificial service of the Temple."

"How, then, could the sacrifices be a foreshadowing of His own great work?"

"They were not. Neither the Levitical Code nor the rabbinical interpretation of it bore any trace of such a suggestion. The Messiah expected by the Temple was an all-conquering monarch, who was to restore the glories of the reign of David and himself sit for ever on the throne set up by the Shepherd-psalmist. The opposition the priests and rulers offered to the Christ, which was carried to every possible extreme until the crucifixion was accomplished, sprang from the fact that the character He assumed was so contrary to all their claims, expectations, teachings and interests. The relative positions occupied by Christ and the Temple were as far apart as those which were assigned to Dives and Lazarus in the suggestive parable, and all attempts at reconciliation were impossible unless the cult of the Temple was spiritually advanced and lost in the new birth of the eternal kingdom. Nothing can more clearly show this division than the utterance of the Christ, 'It is written My house shall be called the house of prayer, but ye have made it a den of thieves.' You can commit no greater error in this respect than to imagine that the priests of Israel considered their cult and service to be anticipatory of the sacrificial work of Christ; the Levitical Code abounds in assurances that the priesthood shall be an everlasting institution, while all the prophets are equally emphatic in declaring that the cult was a purely human one and lacked divine authority. Jesus was neither Priest nor Levite. He came of neither of the sacerdotal clans, nor was He one with the spirit of the fraternity. He was through and through a prophet, and upon Him rested the undeniable mantle of prophetic inspiration."

"But did not the prophets also offer sacrifices?"

"No!" was the laconic but emphatic reply.

"Have you forgotten Elijah on Carmel?" I asked.

"That was not a sacrifice, but rather a test to prove whether the God of the prophet or the god of the priests was the true God. It was a demonstration to Israel in a time of national danger that organized religion, however punctiliously its ceremonial may be carried out by a united people and a hierarchy of priests, has not the influence of a single consecrated life in an appeal to Heaven. It was a declaration once and for all, such as Paul afterwards put into words on Mars Hill when he said, 'God that made the world and all things therein, seeing that He is Lord of Heaven and earth, dwelleth not in temples made with hands; neither is worshipped with men's hands as though He needed anything.' What more need I say to prove that the God men have fashioned and moulded into the creeds of systematized theology is not the God the world has so long been stretching out its hands to find? The God of Christ is the God the world is waiting for. He who has been put forward as a god by the priests-a god subject to all kinds of petty caprice, who can be bribed into imputing a righteousness which is not attained, who is manipulated by the will of man, and governs his kingdom according to the decisions of church councils-is but a poor substitute for the great Father of the human race, has become an insult to intelligence, and men turn away from the ecclesiastical popper in loathing disgust. Let your first endeavour in your new mission be to give them back the God and Father of our Lord Jesus Christ; speaking a living gospel through the inspired lips of living men, and calling to a newness of life which shall prove its divinity by the fruit it bears. This is the only spiritual authority the world will accept, radiating the power and glory of God, and so safeguarded that the gates of error shall not prevail against it."

* * *

CHAPTER 20

THE MEN OF GOD

Rhamya certainly struck his ploughshare deep into the subject he had been commissioned to expound for my edification. Like the Master, he so fervently counselled me to follow, he spake with no uncertain sound, though behind his fervour it was easy to discern a background of caution to temper the zeal with which the tares were plucked up lest the wheat might also suffer. His confidence was firm in the inherent vitality of truth as contrasted with the transient existence of error. The former must triumph, the latter must fail. He would have the labourer in the harvest field toil that the consummation might not be delayed.

Still, though he would not have the tares carelessly and recklessly destroyed, he was equally determined to do his best to prevent them sowing their seed abroad. The present crop must for the present remain, for the sake of the wheat found to be growing in close association therewith, but so far as he could avoid it, there should be no chance of succession. Other toilers were responsible for the past and present condition; his duty was concerned with the future, on behalf of which he was resolved to show himself a workman approved by God and needing not to be ashamed.

The firm tone and manner he assumed from the first inspired my confidence in him. He made no attempt to distinguish between the relative merits of different religious systems, but finding that all rested upon a supposed authority they did not possess, and that every hierarchy was reared upon a false foundation, time was too valuable for him to use it in pointing out distinctions of detail. He was willing to admit that all possessed a desire to render a certain service for the good of humanity, and so far as that desire honestly reached, he would accept whatever service the institution could render, but the instant any system applied the measurements or limitations of a man to the capacity and attributes of 'the unknown God,' the moment the priest attempted to say what God would, and would not do, on the sole authority of the leaders of his particular school, Rhamya put his foot down, denied the authority, and would have no further association with the aspiring usurper.

The church has a good and useful work to do, but that is first to follow-humbly and faithfully to follow-in the steps of Christ, and let the light of Christ shine through its own spiritual nature to lead a blind and ignorant world into the fold of regeneration. But in doing this the church can never be more than a willing servant, who can know the mind and will of God only in proportion to its likeness to Him. The purposes and secrets of God are revealed to individual souls, not deposited in trust with institutions, so that none can claim any succession in an unbroken line except the common one of human frailty and lack of understanding.

This was the goal to which Rhamya was clearly directing my attention, and in his effort to do so, he had captured the interest of Eilele equally with my own.

"Was not my decision to appeal to Omra a wise one?" she asked as Rhamya paused, indicating the end of that part of his argument.

"I never had the slightest doubt of that," I answered. "My point was not that I objected to a greater teacher, but rather that I should be willingly content with yourself."

"Let there be no thought of greater or lesser between us," suggested Rhamya; "in this life all things work together to supply the best adapted means to every requirement, and it is in accordance with that provision that Eilele asked, and I am sent to your assistance. At the same time I must ask you to guard against any exaggerated anticipation of what I shall be able to do in this way. I wish you distinctly to understand that I can only direct your attention to the way in which truth lies. It is impossible for me to fully expound or discuss in detail the revelation which has already been granted, without attempting to indicate what has yet to be revealed; these expansions must be left to your own study and experience, but you may be well assured of this, that what is left unnoticed of the past, equally with that lying in the future, will be found open and accessible to you along the line of the law of God from which no development can ever deviate. No man in his search for truth need turn either to the right or left, for the path of God is always straight forward and shines more and more unto the perfect day, that the wayfaring man, though a fool, may not err therein."

"I like to hear you interweave those familiar quotations into your arguments; they appeal to me as new and living commentaries by the way you use them, and give to the old book a brilliant significance I have not found before."

"Will you also notice that I only quote from the prophetic parts of the book? In my exposition of truth I have no need for, and receive no assistance from, any part of the priestly system or ceremonial law. If you will bear this in mind, it will help you to understand how clearly and completely the two cults are divided."

"Thanks for the hint. I will keep it steadily before me."

"I need not dwell upon the wild and fanciful postulates of the later religious systems, from the self-evident contradictions and impossible assumptions of which a calmly inquiring mind recoils as being contrary to all intelligent conceptions of God. You have discovered all these things for yourself. I will therefore pass from the negative to the positive consideration of religion. And here I must ask you to give me your most careful attention while I lead you by a somewhat unknown path into that highway of spiritual evolution of which I have just spoken as being 'The highway of holiness' where 'wayfaring men, though fools,' should not err by reason of not being able to understand.

"This new point of view we find in the after-light in which you and I are now standing, from which we look back and see the providences of God as we never were able to understand them from the level of the lower life."

"Will you excuse me if I ask whether this new position is a valid one under the circumstances? Does not the necessity for any religion arise from the peculiar position in which man may be found at a given time, and must it not be truly natural to that condition?"

"I am glad you have asked your questions, because the inquiry will assist you to grasp the central thought upon which I wish to fix your attention. Keep them well in view, and I will proceed to answer them by continuing what I was about to say.

"As seen from this after-life, all creation is a unit working through innumerable successive stages towards a definite and well-defined goal-the production of a divine humanity. In tracing this lineage, however, it will be unnecessary for us to go further back than where we find the ford of the rubicon where man crossed into the consciousness of individual existence. Behind him lay the fogs of oblivion in which all remembrance of the yesterdays of the past were lost. When he sufficiently understood himself and his faculties to begin to make comparisons, the difference between himself and nearest neighbour in the animal world was so great as to lead him to believe he was a new order of being-a new creation. But as he became more intimate with the operations of nature, in the chrysalis was found a link uniting the caterpillar with the butterfly, constraining him to pause and ask if there might not be another absent link, upon a higher stage, uniting himself with the life below. It is not for us, however, to linger here in our present inquiry, but we pass on to more wonderful phenomena which forced themselves upon the attention of the unfolding mind. One of his earliest discoveries inspired him equally with terror and curiosity. He learned by watching and comparison of experience that while he lay quietly unconscious of all around him, he was possessed of other eyes, ears, and senses than those of his body; was able to hunt and follow various pursuits while his friends assured themselves that he was lying quiet in his cave; he met and talked with companions who had long since been eaten, burned or buried. Presently someone brought back from his sleep a memory of something foreseen which afterwards transpired in real life, and others, like Balaam, grew into the habit of consulting sleep-people as to their daily doings, 'And he (Balaam) said unto them, Lodge here this night, and I will bring you word again, as the Lord shall speak unto me; and the princes of Moab abode with Balaam. And God came unto Balaam, and said, What men are these with thee?' (Num. xxii. 8-9). Others found they were able to make requests in their sleep and receive gifts which rendered them peculiarly valuable service in their daily vocations. Let us take the record as given of Solomon's experience as an instance of this. In the Book of Kings (I Kings iii. 5-15) we read:

"*'In Gibeon the Lord appeared to Solomon in a dream by night; and God said, Ask what I shall give thee.*

"*'And Solomon said, Thou hast shewed unto Thy servant David my father great mercy, according as he walked before Thee in truth, and in righteousness, and in uprightness of heart with Thee; and Thou has kept for him this great kindness, that Thou hast given him a son to sit on his throne, as it is this day.*

"*'And now, O Lord my God, Thou hast made Thy servant king instead of David my father; and I am but a little child; I know not how to go out or come in.*

"*'And Thy servant is in the midst of Thy people which Thou hast chosen, a great people, that cannot be numbered nor counted for multitude.*

"*'Give therefore Thy servant an understanding heart to judge Thy people, that I may discern between good and bad; for who is able to judge this Thy so great a people?*

"*'And the speech pleased the Lord, that Solomon had asked this thing.*

"*'And God said unto him, Because thou hast asked this thing, and hast not asked for thyself long life; neither hast asked riches for thyself, nor hast asked the life of thine enemies; but hast asked for thyself understanding to discern judgement;*

"'Behold I have done according to thy words; lo, I have given thee a wise and an understanding heart; so that there was none like thee before thee, neither after thee shall any arise like unto thee.

"'And I have also given thee that which thou hast not asked, both riches, and honour; so that there shall not be any among the kings like unto thee all thy days.

"'And if thou wilt walk in My ways, to keep My statutes and My commandments, as thy father David did walk, then will I lengthen thy days.

"'And Solomon awoke; and, behold, it was a dream.'

"But the gift did not vanish with the waking. The wisdom of Solomon has always been proverbial. Others again were endowed with the powers of interpretation of dreams, as Joseph; or, going yet a step further, we hear of Daniel asking for time to enable him to revisit the realm of sleep and recover knowledge of the king's dream before he made known the interpretation.

"Now, it is no part of my purpose to ask you to believe that all dreams are divine communications-I simply affirm that sleep is a convenient and natural agent to be so employed, and also I wish you to see in the records I have named the origin of the prophetic gift in which we are now interested. Here is to be found another link, this time uniting the natural and spiritual conditions and available for the further carrying on of an unbroken system of evolution. From this crude beginning, the prophetic stream may be clearly traced onward as the divinely appointed channel of revelation. 'If there be a prophet among you', God is recorded to have said, 'I, the Lord, will make myself known unto him in a vision, and will speak unto him in a dream.' (Num. xii, 6) A little later we find the prophet to be a man upon whom, in a normal condition, the Spirit of the Lord descends and changes him 'into another man' (I Sam. x, 6), compelling him to speak not his own words, but as the Spirit shall give him utterance. Here, then, we find the divine and living way by which God has ordained to make His revelations to man, and in this prophetic line we shall presently find the Christ of God."

"Pardon my interrupting, but is not this descent of the Spirit upon the prophet that which I have seen in Cushna's overshadowing of our own psychic?"

"Precisely; and if you have watched Cushna's control you will understand far better than by any explanation I might give."

"I have not only watched," I replied, "but have been permitted to send a message back to earth. But before you go further will you allow me to ask for information respecting one injunction which raises a difficulty in my mind respecting this open communion, to which you are so clearly bringing me?"

"What is it?"

"I refer to the command in Deuteronomy forbidding consultation with familiar spirits as an abomination to the Lord."

"The inquiry is most opportune, and we will at once consider it. The prohibition is an enactment of the priests, and as such, being of purely human origin, has no valid force when directed against a natural phenomenon. It does not deny, but rather admits the genuineness of the communion, or there would be no reason to forbid it. It is not the only time in the history of religion where priests have used the power of the state in a futile attempt to crush the truth. The effort to put an end to this direct intercourse with spiritual powers was a vital necessity to the existence of the priest. Whenever priest and prophet clashed it was always the latter who proved to be superior, and the former were only able to maintain themselves by the support of the throne. So pronounced had this fact become, that the Temple authorities in Jerusalem were at length driven to an acceptance of the prophetic principle, and once a year, the High Priest was supposed to directly consult God by means of Urim and Thummim. But though the form of consultation was observed, its spirit was absent, and there is no record of any priestly success. I must not, however, leave this subject without pointing out that by the possibility of this communion being due to a natural law, access is given alike to high and low intelligences to engage therein, the law of God, in this as in every other instance, being without respect of persons. This, the prophets have seen and recognized from the first, and advisedly laid down this rule concerning the intercourse:

'When a prophet speaketh in the name of the Lord, if the thing follow not, nor come to pass, that is the thing which the Lord hath not spoken, but the prophet hath spoken it presumptuously; thou shalt not be afraid of him.' (Deut. xviii, 22) Such a law bears on its face evidence of its emanation from the truth; it does not insist on acceptance, immediate and unconditional, because declared even by inspired lips, but with all the charity of reason seeks acceptance when its verity has been established. It is the spiritual law at one with the natural-'By their fruits ye shall know them'. Its law works both ways, therefore in your intercourse with earth, let it be known without equivocation, that whoever approaches this intercourse will attract to themselves souls who are in close sympathy with the lives they are living. What they who seek the communion are, they who respond to the call will be. Those who are good will attract the good, and the curious, the deceiver, the hypocrite, the impure, the vicious and immoral will bring themselves into association with characters who are in harmony with their own natures. This law is inexorable, and there is no evading it. Therefore let all who would enter into the enjoyment of this divine privilege approach it with clean hands and pure hearts, for only such have power to ascend the hill of the Lord, where those are to be met with who know and are able to declare the secrets of the kingdom."

"I thank you for your caution," I answered. "I have been with Ladas through the sphere of his work, where I have seen this law of attraction in active operation, so I am not likely to forget."

"If you have seen it, you will not forget it. Now, having glanced at the rise of prophetic inspiration and found it to be a natural provision for supplying an unavoidably existent need, let us go on to see how it is designed to elevate man into the region of the Divine, and thus secure the salvation of the whole race by bringing it into actual at-one-ment with God."

* * *

CHAPTER 21

THE COMING OF THE CHRIST

By this time you will be in a position to understand how closely the school of prophets is allied to the spiritual side of life," Rhamya continued, "and how widely divergent and absolutely irreconcilable is their system with that of the priests. The one operates from the future and above, reaching out and down to guide the race into the ever-unfolding truth; the other is of the past and below, using the energy and the influence of the ages that have gone to restrain the present from moving forward. The one is of life, the other of death; of hope opposed to fear; of emancipation versus bondage; of Heaven in succession of earth.

"When once the divine order for reaching and guiding man had been satisfactorily installed, and began to give clear and unmistakable evidence of being controlled and used by intelligences with power to read and interpret mysteries inscrutable to human eyes, it is not difficult to see how infinitely superior to their fellows became the position of all who chose to work in harmony with the conditions laid down by those who, from their higher vantage-ground, were proffering help to all who were still walking in darkness and the shadow of death. All the infinitude of God was made available for the benefit of men; the supply having no restriction but that of demand, and the transmission without limit, save the carrying capacity of the vehicle placed at the Divine disposal. The prophetic conduit taps the infinite ocean of the water of life, from which the supply and quality of the revelation will always be governed by the channels through which it flows. But, as I have already said, from the time when we see the spirit of the Lord falling upon the prophet and visibly changing his present identity-as you have seen in the case of our own psychic- a sense of satisfaction with results attained took possession of the prophets, further development was arrested, and the stream was allowed to run its own course.

"Now came the opportunity of the priests, who, allying themselves to the state, entered into violent opposition to the prophets, and used all the machinery of the temporal power to destroy the influence of the preachers of righteousness by capturing the senses with ornate ritual and ceremonial.

"The kingdom of God, however, cometh not with observation, and the inflow of revelation being once clearly established, the river continued to rise, since the reservoir of supply lay in the everlasting hills far above any level of temporal opposition or human machinations. None of the endeavours of God are ever abandoned. Whatever truth begins will be carried to a finish. The greatest mistake we can make is to try to measure God's eternity by the span of our mortal existence, and because He does not complete His plan within the clock-tick of our brief day, come to the conclusion that He has failed in and abandoned His project. No greater fallacy ever assailed the human mind. Consider the aeons of the earth's existence in comparison with your own startled swallow's flight across it. All through those immeasurable periods, God has patiently waited for the earth to produce the man He commissioned it to bring forth-it was not long considering the magnitude of the result-and eternity is not yet a pulse-throb older than when the command was given; what then is the thousand years of the Jewish static spiritual age, when all the variations on the stream of prophecy were like ripples, caused by the breath of a passing enthusiasm? The stream was rising, though no one noticed it, and the quiet waters crept higher and higher towards the copingstone of the obstructing dam."

"I wish you would answer a question that has just occurred to me," I interposed.

"Certainly; for I am anxious to leave no doubt behind me. What would you ask?"

"If, as the records state, there had also been a direct

interposition of angelic ministry at the time you are speaking of, how was it, when the prophets became negligent of their privileges, that angels did not take up the work and carry it forward?"

"Because they were unable to do so. There are many occasions where help must be rendered and other duties performed, for which no human agent is available, and in all such cases we are warranted in assuming a physical form and discharging the duty-a little longer experience will show you how often this is done beyond what you might now be inclined to suppose. But wherever the ministry has reference to a rule of life or conduct, the instruction must be given through an agent occupying the same position as the one to whom we speak. For instance, suppose a man to be heroically fighting a fierce temptation, to approach him with all the recognized accessories of an angelic form might excite his reverence and wonder, but it would signally fail where it was most needed-in the capacity of imparting strength. Where we would draw near to strengthen by our sympathy and assurance of success, we should only succeed, owing to men's mistaken idea concerning angels, in provoking the inquiry, what could we-who had been created sinless, who had never felt the power of temptation, who had never experienced the weight of weakness associated with the flesh-know of the daily and hourly struggle a man is called upon to endure? And the result would be that the difference in the two conditions would form a gulf across which the assistance we would gladly render would appear more like a mockery than an encouragement. On the other hand, God has designed, in the prophetic gift, a natural scheme in which the human and angelic conditions may combine and interblend so harmoniously, that he who runs may read and find a certain refuge in every time of trouble.

"If you wish to trace the impotence of any ministry to man, offered through a nature in any way differing from his own, you may find material for doing so in the dogma of the modern church, concerning the so-called procreation and birth of Christ. The monstrous postulate bristles with contradictions from the first thought of it, and when two thousand years of human intellect have been employed in an attempt to adapt it to the common need, nothing has been attained but a confusion worse confounded from which reason and intelligence turns away in weary disappointment.

"That is the reason why the direct ministry of angels has not taken the place of prophecy."

"Tell me," I exclaimed with eager impatience, since he had at length broken silence concerning that name, which is above every name, "tell me-for here lies the goal of all my inquiry—how would you read and interpret that one great mystery of the ages; the personality and the nature of the Christ? If angels in their nature stand so far apart from man, surely He must be immeasurable-unapproachably more so!"

"Let me first of all disabuse your mind of one idea you are in danger of confusing; there are no angels, but those who have entered upon the estate through the portal of humanity. Jacob's vision of the ladder gives the natural order in the generation of angels; he saw them 'ascending and descending'. Until they have reached this condition, they cannot be employed in the ministry. When the earth grasps this fact, then direct angelic interposition will be more effective.

"But it is the idea of the loneliness and isolation of the Christ I am more particularly concerned with for the moment. That He has been forced into this false position I have already admitted, and the natural effect of it is the impotence of the religion called by His Omnipotent Name. But the Christ who consents to be thus disposed of, is only an ecclesiastical lay figure from which I would turn your eyes to a contemplation of the living Christ-the Christ of God.

"In Him we find no desire for separateness or isolation, but rather a Good Shepherd, living among or walking at the head of

His flock, carefully considering all who are frail or weak and nestling the young tenderly in His bosom. If one should by any inadvertence or temptation go astray, He will go after it until He find it, because, saith He, 'this is the Father's will which hath sent Me, that of all which He hath given Me I should lose nothing.' In the execution of this command He identifies Himself so closely with the members of His charge that to touch one of them is to touch Himself. Never was a closer or more ideal and far-reaching union conceived than He contemplated. Hear Him as He supplicates Heaven in their behalf, 'Neither pray I for these alone, but for them also which shall believe on Me through their word; that they all may be one; as Thou, Father, art in Me and I in Thee, that they also may be one in Us; that the world may believe that Thou hast sent me. And the glory which Thou gavest Me I have given them; that they may be one, even as We are one; I in them, and Thou in Me, that they may be made perfect in one; and that the world may know that Thou hast sent Me, and hast loved them, as Thou hast loved Me.' Is there any wish or thought of isolation here? I will grant that of necessity, for the time, He was the only begotten Son of the Father, but the position was only a temporary one, such as must naturally fall to the lot of 'the first-born among many brethren', all of whom are to be joint heirs in the common heritage.

"But enough of these disclaimers of error. Let us rather proceed to a consideration of what is true in relation to Him. And in order that we may not miss His direct descent from the line of prophets who had preceded Him, let me recall how far we had traced the development of the cult. Our last personal notice of it was where Samuel assured the newly-anointed king Saul that as he proceeded homewards at a certain place, the spirit of the Lord would come upon him and change him into another man, thus divinely initiating him into the school of the prophets. From this incident the stream of inspiration runs on with but slight variation for something like a thousand years before we find the majestic figure of John the Baptist, overshadowed and controlled by the spirit of Elijah, preaching in the wilderness and announcing the speedy coming of the Christ."

"Was John a reincarnation of Elijah?" I inquired, glad to be able to receive some authoritative statement on this vexed and difficult problem.

"No! The theory of reincarnation is one of the devices invented by priests to terrify men and women into subjection; it could not possibly be introduced into the natural order of existence without reducing the whole system to chaos. Besides which it has neither use nor purpose; all that it is supposed to effect is far more orderly and expeditiously accomplished by a process more consistent with love and righteousness. John was a prophet upon whom the spirit of the Lord was able to descend, turning him another into man, and speaking the word of the Lord to the assembled thousands who were drawn by the strange magnetic attraction of the mysterious preacher, and the spirit who inspired the utterance was the aforetime prophet Elijah. Hence, the Christ in speaking of him said, 'Elias has come already, and they knew him not, but when John was asked, 'Art thou Elias?' he answered with equal truth, 'I am not'. There is no contradiction here; Christ, speaking not so much of the man as of the mission, lost sight of the instrument in His exaltation of the power behind-forgot the flesh in His recognition of the divinely commissioned herald who overshadowed and controlled it, and therefore acknowledged the presence of the great Hebrew prophet. But John, when his preaching was over and the controlling spirit had withdrawn, being asked whether he was Elias, with equal truth answered, 'I am not!' The incident is full of pregnant suggestion when thus considered, but from every other point, casts a shadow of reflection upon the veracity of one or other of the two great personalities. Again, John was the forerunner of the Christ, sent to prepare the way for Him, and the beautiful significance of the office is entirely lost unless this purely prophetic interpretation is admitted, as you will presently see before I have finished speaking of the greater than

Chapter 21 — The Coming of the Christ

John."

"Yes! I am anxious to hear what you will say of Him," I cried with eager impatience.

"There are many questions I feel prompted to discuss by way of introduction to this pre-eminently unique figure in the world's history," he began with slow and calm deliberation, strangely in contrast to my own excitement. "But I will pass by the whole of them, lest I should draw your mind from the central and all-important issue for the moment. Collateral questions may be afterwards considered, but for the present, we shall find enough to occupy all our attention in finding out the true relationship of Jesus the Christ to humanity and to God. This I now propose to do. And perhaps the most favourable moment for us to make the acquaintance of the Nazarene will be to find Him among the multitude hanging upon the discourse of John, who acknowledged that he saw Jesus but knew Him not."

"Was not that very strange?" I inquired.

"No, and I will show you why. The explanation will be of personal service to yourself before you have proceeded very far in your own ministry. God has wisely ordained that all actively engaged in any mission may not be able to see what its final result will be. While we are at work, our certainty of success must be of faith springing from God's blessing, resting upon our wholehearted endeavour. If we could already see onward to the result of our labour it might tend to negligence, and the Father will not suffer us to be tempted above that we are able to bear, hence He drops the veil, and leaves us to feel that the responsibility of success rests upon our own shoulders. Had John recognized Jesus as the Messiah he might have relaxed his efforts before he had finished his work, therefore his eyes were holden until the hour had arrived for the revelation to be made."

"But the two were cousins, and the circumstances of the birth and early life of Jesus, with the angelic announcement of whom and what He was, must have been familiar to John."

"Your conclusion is a perfectly natural one from the aspect in which you regard it, and makes John's failure to recognize his cousin to be a mystery calling for some satisfactory explanation. But I do not desire to follow our inquiry along ecclesiastical lines, but by a more excellent way-recurring again to the declaration of Isaiah-where 'the wayfaring man, though a fool, may not err therein.' If you will accept my assurance and follow where I will lead, leaving all your old difficulties unanswered for the time, you will presently see that the whole of them are only spectres and creatures of the imagination, haunting by-paths into which you have illegitimately wandered, at which you will laugh when you reach the light of truth."

"Your forbearance makes me ashamed of my interruptions, but I will accept your advice and try to listen to your instructions without further question."

"We must necessarily move with caution that you may clearly grasp my meaning, and your inquiries are only to be expected. I have travelled this way too frequently not to know that these questions will arise, and for that reason, I am determined to avoid everything tending to multiply them.

"In taking our next step perhaps it will be well to remind ourselves of the mission and aim of prophecy in order that we may have a clear conception of the issue. Its simple object is to prepare mankind for entrance upon the next phase of existence on the most advantageous terms. Much of this, of course, has now been made perfectly clear to you, and you will understand how impossible it would be for earth, without some guidance, to reason its way into the truth, hence the just necessity for the prophetic provision. From the dawn of reason and inquiry, man has been face to face with the problem as to whether the hope within of a continuity of existence had any basis of justification. But how was the doubt to be resolved? Who by searching could find it out? The heart yearned for it with a yearning that could not be subdued. The hope had risen spontaneously; was it only a mocking illusion? If in the black beyond there existed a God, why not also a life? So the inquiry gained courage and strength until it rose with the fervour of a helpless race appealing for assistance. In reply to this, God threw open a door of revelation in the corridor of sleep and gave free access to the gift of prophecy, with its almost infinite possibilities. If men only understood the true nature and value of this divine response to human need, they would stand appalled at the awful magnificence of the forces here placed at their disposal. But the thoughtlessness of man is proverbial; 'The ox knoweth his owner, and the ass his master's crib, but Israel doth not know, my people doth not consider.' Think of the value of a bestowal which enables the imprisoned Joseph to interpret the dream of the butler and baker, then throws open the prison doors and leads the young Hebrew to perform the same office for the king, who raises the slave to be only second to himself in consequence, or of the power by which Elisha in Dothan heard the strategic plans of the distant king of Syria, and was thus able to save his country from the invading foe; or the ease with which Daniel is enabled to make an incursion into the realm of sleep and recover the forgotten dream of Babylon's monarch! Who among the sons of men have attached the suggestive importance to these matters they legitimately demand? To what extent may this endowment be developed with systematic study and improvement of the conditions by which it operates? It is to this question I am anxious to give you a reply in leading you to the Christ.

"I must not forget, however, that the Jews failed to recognize Him because of their mistaken conceptions as to the position He would occupy. To save you from this mistake, let us remind ourselves what we may reasonably expect to find when we see Him, and what it will be His mission to accomplish.

"He will be 'God manifest in the flesh.' But I would here caution you to be careful against applying theological or dogmatic interpretation to this or any other quotation I may now use. Christ is not God, but He is all the power of God necessary for the occasion made manifest through the flesh. He is the ambassador of the King speaking through the interpreter necessary to bring monarch and subject into intelligent communication. He is a commissioned servant, and always places himself personally on the level of the servant, assuming union with God only by virtue of His official capacity, where He is always careful to draw the distinction between 'My Father and I,' for 'My Father is greater than I' We have not in Jesus an example of God emptying Himself in order to assume a lower nature, but rather a prophet of an advanced type offering a body prepared for the in-dwelling of the Christ who is the highest manifestation of the divine the flesh can receive. The real phenomenon, therefore, is the elevation of humanity into the region of divinity as an example of the possibility of spiritual evolution; it is the intersphering of the two conditions of adjacent life, where, like a rising tide, the flood reaches further and further inland until it lifts and floats the stranded craft and silently woos it away and carries it out to sea.

"This indispensable development had from the first been seen and understood by us from the spiritual side, who through the prophets had pointed to its coming.

"Then Jesus was born. The child of a holy woman's prayers, accepted from the first conscious probability of His advent as a gift from God to be sacredly set aside for the service of that God, and through the months of His tarrying, saturated and psychologized with the holy aspirations of her who was giving him life and predisposition of character. He stands yet as the highest type of what a mother may produce in her offspring. A man may boast of his intellectual power, but it is a woman only that has ability to build a living temple in which God may incarnate a holy spirit. Heaven indeed sang songs of welcome when it beheld Him come, and joining efforts with the mother, hedged Him round about in preparation for the work He was destined to perform.

"He was born a prophet. Throughout childhood and youth the inspiration of the spiritual life played visibly upon Him, as when in

Jerusalem, the Rabbis and teachers marvelled at His knowledge and wisdom. No wonder that all His sympathies rushed towards the Baptist when His wonderful mission commenced. No wonder He hung spellbound upon the preacher's words. How His heart was stirred as He listened to the appeal to righteousness of life and self-surrender to a diviner service than the ceremonial observance of the Temple, until the contemplation passed to open vision, in the glory of which He trembled while He gazed with speechless awe. He saw His race hopelessly fighting against the powers of the darkness which filled the valley of the shadow of death; heard the multitudinous and agonized cry for help where there was none to save; from the underworld the cry of the slain came like a thunderous peal shaking earth and Heaven; 'Send, send!' Turning His eyes Heavenward, He saw its hosts stand ready but helpless for lack of a prophet who might be clothed upon and become a leader mighty to save. Prostrate before the blinding glory that enveloped the throne, He beheld the type of a redeemed humanity pleading for aid 'with groanings which cannot be uttered,' and from the invisible He heard the troubled inquiry, 'Whom shall I send?'

"Then the soul of the Nazarene leaped upward towards its God, and in a courageous holy consecration flung itself beside the supplicant and cried, 'Here am I, send Me-send Me! and in and through Me, at whatever cost, let Thy will be done on earth as it is done in Heaven.'

"We know what followed. When that consecration was ratified in presence of earth, hell and Heaven at His baptism; 'the heavens opened unto Him, and He saw the spirit of God descending like a dove, and resting upon Him, and lo, a voice from Heaven saying, 'This is My beloved Son, in whom I am well pleased!'

"Such was the order of that first second-birth to which the Christ afterwards called the world-a birth in which Jesus the prophet of Nazareth became Jesus the Christ of God."

"Why have I not known it in this light before?" I asked, as soon as my astonishment would allow me to speak.

"Because, as I have told you, like all the children of men, you have been following the footsteps of blind dogmatic guides, who have missed the path and fallen into the ditch."

* * *

CHAPTER 22

THE WORK AND TEACHING OF THE CHRIST

Rhamya paused, not with the pride of one conscious of the strength of his position, but rather in thoughtful consideration of myself, whom he was leading by such a hitherto unsuspected path into the fortress of a long-sought-for truth. My feet stood in the midst of the entanglements of the tares which choked and attempted to destroy the true grain, and he was reluctant to hurry my progress, but left me to contemplate the network of delusion, and contrast it with the clearly-defined highway he pointed out as we proceeded.

If any doubt or nervousness had troubled me in relation to the good faith of my conductor, it had at length been dissolved. My future path was still shrouded with the veil of mystery, but what of that? Behind me could be seen the unmistakable outlines of the recovered highway-straight, well defined and carefully planned, leading in the desired direction, and furnished with safeguards for all who had eyes to see, that were sufficient to keep the pilgrim from going astray.

While I mused on these things and the many reflections they suggested, like a distant echo, I heard the familiar strains of one of my favourite hymns assuring me that—

> *"His love in times past forbids me to think*
> *He'll leave me at last in trouble to sink;*
> *Each sweet Ebenezer I have in review*
> *Confirms His good pleasure to help me right through."*

It came to me like Myhanene's affirmation that "All is well," and bestowed the benediction of the peace of God.

I afterwards discovered that Rhamya was fully conscious of

what occurred just then, but he made no attempt to direct or disturb me; and as for Eilele-she had so completely isolated herself as to be forgotten. I have never quite satisfied myself whether she followed us on that eventful journey, or whether, knowing the road so well and being confident of the result, she did not give wing to her mind and spend the time among the visions which appear to be ever accessible to her daring flights.

Of all the dreams I have had in Paradise, few, if any, have been more sweetly anticipatory than those I enjoyed upon the occasion of which I speak. I was being led through an altogether novel region, which, from a somewhat doubtful beginning, had opened gradually into most unexpected attractions, where I was utterly unable to attempt a forecast of what might yet remain to be revealed.

> *"If but one step across the threshold*
> *Had shown such sweet ambushed surprise,*
> *What would be found when I should reach*
> *The sanctuary, and, from within, new eyes,*
> *Not yet evolved, behold the God-truth light*
> *Blazing with perfect glory, and my steady sight*
> *Endures as I adore?"*

I know not, nor could I waste valuable time in useless speculation; enough that for the present I was in an enchanted land where new and more divine senses were unfolding within me under the influences native to the condition in which I reposed. I was nearing the truth, and over its fields of glad surprise, swept the gentle breezes of God's soft revelation, bringing to me health and strength.

I was so glad to rest, and yet my buoyant soul was impatient to be away that with my now clearer vision I might behold more of the beauty of the King. I was coming nearer to the Christ! Oh, so much nearer than ever I had been before, and I longed to throw myself

The Work and Teaching of the Christ

at His dear feet, and with the satisfied Thomas exclaim-"My Lord and my God!"

Rhamya patiently allowed the exhilarating anticipation to pursue its course until it had wrought its full effect and the sign was clear that the time for his advance had come. He then re-addressed himself to his ministry and led me forward.

"You will now be prepared," he began, "to look a little more closely at the beautiful interblending of the human with the divine by which God in Christ Jesus was working out the reconciliation of the world unto Himself. And let me here again impress upon you the importance of never losing sight for a single instant of the fact that the whole and sole object of the work of Christ is the reconciliation of the world to God, it is never to propitiate God or to secure His favour on behalf of the world.

"The fundamental difficulty to the establishment of this desirable partnership on the human side was the doubt as to whether man was really immortal or only 'as the beast which perisheth.' And it was just here where the priest was found to be as hopelessly ignorant as the laymen or the heathen. If a system is to be judged by the value of the service it is able to render, then at this all-important point, for which alone religions are called into existence, theologies, ecclesiasticisms and churches become nothing better than broken reeds and empty speculations. Neither priest nor schoolman is equipped for fording this Jordan, and bringing back such a report of the land on the other shore as shall satisfactorily solve the doubt. They,

> *"'Stand lingering, shivering on the brink,*
> *And fear to launch away.'*

'But God hath chosen the foolish things of the world to confound the wise; and the weak things of the world to confound the things which are mighty; and base things of the world and things which are despised, hath God chosen, yea, the things which

The Life Elysian

are not, to bring to naught things that are; that no flesh should glory in His presence.' When learning fails, God has placed the prophet in readiness to serve humanity. And the greatest of all the prophets was Jesus, through whom the Christ came 'to bring life and immortality to light.' Everlasting-an unbroken, uninterrupted-life was the gift He came to bestow, or rather make clear the fact that it existed as the natural heritage of all mankind. This revelation was the God-erected goal towards which the prophetic gift had from the first reached out its hands. Its prize was Messiahship, and the competition was an open one which Jesus alone secured, and upon Him descended and rested the Christ of God. Let me now try to make the certainty of this dual personality somewhat clearer to your understanding.

"Can you first give me any information as to the relationship of Christ to the Godhead?" I asked.

"I can tell you something of it," he replied, "but you will fail to comprehend me because it relates to an exalted condition of life of which I know but little and at present you have no conception. We shall only be able to understand it clearly when we reach it. Still, I may say this. The name of Christ is one which applies to a community rather than to an individual. It is a circle formed by the greatest souls from advanced existing worlds-into which number the earth has not yet been admitted -and what may be termed the rearguard of worlds who have entered upon higher stages of existence I have no power to anticipate. The ideal after which the Christ circle reaches is the union of many worlds (or folds) in the communal spirit of a new order in which the Divine features may be better expressed; but their aspiration also denotes their present imperfection, and if you will bear this in mind in relation to the position from which the Christ descended upon Jesus, you may find it to be a key by which you may open and understand many of His sayings which otherwise must remain mysterious; the ideal He desires His Church to reach 'that they all may be one,' is the natural atmosphere in which He dwells; it is not a prayer for union of personality-that would be impossible-it is rather union of spiritual tone and service, such as He knows with the Father of whom He speaks as being so much 'greater than I.' It would be easy for me to multiply such sayings if it were necessary, but you may easily do so at your leisure, so I will leave this and pass on."

"Permit me one other question here," I ventured further, "that my mind may be perfectly free to follow what you have yet to say."

"What is it?" he replied with kindly indulgence.

"You quote the Scriptures so frequently that I am anxious to know just what amount of authority you allow them to bear."

"In all that I am saying to you," Rhamya answered with a slightly accentuated deliberation, "I am guided by the thought that I am preparing you for your coming mission to earth. If it were otherwise, I should prefer to treat all these subjects on a much higher plane and draw my illustrations from far more satisfactory sources, but such a course would be of no service or assistance to you, and for this reason entirely I shape my arguments for your convenience and guidance. In doing so, I remember how many of the men with whom you will be brought into contact will take their first stand in relation to an open communion between the two conditions of life, upon the traditional interpretation the Church has placed upon the so-called sacred writings, and knowing this, without wasting any time in attacking their position, I have preferred to draw your attention to the clearly evident fact that what is recognized as an orthodox interpretation of the Bible, is itself directly opposed to a far more satisfactory and consistent revelation contained in the self-same volume. With only obligatory references to the sacerdotal system-recognizing that it contains qualities capable of good, and willing to concede that, in spite of its manifold errors and inconsistencies, it has done an inestimable service for humanity in the mundane sphere, and that also it has been a starting point for multitudes of saints who have risen superior to its own environments-I am content to leave its defence and promulgation in the hands of its own champions and simply expound the truth as I know it for myself. In doing this for your assistance and edification I use the Scriptures simply as historical documents recording a stream of events with one branch of which we are closely interested, but in so doing I claim my right to accept or reject what my knowledge or reason dictates, which is a standard of judgement one is bound to erect, especially where records speak with such double-tongued voices as those we are dealing with. Let God be true though by such an allowance we convict every man and book of lying. Men may and always do edit, re-edit, interpolate, interpret and generally deal with manuscripts and books to suit conveniences; the use and meaning of words and phrases change; and even though we admit the highest possible authority for an utterance made under certain given circumstances and conditions, it needs no skill in dialectics to prove that a command vital to the interests of one question might be equally fatal to another. Therefore a living and ever-present God elects to speak through living men -hence the prophetic ordination, 'Thou shalt hear a voice behind thee saying this is the way'; 'He shall give His angels charge concerning thee to keep thee in all thy ways'; 'I will never leave thee nor forsake thee'; 'Lo, I am with you always, even to the end of the world.' These and other kindred assurances through the lips of prophets are infinitely more in accordance with the Spirit of Divine Fatherhood than a thousand appeals to what is written, although we may be assured that such words were in reality the voice of God to other men. It is in this light I make use of the Scriptures. They record, so far as they go, some of the inspirations of the past, enabling us to trace certain evolutionary lines of thought and development; they preserve outlines of the form through which ideas and movements have passed; they give to us a humanly-sketched portrait of the Christ, which is certainly beautiful in spite of its imperfection, misconception, and failure to understand his true relationship either to God or man, but after all, they hand on nothing more than the form of godliness-the life, the vigour, the strength, and its fervid

Chapter 22 — The Work and Teaching of the Christ

inspiration cannot be transmitted through the inanimate channel of any document; they are spirit, they are life, and must needs flow from their source through 'living epistles, known and read of all men.' Briefly then, I use the Scriptures as I use the systems which are founded upon them for the good and truth I find therein. With a fervent desire at all times and in all places to be guided aright, I use my reason in a careful endeavour to 'refuse the evil and choose the good.' No man can do more, and if he honestly does this, he will not go wrong. Have I made my meaning clear to you?"

"Perfectly, but I am afraid you will think my interruptions sadly interfere with what you wish to say."

"Not at all. They come naturally and are necessary for your future guidance. All that I have to say will rather be assisted than otherwise by any inquiries you may wish to make, and when I have answered you, I shall always find myself standing in the presence of one or other of the kindred points I still wish to notice. For instance, while our thoughts are engaged with the sacred writings, we may advantageously linger to learn what they record about the teaching and work of the Christ, reserving my other point for later consideration.

"Now, if it were possible for you to clear your memory of all the teachings you have heard and been taught to believe as a Christian, then sit down and read for the first time what the Gospels record of the teaching and ministry of Christ, and afterwards, listen to the doctrines of what is known as Christianity; you would be astounded to find how the one is at variance with the other, and inquire by what right the Church claims the authority of Christ for any such system formulated and taught by any one of the many sects calling themselves by His Name. In His teaching, Christ took exactly the same position that I have taken with yourself. It would have been easy for Him to have used more learned language, higher arguments and philosophical illustrations, but had He done so, the result would have been by so much a more hopeless misunderstanding. This is well evidenced by His interview with Nicodemus, who as a ruler and teacher of the people should surely be in a position to speak of spiritual things intelligently, yet even from him we hear the disappointed Christ asking, 'If I have told you earthly things and you believe me not, how shall ye believe if I tell you heavenly things?' The Master always had to accommodate His teaching to the gross mental and spiritual darkness which covered the people, in order that from the midst of it, a light might shine-His light which was to be the light of the world. Hence He mentioned no word about theology-He who was in a position to speak so clearly and definitely-but it would only be (to use His own simile) to cast pearls before swine, who would afterwards turn and rend Him. Men are not in a position while subject to the domination of the animal passion consequent upon the flesh, to arrive at a passionless and purely spiritual conception of the nature, perfection, purposes and attributes of God, who is Spirit, and must therefore needs be understood in the shadowless uncreated beam of His own self-emanating light in the region of absolute truth. The Christ found a race of children running about with the preliminary inquiry it is still making-'What is truth?' and He wisely took the kindergarten system of teaching from natural pictures and parables the elementary lessons, which others coming after Him would gradually follow up until the ministering spirits of God would lead mankind into all truth. He began by teaching the human child-race to dismiss the confusing idea of God from their minds and replace it by the conception of a Father whom they might think of, in every good, noble, and considerate way, as being infinitely better than any human father the world had known, and one who-though Himself unseen-heard, saw and knew all men did and even thought. Christ knew this Father -had come from Him to teach mankind the way to the home where God awaited their coming-and if they prayed to Him as 'Our Father, who art in Heaven,' and lived a life such as He (Christ) would live for men's example, the prayer would be heard and the Father would give them whatever they asked Him for, because, while they lived as He would show to them it would not be possible for them to ask anything but what the Father intended them to have. Throughout this typical life He was always drawing attention thereto to illustrate all He said, in which He summed up the whole duty of man in one sentence, 'All things whatsoever ye would that men should do to you, do ye even so to them; this is the law and the prophets.' This command is to be so literally carried out, or honestly aimed at, that when the child prays to his Father he need not fear to link with his petition the plea 'forgive me my trespasses as I forgive them that trespass against me,' and he who can fearlessly make this request has nothing to fear."

"Did He not also teach 'Thou shalt love the Lord thy God with all thy heart'?" I inquired.

"Certainly! But love to God is not to precede, but be the outgrowth of love to man. 'If a man loves not his brother whom he hath seen, how can he love God whom he hath not seen?' In his humanity, Christ represented the door by which alone entrance is to be found into the higher-the truly spiritual-life, and whoever tries to enter by another way 'the same is a thief and a robber.' Notice how stringently Christ lays the rule down: 'If thou bring thy gift to the altar, and there rememberest that thy brother hath ought against thee (not that thou hast ought against thy brother), leave there thy gift before the altar, and go thy way; first be reconciled to thy brother and then come and offer thy gift.' The passport to admission into the kingdom of Heaven is righteousness of conduct towards men. This is the scope of the teaching of Christ which is strenuously enforced in His sermon on the Mount, in parable, in prayer, and by every aspect of His ministry. He came to save the world from the inevitable consequences of sin, and this He does by repentance and a new life in which rightness rules supreme. But repentance towards God can only be approached by repentance towards men accompanied by reconciliation. Salvation came to Zaccheus by his repentance and restoring fourfold that which had been unrighteously acquired; and the rich young ruler's acceptance depended on distributing his wealth among the poor. 'If thou wilt be perfect, go, sell that thou hast, and give to the poor, and thou shalt have treasure in Heaven, and come and follow Me.' The instinct of selfishness which is legitimately dominant in the brute, becomes not only unnecessary but woefully injurious in the man, and the coming of Christ is to save both from the evil of the natural passion and the consequences its indulgence will entail."

"Will you allow me here to suppose that such an incarnation as that of Christ had not taken place-what then would have been the fate of humanity?"

My teacher smiled good-naturedly as he heard my query.

"Such a supposition would be impossible to realize. Given a humanity, the manifestation of the Christ is a sequence as inevitable as death following the birth of the body. It would be just as futile to attempt to take the noon from day as Christ from the race. He is a natural stage in the divine order of ascent. He is not an interpolation to rectify the effects of a supposed fall-Christ has no connection with any scheme necessitating interpositions or corrections-but the orderly revelation of the next step to be taken in creation's return to God. But this does not exactly answer the true path of your inquiry, which is, 'Had Christ not been made manifest, would the race have been lost?' No. God is in no sense confined to one particular mode of action to accomplish His determined purpose. To argue that He is would be to assert that He is limited in His operations and hence finite. But without rising into any such debatable sphere respecting the nature of God, which neither of us understands, I have full authority for all I have said when I consider the condition of those souls who passed hither before the advent."

"Were they not in prison?" I inquired.

"Let us very carefully see what the Scriptures record of the teaching of Christ," he replied, "for I must not forget that I am now drawing all my argument from what is written. In the parable of Dives and Lazarus, Christ speaks of Abraham's bosom as being a place of comfort, compensation and blessedness to the erstwhile beggar; and when Jesus was transfigured, Moses and Elias 'appeared in glory' and spake to Him of His coming decease. Now if Abraham, Moses, Elias and the beggar Lazarus were not in prison, but rather in glory, the principle is established for which I contend. But God is love, and the essence of love is to lavish benefits upon the object of its affection, as far as possible to throw a protecting care around it, and save from the slightest approach to misfortune. Now, 'God so loved the world that He gave His only begotten Son...not to condemn the world, but that the world through Him might be saved' from the consequences of the evil which is so closely allied with human nature. The descent of Christ was the expression of the God-paternal consideration and regard for the welfare of His children. They must ultimately reach His abode because He 'will have all men to be saved,' and He, being Lord, than whom there is none beside, whatsoever must come to pass. But love constrains itself to devise a means to bring about the early consummation of its own dear desire, and so God cannot leave to nature what may be more rapidly reached through the avenue of grace. Here is the needs-be for the work of Christ, who descends with the revelation of a moral law which brings a power of salvation to everyone that believeth and accepts it as a rule by which his life is to be henceforth governed.

"So far I have confined myself to the teaching of Christ as a law binding upon human life, but no wise ruler-no loving and tender father-issues any command without some good and sufficient reason for so doing. We have now to find the reason for which this new law, as promulgated by the Christ, has been established. I have already spoken of the universal disquietude concerning the fate of man, of the unanswered inquiry, 'If a man die shall he live again?' The coming of the Christ is God's response thereto, and the law He proclaims is the love-appointed way by which the best-an abundant entrance-may be made into the entailed heritage of immortality. For the discharge of this embassage, he was in every way adequately qualified, since He had passed through identical developments and won His way to a spiritual condition beyond the reach of any soul newly passing from the earth, although He was not so far away as to be out of sympathy with the frailties and weaknesses of the flesh. From this elevation He was able to declare the whole counsel of God in so far as men could receive and appreciate it, but when He had accomplished His mission, He was compelled to assure His disciples that much yet remained to be disclosed, though He could not tell them then. This rule of life, by a master-stroke of matchless genius, He reduced into a single sentence sufficiently simple for a child to understand, and which cannot be too often repeated 'Therefore all things whatsoever ye would that men should do to you, do ye even so to them; for this is the law and the prophets.' Nor does He lay this down as a basis of conduct desirable merely for religious, social or political reasons, but speaking from His own intimate acquaintance with an inexorable law, He reveals the natural sequence of all conduct in His eloquent warning, 'For with what judgement ye judge, ye shall be judged; and with what measure ye mete it shall be measured to you again.' For this reason, then, He insists that life shall be so regulated that when one lays his petitions and needs before the Father, he may confidently ask to be forgiven as he has forgiven others.

"Men miss the awful emphasis Christ places on character because they forget that speaking from the immortal side of life, death to Him was simply an incident in existence and not an end of it-a veil He could thrust aside, passing in and out at will. Neither King of Terrors nor Valley of the Shadow exists for Him, but His eyes look calmly forward from earth into the shadowless light of the eternal day, and He carries forward into that to-morrow the unbalanced account of life's to-day. It is this thought in His teaching that should make men pause. There are many nights and days between the sowing and the reaping, but whatsoever a man soweth in the spring he shall reap in the autumn. There is only one accessory death has no power to confiscate as the soul passes forward-character. Beliefs, dogmas, creeds and professions will all be left behind, but character will furnish the only possible clothing with which it may step into immortality. Its works have preceded or will follow on and be produced in evidence in the judgement where 'except your righteousness shall exceed that of the scribes and Pharisees, ye shall not enter into the kingdom of Heaven!'

"I wish you to notice here again how inseparably the Christ insisted on the union between cause and effect-sowing and reaping-as He here blends it in God and humanity. This law He promulgates takes the veriest outcast of a depraved humanity and makes its loathsome exterior to be the unattractive casket in which reposes a divine gem. It has been taken at its sight value on earth-'despised and rejected of men'-but in that judgement hall every fragment of humanity must be gathered up that nothing be lost, and the King shall say to those who stand before Him, 'Inasmuch as ye did it to one of the least of these, My brethren, ye did it unto Me.' It is so far the Christ declares God to outreach to bring the whosoever unto Himself.

"This essential purity of life, in the struggle for the acquirement of which neither ceremonialism nor priest was necessary or admissible, but only God and the aspirant can have any part in, was a revolution not lightly to be tolerated by the conflict that ensued, in which Christ never for an instant yielded a single spiritual claim to His persecutors, and God only used their wrath for His own praise, but would rather direct your attention to the steady purpose of the Christ to fulfil His mission, and by successive stages-clearly visible and well defined in the after-light from which we may view them-led to the great and all-important demonstration for which He came, that of bringing life and immortality to light by the resurrection of Jesus. Have you ever noticed how orderly and systematically this evidence is marshalled?"

"I scarcely understand your meaning," I replied.

"Let me help you to do so by briefly reviewing some of the facts. The definite mission of the Christ, as we already see, was to establish the certainty of existence after the death of the body. 'I am come,' He said, 'that ye might have life, and have it more abundantly.' Whether the surmise, the hope, of this was true or not, was the greatest unsolved problem of the ages, and He had been sent with the definite purpose of answering it. With the success of His demonstration the collateral doubt would also be settled as to whether man possesses a dual nature, and Christ established His claim to speak as to the best method of preparation for entering upon the life invisible to earth. But until the demonstration had been satisfactorily concluded, that man did actually exist after death as the same conscious and intelligent personality as before, all other issues were beside the question and irrelevant. The old prophetic standard was raised as the arbiter of truth in the matter: 'If the thing follow not, nor come to pass, that is the thing which the Lord hath not spoken.'

"From the instant of His descent upon the Nazarene, the latter 'was changed into another man.' 'Old things had passed away and all things became new.' There were visible in Him new powers, new purposes, new lines of conduct, new recognitions, new everything. The point of contact with humanity had been changed, and He spoke 'as One having authority,' and not as the scribes and Pharisees. Perhaps in no instance was this more marked than in His attitude towards the members of the family of Jesus. The Christ refused to be subject to a blood relationship, 'Woman, what have I to do with thee?' Or again: 'One said unto Him, Behold Thy mother and Thy brethren stand without, desiring to speak with Thee. But He answered and said unto him that told Him, Who is My mother? and who are My brethren? And He stretched forth His hand toward His disciples and said, Behold, My mother and My brethren! For whosoever shall do the will of My Father which is in Heaven, the same is My brother and sister, and mother.' (Matt. xii, 47-50) From the outset He assumed the spiritual position, and lived that for which He prayed—

'Thy will be done in earth, as it is done in Heaven.'

"Such an assumption, so far removed from and opposed to the empty ceremonialism of the established religion, could not be allowed to go unchallenged, and soon He is beset by carping critics who wish to know by what authority He speaks and performs His mighty works. The reply of the Christ fixes the attention of the whole world upon His one great purpose-He will stand or fall by the test of the resurrection, 'What sign showest Thou unto us, seeing Thou doest these things?' Jesus answered and said unto them, 'Destroy this temple, and in three days I will raise it up.' Then said the Jews, 'Forty and six years was this temple in building, and wilt Thou rear it up in three days? But He spake of the temple of His body.' (John ii, 18-21)

"So throughout His whole ministry He keeps all eyes fixed hopefully upon the reawakening hour. His teachings are full of references to the harvest of life that must then be reaped and garnered; His parables abound with cautions as to what is sown because of the harvest time which lies ahead; and between the lines of every illustration He used, may be read awful significances of the reward of conduct.

"And all the while He worked and preached He also lived the life-the typical life to which He called all men-which bore evidence to its alliance with God in this world and secured the best results in the world to come. Let us follow Him along the pathway of His works to the great consummation.

"He began the demonstration of the superiority of the spiritual over the physical man by the cure of diseases of a temporary nature, proceeding afterwards to those of more chronic form. Presently we hear Him hurriedly summoned to the bedside of the daughter of an alien who lies at the point of death. In His attendance on others He allows the girl to cross the river, from whence He almost immediately recalls her, and gives her back to her consternated parents.

"At last the Christ had met the adversary He had come to destroy-had caught him in the act of spoliation; and Death was overthrown.

"They next meet at the gate of Nain. Death may well be sure of his prey this time, for the cortège winds its way to the burial; the broken-hearted mother following in the wake of the bier. But Christ had been sent to bind up the broken-hearted. The tyranny of death had already been destroyed in the chamber of the centurion, and the Christ restored the lad to his mother.

"In the third encounter the tomb joined issues with death to hold the sleeping Lazarus. But all in vain! 'Christ is the resurrection and the life.' All power is given unto Him! Therefore at His call he that was dead comes back to life again, and the claims of Christ gain cumulative evidence as to their veracity.

"There yet remains the last and all-decisive contest between the Prince of Life and the King of Terrors to be considered, but before proceeding to this, let us make sure we clearly understand what it is the Christ is making manifest. Jesus of Nazareth, 'a man approved of God,' has placed Himself unreservedly at the Divine disposal, that in and through Him God may answer and supply the world's great need. He was 'in all points' a man as other men, save in His whole-hearted consecration to the cause He espoused. Had He been otherwise-gifted with a peculiar nature, born under abnormal conditions, or conceived as the councils of men have determined-all that was accomplished would have been of no avail; it would have borne no manner of relation to the salvation of men who had come into existence under other circumstances. It is this conception of the Christ that has made Him to be so solitary and unapproachable to your mind. For Jesus was 'a man in all points tempted like as' other men, one chosen from the common brotherhood of humanity because He had been prepared by a holy mother's efforts and His own spiritual aspirations to be the chosen

Chapter 22 — The Work and Teaching of the Christ

messenger of God. Upon this man among men, this body which had been prepared; this temple made meet for the indwelling Spirit of the Lord, the Christ descended and by many mighty works gave evidence to the world that man possesses a nature capable of being elevated into a union with powers greater than the physical, possessing knowledge beyond the limitation of philosophies, and of directing forces which hold the material universe in subjection. This indwelling Christ who is first revealed to man through Jesus of Nazareth, blends the human with the divine, and carries evolution forward into another stage, becoming a second Adam of a new and nobler race. For though He is the firstborn, He is only the type of what the succeeding race shall be, which shall enter into the heritage He already enjoys, and by the powers they wield and the works they perform, make their title clear to be called the sons of God. 'He that believeth on Me, the works that I do shall he do also.' 'By their fruits ye shall know them.' The feeling after immortality which has hitherto met with such unsatisfactory response is but the prenatal struggle of a man fighting his way to the second birth, which having been attained, both death and the grave shall be vanquished, and the first-born among many brethren shall bear away the captured keys into the region of an ever accessible immortality. It is to this last combat and the victory of Jesus I now invite your attention."

"Why do you lay such marked emphasis on the name Jesus?" I inquired, as I noticed the peculiar significance of its mention.

"Because it is very essential that you should distinguish here between the two individualities at a point where they again separate. The Christ was not born, but descended upon Jesus at His Baptism; nor could He die; therefore, having finished His work, He re-ascended before the crucifixion. For Christ to have gone to the death would be as valueless to humanity as the miraculous birth. What man wanted to know was whether, if a man die would he live again, not whether if an immortal pass through the semblance of the event-which by the nature of the case could not be a reality-he would afterwards survive. The work and teaching of the Christ was to give an affirmative reply to the universal inquiry and at the same time lay down the most favourable method of preparation for the event, which typical life He co-operated with Jesus in living, and then withdrew, that the man might enjoy the reward His sacrifice to the will of God had secured. In preparation for this, it was Jesus, and not the Christ, who was transfigured on the mount when Moses and Elijah appeared to make Him acquainted with the nature of the death which lie before Him and give assurances of the victory. Had it been the Christ and not Jesus, there was no necessity for the two to have spoken with Him, for the Anointed One had direct access to the Father, and needed not that any should come between, but Jesus had not passed that way heretofore, and for Him, help and assurance was both needed and encouraging.

"Let us now approach the death on our way to the resurrection, which is to be the decisive test of Christ having been the one sent of God, and in doing so I wish to call your very close attention to the moment when the work of Christ comes to an end, and He re-ascends, leaving Jesus to enter into the reward of the life to which He had so willingly and wholeheartedly lent Himself.

"Will you recall that scene as recorded in the upper room; the consternation and distress of the disciples, and the effort He made to comfort them, 'Let not your heart be troubled; ye believe in God, believe also in Me.' And presently, in the possession of that 'peace of God which passeth all understanding,' we hear Him say, 'Peace I leave with you, My peace I give unto you.' Shortly after the bestowal of this divine benediction we find Him under a tree in Gethsemane in an agony to which that of His disciples bore no comparison. In His terror He sweats 'as it were great drops of blood falling to the ground,' and we hear Him cry, 'Father, if Thou be willing, remove this cup from Me; nevertheless not My will, but Thine, be done.' What has become of the peace which the world could neither give nor take away? How is this change in the attitude of the man to be accounted for?"

"How?" I answered by repeating his own inquiry.

"There is but one reply. The words of comfort were part of the valedictory address of the Christ, in which He promised another Comforter, who would be to the disciples what He had been to Jesus, and by His controlling guidance, lead them into all truth; the conditions being that they continued to love Him (the Christ) and keep His commandments. His farewell was concluded or followed by a paper in which, in more unmistakable language than any previously used, He made known the difference of identity between Himself and Jesus. The work of the Christ is over-'I have glorified Thee on the earth; I have finished the work which Thou gavest Me to do'; on the contrary, Jesus, the man, had to go forward to the death, in order that He might attain to the resurrection, and towards this He went alone, uncontrolled, into Gethsemane. Christ has finished His work, and re-ascended; we shall only catch one other brief glance of Him, for He will come again to roll away the stone from the door of the sepulchre, that the man who has so completely effaced Himself that Christ might be all in all in His life may rise victorious into the glorious immortality His sacrifice has secured. At present your experience has not taught you what amount of nervous exhaustion even the moderate control of Myhanene entails upon his prophet, it is therefore impossible for you to conceive the indescribable condition of collapse to which Jesus returned when the Christ had left Him after His final farewell to His disciples. The agony of the garden was not occasioned alone by fear and dread at the thought of the painful death which stood so closely to Him; the intensity of the suffering was increased a hundred-fold by the physical weakness in which it found Him. Nor was it simply because 'it pleased the Lord to bruise Him' that this bitter cup was held to His lips to drain, it was rather that the world in looking back might see that come what sorrow might there would be none like unto His sorrow, and His obedience and sacrifice sounded deeper depths than other souls would be asked to sound. He swept life's full gamut by the purity and self-abnegation of His life; He made His body a temple meet for the use of the Christ-bore the tension of a physical exaltation up to the highest possible limit of mortal endurance through a protracted ministry which is still the wonder of all in Paradise who are in a position to understand it; then, when the strain was over, the rebound dashed Him to corresponding depths, so that it might be truly said, 'He was in all points tempted like as we are, yet without sin.' But 'He shall see the travail of His soul and shall be satisfied.' You remember the words with which I pictured His volunteering for this work. 'Send Me, and let Thy will be done in and through Me on earth as it is in Heaven?' In the depth of that awful agony His consecrated soul is true to its vow, 'If it be possible let this cup pass from Me, nevertheless, not My will but Thine be done.' It could not pass! Through the valley of the shadow of death humanity had for ages been trying to find its way to a joyful resurrection, but had failed to do so. Someone must find it. God had long been waiting for the pioneer He unseen could lead through the awful terrors of the most painful dissolution. So far the life of Jesus had been placed at the Divine disposal, and the Christ had utilized it to manifest what the highest, truest type of humanity might be. Was the Christ-divested man willing to tread the winepress of the last great sorrow alone? The way was dark, and the guiding hand was gone! Still when the terrors of death seized Him and He could not see His way, He cried, 'Not My will, but Thine be done,' and His feet felt their way forward while the 'bloody sweat' started and ran from every pore. The Christ had come to 'bring life and immortality to light'; the law relating to it had been made known through Him, should not the consummation also be attained? This gave Him strength. In His loneliness and terror He had still the memory of what Moses and Elijah had made known to Him at the great Transfiguration. By His endurance God's will would be made known to man, and not only one life, but the life of all humanity would be transfigured by the sun of truth shining through the darkness in which He struggled forward towards the immortal and eternal day. The flesh was weak, but the spirit was willing, and that spirit was the harvest-producing seed which is endowed with potential omnipotence. In the consciousness of this He pushed His feet further forward, and with outstretched hands felt, if haply He might touch, the everlasting doors.

"He had not, however, reached the bottom of the valley yet. Behind Him lay the betrayal, arrest, scourgings, judgement hall, the forsaking and denial. He had torn the flesh of His hands and feet upon the nails of the cross, the gibes and sneers of priests and high-priests were falling away upon the deadening sense of His ears, the torture of His thirst was overpowering Him, and still the road went down. It was intolerable! Oh, it was impossible that there could be a sorrow like unto this sorrow. He could not go further. Why had the Christ forsaken Him? Why was He thus left alone? He might ask, but there was none to reply. Then He stood still. Stood still to gather what strength He might, and from the depths of His despair sent up such a prayer that would compel an answer. Whenever the Christ (the God) had left Him for a space before He had but to cry and the return was immediate; He would cry again, and the valley of death, with the impinging regions of earth, hell and Heaven, rang with the heart-breaking shout, 'My God, My God, why hast Thou forsaken Me?' He could do no more; but fainting fell and burst the everlasting doors! He had found the way for all mankind into the immortality they sought, from which, after a necessary rest, He would shortly return and make the truth of his discovery known."

"I never felt the awful nature of His death so keenly before," I gasped with relief when he came to the climax, "but have you not carried away somewhat of its importance in favour of the resurrection?"

"No, the resurrection is the all-important fact and the death only an incident necessary thereto. We may now go back to the teaching at the point where we left it by the resurrection, or rather the recalling of Lazarus from the dead."

"But resurrection and recalling are one and the same, are they not?"

"By no means. Christ recalled his three persons in their natural bodies, but the resurrection must be in the spiritual body, which is no longer subject to physical law. It appears and vanishes at will; it is now mistaken for the gardener by Mary; and again it takes 'another form', and is unrecognized until Emmaus is reached and the breaking of the bread discloses the identity of Jesus; Thomas must see the print of the nails before he is satisfied, and by all these changes we discover how different is the spiritual (even when rendered tangible) from the natural body. After the conquest of death in the case of Lazarus the only other sign Christ would give was the resurrection of Jesus, by which alone Paul says light and immortality was brought to light. Death was a phenomenon too common to attach any significance to, but to announce a resurrection from the dead was both a stupendous and incredible occurrence. Therefore the Apostles went everywhere 'preaching Jesus and the resurrection,' claiming it as the very foundation-stone upon which the Christian faith must rest-'If Christ be not risen from the dead, then is our faith vain?' Paul's ambition everywhere was 'That I may know Him, and the power of His resurrection, and the fellowship of His sufferings, being made conformable unto His death; if by any means I might attain unto the resurrection of the dead.' (Phil. iii, l0, ll)

All the careful precautions of the priests and Romans to make sure of His death and to keep the grave intact was to prevent the resurrection, but the demonstration was one of the power of God, and all these precautions of the wrath of man were to be pressed into service to testify to the fact they were so futilely determined to prevent. Therefore you may go on with your new ministry with this clear certainty, my brother, that the demonstration of the return from death is the great corner-stone of the faith of Christ."

"What, then, of the atonement?" I asked.

Chapter 22 — The Work and Teaching of the Christ

"The doctrine of a vicarious atonement is one I must leave for priests to reconcile as best they may, but since it is a purely human dogma, it is also one with which Paradise does not concern itself, being also entirely opposed to the teaching of the Christ. Think for one moment of what He taught. 'Every tree beareth its own fruit; with what measure ye mete it shall be measured to you again; whatsoever a man soweth that shall he also reap.' Zaccheus extorted, and he had to restore; the prodigal squandered, and he had to hunger; Dives neglected the sick pauper at his gate, and he had to endure the torment of hell; the unfaithful steward had to go to prison until the last farthing was paid. There is no room for vicarious atonement in the gospel of the Christ, but it is always the soul that sinneth that has to bear the penalty. So also in regard to sacrifices we may accept the words of the prophet-psalmist, 'For Thou desirest not sacrifice; else would I give it: Thou delightest not in burnt-offering. The sacrifices of God are a broken spirit; a broken and a contrite heart, O God, Thou wilt not despise.' I know the discrepancy between this and other passages in the Bible which might as easily be quoted, but God and Christ at least must be consistent —'a house divided against itself cannot stand.' Outside these we have priest divided against prophet, but Jesus was greatest of the prophets and always opposed to the priests and their law. The Scriptures contain a record of the history of both, and therefore need to be rightly divided to ascertain the truth.

"So we come to an end of our inquiry," continued Rhamya as he rose to leave, "and as a spirit who is to be sent forth for the inspiration of a prophet, I counsel you to be wise, and only speak to earth the things you know and see and understand, and then you need not be afraid. Peace."

* * *

CHAPTER 23

THE COMMUNION OF SAINTS

Rhamya had finished his work and taken his departure, but how shall I speak of the effect his visit had produced? I can well understand you, my reader, regarding the result as very unsatisfactory; all along his argument, as I have traced it, you have detected weak points, false conclusions and unwarrantable inferences. I allowed him quietly to assume positions you would have contested stoutly, and consequently, had you been in my place, Rhamya's whole argument would have taken another complexion. That is, supposing the record is one of an actual event and not the creation of a mind inventing a hypothetical programme upon which to build another creed.

Had you been in my place, it is there where all the difference lies. Let me for a moment suppose that such had been the case. What would have happened? I can tell you perhaps better than you can imagine; all your present prejudices would have vanished; a thousand experiences which now lie between the two positions you and I occupy would have broken up your shallow knowledge of the things of God, and prepared you to receive the truth in furrows of deep expectant desire; the spiritual atmosphere in which you sat would be so clear and your powers of discernment so quickened that you would recognize and hail each truth in its approach, and lose the power to cross-examine or seek to evade it in favour of a cherished but erroneous opinion. You, as myself, would have joined hands with Thomas and when the evidences were seen, would neither have waited to touch or handle, but fallen at the feet of the all-too-certain Saviour and exclaimed, "My Lord and My God!"

That is what would have happened had you been in my place. Rhamya had said he intended to do no more than sketch the outline of the highway of the Christ. It was not necessary for him to attempt more. His simple indication of its direction made the whole course to shine with the radiance of divinity. It reduced a previous chaos to calm, and before my astonished sight, lay the way along which the ransomed of the Lord might return with songs and everlasting joy to the fatherland and rightful heritage of divinity. In his mission of enlightenment Rhamya had broken down the cross-entanglements of theology, pushed his way through the contradictions of dogmatics, regarded as of no consequence the definitions of Fathers and Councils, ignored the confusing battlegrounds of schoolmen, found no occasion to discuss theories of Eden, man's first estate, the fall, original sin and cognate subjects; if he knew that Israel were a peculiar people more dear to the heart of God than any other nation, he failed to mention it, nor did he call any by the name of heathen, or point out where they had been divinely appointed to be the bond-slaves of others. The God upon whose shoulders he found the government to rest was truly no respecter of persons, but in every nation, he that feareth Him and worketh righteousness is accepted of Him; a God who is not to be worshipped only in temples made with hands, but rather in the purity and holiness of consecrated hearts, cleansed and set apart as the appointed and guarded trysting-place where earth and Heaven blend in one. This, the only truly divine and appointed temple for the worship of Him who alone is God, can only be approached by the one ordained and Heaven-elected way which Rhamya had discovered to my mind, and as I scanned its course, after his departure, I understood with a vividness and beauty I had never discerned before, the fullness of the inspiration of the psalmist when he exclaimed, 'The path of the just is as a shining light, that shineth more and more unto the perfect day.'

As I contemplated what had taken place I was more than astonished to find how closely associated was the question of the personality and work of Christ with every conceivable subject and

Chapter 23 — The Communion of Saints

detail of a religious nature. Rhamya had directed his attention to the very heart of things, and having made the one point clear, the mists had apparently rolled away from every quarter of the spiritual horizon until no cloud remained, not even so large as a man's hand.

Especially was this so with respect to the question of intercommunion. Rhamya's interpretation had placed this upon an unassailable basis, and I could go forward to my work with a confidence and authority of which I had never dreamed. The communion of saints now appeared in a new and deeper sense than before, needing no commentator to expound that doubtful passage in Hebrews xii., "Ye are come unto Mount Sion, and unto the city of the living God, the heavenly Jerusalem, and to an innumerable company of angels, to the general assembly and church of the first-born, which are written in Heaven, and to God the Judge of all, and to the spirits of just men made perfect, and to Jesus the mediator of the new covenant, and to the blood of sprinkling, that speaketh better things than that of Abel. See that ye refuse not Him that speaketh." In the light I had just received I could read and understand this and many other hitherto mysterious passages for myself, having reached that highway to which Rhamya had so frequently directed my attention, where 'the wayfaring man' need not wander from the truth.

But speaking of the communion of saints suggests to me an incident which took place at this time, and placed in close relationship with the work of the Christ will pleasantly illustrate how the great law proceeds to its almost infinite adaptations. We have seen it working in its highest aspect between Jesus and the Christ; the case I have now to record is of a very different degree, but it shows the same Spirit and the same Lord to be directing it.

I had but recently returned, and was speaking with Vaone of all I had heard from Rhamya, when Jack and his friend Dandy joined us.

"Did Eilele come back with you?" inquired the former at once.

"No. Why; do you want her?"

"Yes, I want her to talk to Dandy."

"Is it anything that I can do?" I asked.

"There ain't anythin' to do at all," the culprit explained. "I o'ny sed as things ain't as they ought ter be, an' if Jack ses they are, 'e don't know, that's all."

"In what way are they wrong?" I asked, interested to know such a curious point of disagreement.

"Dandy says he ought not to be here," said Jack.

"No, I didn't say it like that," cried the other. "I said it warn't right ter make me come away an' leave Bully Peg wi'out anybody ter look arter 'im."

"But does not God know what is best?" I asked.

"I don't know what God knows or what 'E doan know. But if I'd been God, I shouldn't 'a' done it that way."

"Which way?"

"If I'd been 'im, I should 'a' knocked the box on the little kiddy, an' killed 'im; the big un could look arter 'imself."

"But God will look after Bully Peg," I replied, catching the drift of his grievance. "He will be all right."

"But 'e ain't all right," he affirmed with something very much like defiance. "He's about as wrong as they meks 'em. An' that's where yer mek yer mistake!"

"What is the matter, Jack?" I inquired, anxious to gain some insight into the perplexing situation.

Whereupon I was informed that the lads had but just returned from a visit to the 'College' where they had met Bully Peg and learned how the little fellow had fallen on evil times, and for the whole of the preceding day had been without food. At the best the lad had but very indifferent health, and Dandy resented the additional hardship he had to endure on account of the death of the elder. Had he been alive, Bully would have been fed somehow. This was the extent of Dandy's grievance, and he stoutly refused to accept the fact of his removal as absolving him from responsibility in connection with his friend. In his rough untutored logic, the lad had worked out the proposition that the goodness of God was at fault somewhere to allow Bully Peg to bear this additional suffering under the circumstances of his bereavement.

As I heard the touching story, my heart went out in genuine sympathy towards the distressed Dandy, but where the lad only saw a hungry child, he considered it to be his duty to feed, and that at once, I saw a yawning gulf, impassable to such a physical ministry, or so it presented itself to my doubtful and inexperienced mind.

It was a new and apparently unsolvable problem to me, how to secure and then transmit to Bully Peg that which Dandy had thoroughly made up his mind the child should have.

In my perplexity I recalled Myhanene's counsel to do the best I could where I could not do all I would, and leave the rest to God. I would act upon it, though I knew how impossible it was for me to satisfy the demand that would not accept denial, for I saw the intense determination upon the face of the supplicant, who was ready to give up Heaven, if need be, that his friend might be fed.

"Try to be patient, Dandy," I began, drawing the lad closer and laying my hand upon his troubled head. "It will be all right, though you nor I see how it can be so for the present. God will take care of your little friend for your sake as well as His own, since you are so very anxious about him. Who knows but that Bully Peg is coming to be with you and Jack shortly, and this is the beginning of the end of all his suffering?"

"But I thought God was very good and kind?"

"So He is-more good and kind than any of us know or can imagine."

"But it ain't good an' kind o' the butchers to keep calves wi'out anythin' to eat before they kill 'em."

"I did not say God was doing so. Only that..."

"I know all abart it," he interrupted impatiently. "But Bully Peg wants summat t' eat, an' I wants 'im t' 'ave it at once. Can't yer go an' see God, an' tell 'im 'ow 'ungry Bully is?"

"He knows all about it without our telling Him."

"Then if 'E's as good as yer say, why doan 'E let im ha' some?" Then with a flash of child-like inspiration he suddenly exclaimed, "Oh! I know, p'raps 'E ain't got anybody ter tek it! Come on, let us go an' tek it for im."

It was no use. The determined importunity, sympathy, precocity and artless faith of the lad were too much for me to attempt to cope with. I was worse than helpless-afraid that my incompetence would prove to be harmful to the lad, and in my perplexity I called for Myhanene.

In this I found the relief I so sadly needed.

Dandy recognized him in an instant, and accosted him before I had a chance to speak.

"'Ere! You killed me-didn't yer?"

Myhanene patted his head, and smiled affectionately.

"No-no! Not that," he answered. "Dead boys do not talk excitedly, do they?"

"Well, yer brought me here away from Bully Peg, didn't yer?"

"Ah yes, I will admit that."

"An' do yer know 'e can't get anythin' t' eat-all day yesterday 'e didn't 'ave a bite."

"Poor little fellow! How did you learn this?"

"We have just come from the 'College'," replied Jack, "where he told us so himself."

"Yes, an' I want ter know 'ow God can be good an' let Bully Peg be 'ungry all because God sent you to kill me. Why didn't yer kill Bully and let me live?"

"I was not sent to do that."

"But why warn't yer? That's what I should 'a done."

"Perhaps so, but God knows what is best much better than we do."

"It ain't better ter let Bully be 'ungry. Can't yer gi' 'im summat ter eat?"

"Yes. God will give him something to eat," replied Myhanene, sitting down and drawing the interceding Dandy close to him, "and when he gets it, you will be able to see how very much better everything has been than if you had had your own way. God knows more than we, and what He does is always for the best."

"But it isn't best for Bully to be 'ungry."

"Yes it is, for a little while."

"Well, how is it?"

"That I do not know for the present, but I know God well enough to say that both you and I will see it has been for the best presently."

"When?"

"Almost directly."

"How shall I know?"

"We will go and see your friend as soon as I learn what to do, and you will see how God will find a way for him to be provided for."

"Are you sure?"

"Yes-confident."

"All right, then. But I wouldn't be 'appy 'ere if he was goin' ter be left 'ungry there."

Waiting for God is never a long or trying ordeal under such circumstances. Dandy was most intensely earnest. He was asking help for his friend, and to secure it, if necessary, he was prepared to sacrifice everything, willing even to give up his own heaven for the time that the hungry one might be fed. Such importunity had to be answered. Myhanene knew it as soon as he saw it, and almost at once received his commission to proceed to the relief.

"Come with me," he said with more of command than invitation in his tone, as his alert and ever-ready self was caught up by the urgent mandate. And in a flash of thought we found ourselves beside the hungry lad, who with unshod feet and tattered clothes was doing his best to sell matches among the passers-by in front of the Royal Exchange.

"'Ere we is, Bully," cried Dandy joyfully. "Now yer can ha' some..."

But his exclamation was cut short, for the eager little fellow darted past him, without taking the slightest notice, in answer to a call for "Matches" from the top of a 'bus just pulling up at the kerbstone.

"Well! If that don't tek the cake," gasped Dandy. "But p'raps 'e didn't see us in the fog." Then he added with anxious sympathy, "Fogs don't do for Bully."

Myhanene smiled and drew the little protector to him in a tender embrace, which spoke more eloquently than words.

"What are yer laughing for?" he asked naively.

"At you thinking there is a fog," he replied. "You forget that you have changed your eyes, and see what your friend cannot see, while he is not able to see that we are here."

He started as he grasped an idea that had not occurred to him before.

"Yes, I forgot that! My eyes are dead uns, ain't they? What shall we do?"

His appearance at this discovery was at once droll and pitiable. At length he realized what I had before seen-the apparently impassable gulf across which he wished to reach his friend.

"You must be satisfied for the present to let me do what I can to help your little friend," said Myhanene. "I have not time to explain, but when we get back Eilele will tell you all about it, if you ask her. But let me say that while I have come with you to let you see that Bully Peg has some breakfast, many other angels of God have gone away to bring someone here to give him what you wish, and perhaps more than you expect."

"That's all right," he answered, willing to consent to any arrangement for the moment that would lead to the supply of Bully's need. "But yer'll g' me a chance ter tell 'im who yer are, won't yer?"

"You could not do that, my child. Your friend can neither see nor

Chapter 23 The Communion of Saints

hear us."

The astonished incredulous doubt that is born of ignorance again swept across his face.

"But why can't 'e see us as well as we see 'im?" he asked.

"Did you never look from a dark hiding-place at people passing along a lighted street?" asked Myhanene.

"Many a time."

"Did they see you as plainly as you saw them?" No! But we ain't in the dark."

"Not as we know darkness, but to your little friend we are in the blackness of death, and it is impossible for him to see us."

"Then we can't do nothin' for 'im arter all."

"Yes, we can. We shall perhaps be able to do more than you hope or expect. God is always far better than we anticipate, and if you will be content to wait until I and my friends have done all God will help us to do for little Bully, I am sure you will be more than satisfied."

"Shall I?" he asked in eager acquiescence.

"Yes, I am sure you will."

"Then if my tongue tries to speak agen, I 'ope my teeth'll bite it off."

As I listened to the anxious concern of Dandy for his friend, I wondered what would happen if the eyes of the hurrying, surging crowd around us could for one moment be opened, as were the eyes of Elisha's servant, and our ministering presence be discovered. Ah, brethren, how little do even the wisest and best of men know of the invisible agencies which are continually being employed around them; how little do the most spiritually-minded know of the secret actions of the Lord, moving to correct the errors, frustrate the evil or accomplish that which is for their good? From a human computation in all that Mansion House throng, there was no other person so insignificant or neglected as the little vendor of wax matches, and yet, in the estimate of God and salvation, the commercial interests of the world's centre occupied a secondary place for the moment to the welfare of that lonely and neglected child. Had the veil been lifted, what Prince of Finance would not have forsaken the Exchange in favour of the lad, and wealth would have been laid at the feet of the pauper, in anticipation of the commendatory reward, 'Inasmuch as ye did it to one of the least of these, My brethren, ye did it unto Me.'

But would a service so rendered secure such approbation? Would it not rather be tendered more for the angels than the child and have its only reward in the vision granted? To secure the Master's commendation needs the spiritual sight that can find the Christ in the rag-clothed, starving outcast, and the ministry must be in sympathy with need. This constitutes true and genuine service to the Master-to do good in all places, at all times, and without respect to person; to stand ready for whatever service may be required—if it is to carry a message for an angel at the sepulchre to absent disciples, well, if to bind up the wounds of an outraged Lazarus, pouring in oil and wine, better. It is for God, and God will acknowledge it. No service rendered on His account shall pass unrecognized. God who seeth in secret will assuredly acknowledge each ministry with the reward inseparably linked to the action, which outcome is always to be foreseen in the seed of motive prompting the deed.

God's justice never miscarries.

The veil, however, was not lifted, nor did our little protégé affect the sale he had hoped for. A fellow-traveller had offered his matchbox, the penny was returned to the pocket, and Bully was no nearer, apparently, to his breakfast than ever.

As the child turned from the 'bus with weary dejection, I sorrowfully sighed at my own inability to help to ease his little shoulders of the weight of trouble that was so visibly crushing him, and this in spite of the fact that I knew it was so near its end. If I could only make him know that we were present and that relief was at hand!

But this could not be. Though so near, we were for the present destitute of the necessary means to reach him and make him

Chapter 23 — The Communion of Saints

understand.

"Have you to wait?" I inquired presently of Myhanene, who seemed to be looking for assistance in every passing vehicle and pedestrian.

"Yes! I await the arrival of someone through whom the distress of our little friend may be relieved."

"Do you know who it will be?"

"No. When I received my commission, many other friends were sent forth to find servants of the Master whom they could impress with the idea to come to the Bank. Someone of the number will find a Christ-like soul who will be moved to respond. In some cases, I have known two or even three answer the premonitive summons, but as soon as one sets out the fact is made known to the whole band of workers, who then relinquish their efforts with the many and concentrate their influence on the one, until in performing the service he presently recognizes how wonderfully the hand of the Lord has guided him in the matter."

"Is that the work and purpose of premonitions?" I asked, as his explanation lifted the corner of another veil of mystery.

"Yes! At least it is so for those who stand with their loins girt with loyal readiness to do the Master's will."

"Suppose, as you say, it sometimes does happen that two or three equally respond to the same call?"

"Then he who arrived first would perform the service."

"And the others would conclude that their feelings had deceived them?"

"I am not so sure of that, though it is quite possible it might be so. The ministers working the premonition would readily be able to determine which of the three would first reach the desired destination, and the pressure would at once be withdrawn from the others, who could also be apprised of the fact that the particular purpose had been accomplished, while in the result their ready response to the call will be accepted as equivalent to their having rendered the sole service, and the reward will be equally to each for having done what they could."

"Would it not be possible to foresee who would respond to the call and thus save what I may call an experiment with many?"

"That is, no doubt, foreknown to those who stand at a distance above and are not actually employed in the mission. But God never makes scant provision for the success of any service. Where omnipotence is available no result must be placed in jeopardy. Every agent employed knows that the mission cannot fail, but it requires energy, concentration and whole-hearted effort on our part, for no one of us can foresee how much our particular service affects the whole. Again, these summonses to action serve to ascertain the value of the professions of those who pray to be used in the work of the Lord. Some men cry so loudly as to be unable to hear the still small voice calling them, and their lives pass by in workless praying. God has many devices for testing the genuineness of faith!"

"But are not premonitions rather unreliable tokens to act upon?"

"That depends entirely upon the reality or otherwise of a man's profession. He who lives in unbroken communion with God will hear, and need not be afraid to follow the 'still small voice,' but he whose life is but as a tinkling cymbal will easily be carried away by the imaginations of his own heart, which will drown the true voice of God. The operation of the law speedily draws the dividing line. 'Many are called, but few are chosen'."

"The opportunities and responsibilities of life are terrible realities," I answered, as I saw how important the undercurrents become when thus converted into standards of trial by which so many unsuspected, but terribly appalling, judgements are recorded.

"They must needs be so, my brother, where every act and thought may become a factor in fashioning either an angel or a devil. There is no possible fibre or shade in the whole construction, but is laden with inestimable potentialities. Who can tell the extent to which any single service or mistake may be developed? When eternal results may be concealed in an incautious moment, ought Men not to be ever on the watch-tower? Can we not understand with what significance the Christ said, Watch? But, come, our fellow-worker approaches." Then he spoke cheerily to Dandy. "Now you shall see the answer to your prayer for your friend."

The child in whose welfare we were specially interested had, during this time, been busy plying his wares persistently as each new bus drew up at the kerbstone, but in his efforts he was sadly handicapped by the presence of a bigger and stronger lad, who ruthlessly thrust the child aside and always secured for himself what business in the match-vending was to be done.

Again and again did I see the little fellow dart forward in the hope of affecting a sale, but at each attempt he was forestalled, and his rival danced a joyous step at his easy victory over the starving lad.

As Myhanene made his announcement to Dandy, a Blackwall bus drew up, and a gentleman on the top calling for matches, Bully dashed forward only to be encountered and pushed aside again by his more successful rival, and what was infinitely worse, his two remaining boxes of goods fell from his hand in the struggle under the moving wheel, ignited, and in a moment the broken-hearted Bully was a hopeless bankrupt, without resource or hope.

The heroic fortitude he had hitherto displayed now forsook him. Such a catastrophe was sufficient to crush a man under the painful circumstances, and while the jubilant rival howled with delight at the result of the scuffle, Bully broke down in his hopeless extremity and wept piteously.

As he looked upon the still blazing matches through his tears, an elderly man cautiously stepped out of the bus and noticed him.

"Here, here! What's the matter-what's the matter?" he inquired with a pompousness that was more assumed than real. "What's all this crying about, eh?"

The little fellow looked at his burning capital, but could not speak.

"Dropped your matches, eh? Well, never mind-never mind! It's only a penny, and-here, I'll buy them."

"It's two boxes!" exclaimed the partly-consoled Bully.

"Two boxes, is it? Well, that's only two-pence. Here you are. I'll buy the two. What's your name?"

"Bully Peg, sir," he replied with the sign of a smile breaking through his tears at the unexpected turn events had taken.

"Bully Peg!" repeated the gentleman. "Wherever did you get such a name as that from?"

"I don't know; but that's what it is."

"Nor I don't know either. Where do you live?"

"I don't live nowheer."

"But you have a home."

"No, I ain't."

"Well, where do you sleep?"

"Anywheer."

"Have you a mother or father?"

"Not as I knows on."

"Really me! This is very sad for one so young. What did you have yesterday?"

"Nothink."

"And nothing this morning?"

"Not yet."

"Now I know why the dear Lord put it into my heart to come to the City. Come on, my child; come and have some breakfast at once."

"That's all right," joyously exclaimed Dandy; "I don't care now Bully's got 'is tuppence an' goin' to 'ave some breakfast. I'll go back now if yer like."

"Not just yet," replied Myhanene. "Your little friend has all you asked for him, but while we are here I want you to see how God frequently gives much more than we ask."

"What more do you expect to accomplish?" I inquired.

"We shall do no more," he answered, "our part in the ministry is over, but did you not hear our fellow-labourer say that he recognized a Divine interposition in bringing him to the City? The question now remains as to how far he will go in helping the lad. Let us watch him, but we have no commission to influence him further-that must be entirely a matter of free will."

The little arab was by this time comfortably seated at a table in a café close at hand. The waitress eyed him suspiciously, but his guardian was ample protection, and presently the child was devouring, with all the zest of starvation, a breakfast such as he had never faced before. The gentleman took up a paper, not to read but rather to leave the lad more free to eat apparently unobserved, but the stealthy side-glances afforded full confirmation of the long fast, and we were able to read what the world never knew-a thankful return for God's goodness in enabling him to perform such a service.

Presently he dropped the paper and asked, "Wouldn't you like to give up selling matches and have a nice bed to sleep in?"

"Yes, if I could have summat to eat as well."

"Of course I mean that, and nice warm clothes to wear."

"An 'ave a 'ouse?"

"Yes, live in a large house."

"Yer don't mean a prison, do yer?"

"Certainly not. That is what I am very anxious to save you from."

"Are yer? Well I should like it."

"If I could get you into a comfortable home, would you promise to be good and not try to run away?"

"What should I want ter run away for?"

We need not follow the details further. Sufficient to say that as soon as the lad had finished his meal, his friend took him eastward, where he knew he could find 'an ever-open door for waifs and strays,' and when Dandy returned to his home in Paradise, he had the consolation of knowing that Bully Peg was fully provided for by reason of an importunate prayer and a Father's loving response.

Such is another aspect of the communion of saints in practical operation. We have already seen how the uncontrolled grief of those left behind may disturb the rest of friends in Paradise; here we have the answering sympathy and see how it is possible for those in advance to continue a loving ministry for the protection of those they have left behind. What a service it might render to the world if properly cultivated!

* * *

CHAPTER 24

THE MISSION OF PAIN

When all arrangements were concluded, and Bully Peg finally assured of far better protection than Dandy could possibly have anticipated, the unbounded delight of him whose prayer had wrought the miracle was very touching to witness. He was in a wonderland of bewildering amazement, uncertain whether to show his gratitude by laughter or tears-doubtful whether he was awake or dreaming. His eyes started and blazed with the feverish excitement that shook him; his lips trembled with speechless eloquence and his hands worked with restless incertitude, while he looked from Myhanene to Bully and back again.

"I doan know what ter do, or 'ow ter do it, Jack," he cried in despairing tones presently. "Why doan yer 'elp me?"

"How can I help you?" replied the equally uncertain Jack. "It's quite as bad for me as it is for you. It's more than anything I ever knew before."

"But I must do summat or I shall bust. Why doan somebody tell me what I can do?" and the little fellow literally danced with grateful excitement.

"What would you do?" queried Myhanene with that quiet sympathetic persuasiveness he so effectively employed in soothing paroxysms of emotion.

"I want ter..." But with a jerk of his arms and stamp of his foot, Dandy had to leave his desire otherwise unexpressed.

"Well, what is it you do want?" Myhanene knew that the real relief of the lad's feelings lay in some form of expression, and he encouraged him to find the best available.

"I want-I must say summat! An' it ain't 'thank yer!'-that ain't 'alf enough-it ain't a bit o' what I mean! An' I can't say nuthin'!"

"Then suppose you wait awhile. I know, and God also knows and understands better than you can tell Him."

"Does He?"

"Yes, much better."

"But I wish I could see 'Im; I should like to tell 'Im both for me an' Bully, an' yer can't say nuthin' if yer can't see Im."

"Oh yes, you may, and He will hear you. He heard when you wanted Bully to have some breakfast, and sent us to do all that has been done."

"Did He? Oh, yes! I forgot that, an' all the while I wanted ter say 'thank yer' for it! Well then, 'E knows 'ow glad I am."

"Yes; He knows far better than you can tell Him. Now we will go."

"Yer sure Bully'll be all right?"

"Quite sure, but you can see him at the 'College'."

"O' course! Why, I am forgettin' everything. Come on, I'm ready; and if Bully's all right, I shall niver want ter come back 'ere agen."

So this mission to earth ended-a mission comparatively trivial in itself, but laden with suggestion and illustration capable of being applied to some of the deeper problems of life, and carrying many more lessons than are found floating upon its surface.

I found it to be so in my own case, and trust others may find it to be equally serviceable upon reflection.

Let me mention one of the revelations it afforded me; perhaps the record may contain a suggestion for you, my reader.

As we were leisurely returning, Myhanene and I found ourselves somewhat apart from the rest, and presently throwing his arm around my shoulder he said, "Now that our pleasant duty is at an end, permit me to compliment you upon its very complete success."

"Compliment me!" I exclaimed, as I started from his embrace and scanned his face, expecting to discover the trace of a delicate sarcasm he knows so well how to use upon occasion.

"Yes, my brother. I have to offer you my sincere and hearty

Chapter 24 — The Mission of Pain

congratulations. You have done well, so continue, and your mission to earth will result in a most glorious harvest."

"But what have I done? I have played a less part in this business than Jack, by far."

"Have you?" he inquired, lifting his eyebrows with one of the nervous twitches he employs to express a feigned astonishment. "How strange that I should commit such an error!"

"What do you mean, Myhanene?" I asked persuasively as I caught the smile lighting up his face.

"I mean all I have said, and more," he replied. "The incident we have just so happily concluded has been pressed into service for a double purpose, the one lying upon the surface and now so happily ended being by far the least important of the two."

"And the other was—May I know it?"

"Yes! Now it is over you may do so, and as I have already said, I most sincerely congratulate you upon it."

"Upon what?"

"The course you took. When Dandy saw his friend's extremity and determined to do something to help him, a splendid opportunity was foreseen to test what course you would take if called upon to render assistance under the circumstances. Would you, with your imperfect knowledge, attempt to satisfy and overrule the lad's anxiety, or have the presence of mind to call someone to your help, as I had previously counselled you to do in all such cases? You did admirably, and now you see the result."

"But suppose I had not called you?" I asked startled at the thought of the responsibility I had so unknowingly escaped.

"Then other means would have been utilized to answer Dandy's prayer and you would have missed its reward."

"But I might have lost it so easily."

"Most of life's opportunities are so lost! Unless we are always on the watch-tower they slip by, and we only see them when too late. It is this yielding to the wooing of slothfulness—this coquetting with the plausible excuses of indifference—that suffcocates the spiritual life of earth, and sends such multitudes hither empty-handed from the harvest-fields. The accounts which have to be balanced here are as numerous and heinous in omissions as in commissions and men are astonished to find the reward of both is an equal one, until reminded that Christ had so asserted the law in His parable of the last judgement."

"I can only think of my own providential escape," I answered. "It was far more of the mercy of God than my own deliberate choice."

"That I am always willing to admit," he said. "But you must not forget that the exercise of the mercy of God is not an arbitrary act. Every soul consecrated to the will of God becomes so sympathetic with the Divine mind as to respond intuitively to its desire even before our consciousness has understood the command. Full and complete consecration keeps us in constant nearness to the Father, who is so clearly reflected in ourselves that His will forms the motive power of every action. We are encircled by His guardianship, guided by His eye, so easily moved by the impulse of His love that by the time we come to understand the nature of His will, we also find that we have been already constrained to perform the duty."

"I cannot understand such a relationship," I replied; "I can only fear and tremble at the thought of occupying the position, and almost wish I could escape."

"Do so, Aphraar! Do so by all means."

"How can I escape?"

"There is one way-but only one."

"How? Where?"

"Draw nearer still. There is no safety but with God-no place of rest but the eternal peace His bosom affords. In that nearness you will ascertain the fullness of His strength and love while you will also lose the sense of the awful majesty with which He is girded. If a microbe living in the blood or tissue could form any adequate conception of what a man really is by comparison, it, too, might reasonably fear and tremble, and yet where would be the need so

Chapter 24 — The Mission of Pain

long as the interests of the two remain identical?"

"I like that thought," I replied.

"Of the microbe?"

"Yes! It is so full of pregnant suggestion, and at once appeals to me as containing revelations beyond the power of words to convey. With your clear insight into the working of Divine love, you cannot understand how cheeringly welcome such significant illustrations are to me in my confused bewilderment. I am very much like poor little Dandy-overpowered and utterly helpless."

"I can understand what you mean," he replied with a wooing tenderness that strangely soothed me.

"Can you? Then you know me better than I know myself."

"Even that would not surprise me," he answered with one of his significant smiles. "But then I have been here so much longer that I ought to be more acclimatized to the natural wonders of this transcendent life than you who have so recently arrived."

"I have been here some time now," I responded.

"Not long enough to remove all your earth ideas and conceptions; though I am not sorry they keep surging up and making their influence felt. The experience will be valuable to you in your ministry, and help you in many cases you would otherwise be unfitted to deal with. The unseen God leads us forward with unerring wisdom."

"You well say unseen. Gross blindness is perhaps the best definition I could give of my condition, and yet all around me seems so light, so beautiful and full of hope. I cannot understand myself."

"Let me advise you not to attach too much importance to your condition of uncertainty for the moment. God frequently interposes such a veil while He is passing by, and it may be that He is granting you such a favoured experience just now. Come nearer to me and let me lead you until the shadow of your indecision has passed, then we shall be able to rejoice together, and you will find, while travelling again in a way you know not, you have been drawing nearer to God."

"Direct me as you see to be best, Myhanene; I can trust you, but in myself I have no confidence at all. I feel exhausted, confused and altogether incapable of helping myself."

"I know all about it," he replied encouragingly. "It is the natural strain of responsibility connected with the mission you have so happily concluded."

"But I have played the least important part of anyone—even less than Jack-in what has taken place," I answered, filled with astonishment at the importance he continued to attach to my call upon him to help me out of a difficulty.

"That may be your interpretation of the matter," he replied, "but from this life we regard the issue as a duty nobly performed. What the outcome will be rests entirely with God. Events turning apparently upon insignificant trifles sometimes prove to be of mightiest consequence, and the result of your calling for me will only be known when the Master counts up His jewels. For your encouragement and guidance, however, I may say that the exhaustion you feel indicates to me that the harvest of this mission will be one of which we shall all be glad."

"I sincerely hope it may be so, and there I will try to leave the matter. But the incident generally raises the whole question of prayer in my mind-may we speak of it?"

"With pleasure. What is the particular aspect that presents itself?"

"In this case the answer to Dandy's request has been so prompt and complete as to be in startling contrast to general experience. Why is this?"

"The reason lies altogether in the prayer, not in any arbitrary action on the part of God. Eternal law decrees that any soul enjoying consecrated union with God may ask what it will, and it shall be done, and this because such union will exert a restraining power from asking what is opposed to the Divine will. In every case the prayer will be a spiritual exercise employed specifically

Chapter 24 — The Mission of Pain

for matters touching the kingdom, and not resorted to until every possible natural effort has been employed and failed. Only a fractional percentage of what earth calls prayer falls within this definition, hence the large amount of wasted time and breath-telling God so much about Himself, asking Him to do what men are either too lazy or too selfish to do for themselves, seeking a Divine blessing upon some act of tyrannous oppression against a weaker people, or supplicating Heaven to arise and crush the natural instincts of the starving masses and shield the ill-gotten gain of sweaters from molestation-fall outside the domain of the law and meet with the legitimate reward of oblivion. In opposition to all this, let us carefully look at the nature and circumstances surrounding Dandy's prayer, then you will at once see why it produced such a different result. Having voluntarily assumed a kind of guardianship over Bully Peg, discarnation stepped in and placed a difficulty in the way of exercising the office. Dandy, however, refused to accept the new condition as absolving him from responsibility, and on learning of his friend's extremity, he at once set himself to find some way of securing the necessary relief. The whole circumstance erects a monumental demonstration of fidelity to trust and faith in an existing power of right. As the connection between the lads, from the first time we met them to the present, is reviewed, it will be seen that every condition required by effectual prayer has been faithfully regarded, so that when the crisis came, the petition assumed the God designed omnipotence of prayer and worked its own sovereign will with Divine munificence."

"I see and understand it now," I answered as the inner light bore witness to his patient exposition. "I shall not trouble you so much with these inquiries when once I grow accustomed to study matters from my new position. But, in the meantime, there is yet another kindred question I should be glad to hear you explain."

"You refer to the vexed problem of pain and suffering?"

"Yes! I should be very glad to hear how you would meet an

inquiry respecting it."

"I should begin by divorcing the two as being unequally and ignorantly yoked together. Pain, like the Satan of the Book of Job, has to be ranked among the sons and ministers of God, rather than classed with the emissaries of evil. Its appointed office is to guard and protect the welfare of man and instantly to give warning of any departure from the path of health—physical, mental, or spiritual. They who hear its voice and instantly obey are thus saved by the angel of His presence, but those who refuse and rebel must take the consequences of their foolhardiness. Thus Pain, as every other angel of God, speaks first to man in a still small voice of kindly intimation, for 'the Lord loveth whom He chasteneth,' and the minister is ever of the same nature as the Father. But for the careless, the negligent, the defiant and the deaf, there remains the alternative of the law: 'If ye will not obey the voice of the Lord, but rebel against the commandment of the Lord, then the hand of the Lord shall be against you.' (1 Sam. xii, I5) It is here that Pain hands the sinner over to Suffering. Still, so far as Suffering continues to be the agent of God, its function is remedial and altogether beneficent, as the Christ declared of the man who was born blind. You have just seen an instance of how providences intertwine, and here we may find another illustration of the same law. The man born blind had been deprived of some of the ordinary advantages of life, but in his darkness-not being able to estimate the value of what had been withheld-he enjoyed compensations which others who were normally endowed could neither estimate nor understand. These compensations were withdrawn when the more ordinary faculty was bestowed. But this is only by the way. What I wish you to grasp is the provision of God to endow all joint-heirs with Christ with the power which He possessed to put an end to all suffering of a legitimate nature. You will remember how all manner of suffering fled at His approach, but we too often forget that He intended all who followed after Him to wield the same Divinely merciful power. 'He that believeth on Me, the works that I do shall he do also.' (John xiv, l2) 'As ye go, preach, saying, 'The Kingdom of Heaven is at hand. Heal the sick, cleanse the lepers, raise the dead, cast out devils: freely ye have received, freely give.' (Matt. x, 7-8) 'These signs shall follow them that believe; in My name shall they cast out devils; they shall speak with new tongues; they shall take up serpents; and if they drink any deadly thing, it shall not hurt them; they shall lay hands on the sick, and they shall recover.' (Mark xvi, l7-l8) I need not quote more of the promises to you to show that God gives to children of the Christ, or second birth, power to put an end to all legitimate suffering, making the display to be a testimony to the Christ-life in His true disciples ('by their fruits ye shall know them'), and also a manifestation of the power and love of God to all who are in need."

"But all these gifts have long since ceased to exist," I exclaimed, wondering at his reference to powers which were only intended for the Apostles.

"Let us rather say they have ceased to be employed. God never changes, never corrects, never withdraws. The endowment is still the same. You saw it recently in operation through Cushna in the case of the child with the withered leg, and it is always available for all who are able to use it. Its cessation is something yet to be accounted for by the Church claiming the name of Christ-a dereliction of duty-a sin of omission for which the penalty will fall heavily somewhere.

"But by far the larger part of suffering is illegitimate, and springs directly from unrighteousness of life. I speak now of the starvation, want, misery and wretchedness of every form which characterizes the progress of what is called civilization. This is altogether the product of sin, and is an abomination to the Lord. It need not exist, ought not to be, but for greed, selfishness and inhumanity, for which every man and woman is more or less responsible, and every one of whom will have to reap his just reward according to his definite and active life attitude towards it. The law of Christ-

'whatsoever ye would that a man should do unto you, do ye even so unto him'-would stamp out the condition with the celerity of a revolution if but honestly applied, and the neglected masses of humanity-raised at once to a condition in which the necessaries of life were secure-would be placed more favourably for receiving the moral and spiritual training, which they are incompetent to appreciate where they lie. God is able and willing to deal with the problem if Politics and Trade will step aside and leave it in His hands. But the powers of earth must sport themselves while life's morning vapour is rising. And God is patient, knowing all the compensations He holds in reserve. In the moment between immersion and unconsciousness, the drowning man lives a whole life of agony-and so the robbed and outraged sufferer drags out a weary existence. Still it is only a spark flying upward by comparison with what is to be when Lazarus shall be comforted and Dives enter upon the inheritance he has purchased."

"Do you think it possible that every transgression will ultimately be traced to its particular source?" I inquired.

"Every dove will return to its own window, my brother, and every cockatrice will come back to its own den. God is fully able to carry out His schemes of justice with a perfect balance. Neither you nor I am able to understand how this is possible, but the law of God is perfect and will inexorably ensure that every soul shall bear its own legitimate burden."

"Who, then, shall escape?"

"God in His love and wisdom has planned a scheme whereby the vilest and most depraved may ultimately find his way to peace. It lies through the purifying fires of hell and the innumerable stages of the plains of Paradise, where 'him that cometh shall in no wise be cast out.' But the debt, though great, shall ultimately be paid, the extortion required, the inhumanity atoned for and the sin forgiven. Eternity is long enough to secure all this, and finally the family circle will be complete and God be all-in-all."

Such a glorious prospect so confidently foreseen and

prophesied by Myhanene left nothing more to be said or hoped for, and we finished our course in solemn silence.

* * *

CHAPTER 25

AU REVOIR

On several occasions in the foregoing record, I have been constrained to speak of the limitations imposed by earth, time and the flesh, but just now I find myself face to face with one for which I was altogether unprepared, and the force of it fills me with something like consternation.

One by one I have been dealing with questions arising out of the mass of correspondence still lying before me according as my experience in Paradise has qualified me to do so, but so far I have been scarcely able to commence the real pleasure I was looking forward to when my Recorder astounds me with the information that the volume already assumes somewhat large proportions, and I am compelled to make another break in my recital.

The intimation has brought me to a sudden stand that I might carefully go over the mass of correspondence I have left untouched, and examine my MS. to make sure I have not given space to details of secondary importance at the expense of weightier subjects. I have even sought counsel of friends with much wider experience in the hope of being able to do more in the space at my disposal, but it is all of no avail. I cannot find a teacup that will approximately hold the ocean. The review, however, has afforded me this consolation; my most frequent inquiries range themselves in the following order-Christ, Hell, Sin, the family in Heaven, the future of children, and the relative value of the different religions. On all these subjects I have had something to say in the foregoing pages, giving to the Christ the paramount importance He so necessarily deserves; at the same time I most freely acknowledge how conscious I am of my inability to do the subject the justice I would so willingly have rendered. But though my exposition may seem strange and even unnatural as it is looked at through the theological fogs of earth, and perhaps, on the other hand, to those friends who occupy higher planes of life to which I have not yet climbed, it may seem a weak and unworthy sketch of the Divine portraiture. I have the consolation of knowing that 'when the mists have rolled away' earth-clouded eyes will see as I now see Him, and also that the greater, nobler souls above me will recognize that I have done what I could-'the spirit is willing, but the flesh is weak,' and there I am content to leave it for the present.

Chapters relating to Prayer and God, I have been compelled to withdraw for the present because it was impossible for me to add the illustrative experiences necessary to convey the suggestive ideas and information I wish to set forth. But these with all the other inquiries I have, or may receive in answer to this, shall have attention, if I still feel warranted in continuing my labour of love. Again, though at the risk of being thought wearisome at the reiteration, and altogether apart from the question as to whether my return to earth is ill advised or not-let me repeat that in all I have said I have been guided alone by one motive-to make known to you, my reader, the truth as I have found it by practical experience, as I myself should have been glad to know it when I was standing where you are standing now, and as you must know it when presently the veil shall be withdrawn and admit you to where I am.

If I have touched upon sensitive points in respect of creeds, churches and religion; as institutions, I have not wished to do so in any sense of bitterness, but at all times willing to concede the valuable help they have rendered in their legitimate sphere, while compelled to deny their claim to Divine authority for their limited conceptions of Christ, God, and eternal punishment.

To refuse to admit their utility and service to humanity within their legitimate sphere would be to proclaim my mental incompetence to recognize an obvious fact. What I do deny is the right of any church or conclave of men to assert that their dogmas or decisions mark the finality of God's action, and the assumption that beyond the limit they erect there exists nothing but irretrievable doom. The Church, as an ecclesiastical or theological institution was called into existence to supply a recognized need for an institution that would assume the office of nurse to the infant generation of the day; but the child must always grow and pass from the nursery, first to the school and afterwards through every different sphere of life. As the infant outgrows the swaddling clothes, and the boy the childish garments, so the soul will ever be entering into the heritage of the many things which remain to be told when we are able, by development, to bear them. It is a sad mistake to imagine that 'the faith once delivered to the saints' was God's final word of revelation. There is no finality with God! Such a proposition would also predicate that He had a beginning: ergo, He would not be God. Any formulated eschatology of doom must of necessity be closely allied with death, and can only be experienced by that which is subject to death or termination. Now, such a fate is not the future of immortal souls created in the image and likeness of God, but it may well be the inheritance of the institution itself.

There are no temples in the immortal. All these establishments, with their equipments of professors, priests, rabbis and masters, furnished with laws, dogmas, decisions, racks, faggots, crosses, excommunications and other machinery for ensuring conformity, will be confiscated as being interdicted merchandise on the frontier of Paradise. However useful or essential you may hold them to be, no matter how divinely authorized you may esteem them, if you possess no deeper religion than an institutional certificate, it will be bad for you, for that will be taken away as contraband rather than regarded as a passport, and you will be left alone.

I speak of that I know, and therefore, while I am anxious to give to every aid to the betterment of men its legitimate recognition, I wish to raise a warning voice against your placing too much confidence in what, after all, is nothing more than an arm of flesh.

The only authoritative passport to the abundant entrance into immortality which all desire is the radiance of the Christ shining from within, and it needs no countersigning by any church.

From henceforth to the hour of your departure, let your life be a walk with the Master towards Emmaus. Hear Him and obey; watch Him and do likewise; live-or rather allow Him to live again in you; then you will leave life's Gethsemane behind, as you climb up its Olivet, and from its brow you will ascend with Christ, as the everlasting doors lift their heads, while earth will seek in vain to find you, who will be for ever with the Lord.

In the foregoing, I have also tried to profit by the kindly suggestion of certain of my generous critics, and have refrained from attempted flights which might tax anyone to follow me. I am content for my gospel to appeal by the home force of its own reasonableness. Hear me and judge: if what I speak commends itself to your intelligence as bearing the weight of truth, accept it; if not, then you are equally warranted in rejecting it. Whether I am in the right or otherwise will be certainly determined presently, and if your rejection of it is as honest as my statement, you will commit no sin, nor incur any punishment by hesitating to accept what you cannot understand or believe. The God I serve is not so unjust as to expect you to accept anything against honest conviction.

This brings me to my au revoir, in connection with which I would, for a moment, return to the subject of the reunited family in Paradise. It is always a difficult and delicate task, and oftentimes a most unwise one, to touch or attempt to destroy a cherished superstition. But truth, however unwelcome its first appearance may be, is far more beneficent in the end than an unfounded fiction, and though the shock of my communication may be at first resented, a little quiet reflection will change the balance of opinion; then when the whole circumstances are taken into consideration, and the contributing issues of the life of Paradise are borne in mind, the old idea will melt away and we shall all rejoice together in the wider and eternal hope of God's greater gospel.

I do not make this reference, however, as preparatory to rearguing this point, but rather as introducing a final experience which will illustrate another side of the same subject.

Let me preface this by reminding you of the chronic gloom and melancholy which so completely dominated and destroyed all idea of pleasure in my own earth life. My transition ended this intolerable burden, and restored to me her, whose absence had caused the joy effacing shadow. Have I disappointed you, my reader, in saying so little about this long-delayed and all-important reunion? What did you expect? What could I say? Is the sacred communion and enjoyment of such love a public affair that I should publish its detailed programme for the world to study?

Have you dreamed that the little I have said of Vaone indicates that she proved to be less loved and loving than I had anticipated; that my silence concerning her denotes disappointment; that my long and frequent absences suggest coolness or indifference; that I found her to be no more than others in her claim upon my affections? If so, you have been the sport of wild inferences and an erratic imagination, for I would solemnly assure you that my sweetest anticipation of that meeting fell very far short of what the actuality proved to be.

My silence has been governed by the sacred solemnity of the occasion, nor was the afterwards of our communion so much a matter of public discussion as to warrant my continual exhibition of its details. I could not prevent your eyes catching a glimpse of her as I thrust aside the curtain and fell upon her heart, but I could not hold it aside that you might satisfy your curiosity when I had so long hungered to clasp her in my arms. These divine compensations are always bestowed in secret, nor can any know or understand how supremely divine they are until God calls a soul to know them for itself.

Another reason why I have been so reticent in reference to this most heavenly of all my experiences, has been the knowledge I have gained that love, free from any admixture of sensuous passion or selfish consideration, is altogether unknown on earth, and to attempt to speak of it as it is enjoyed above the earth-conditions of Paradise, would only be to desecrate the most sacred attribute of Divinity. The love of earth is always tinctured in some form by desire, but that of Paradise is the rich ripe fruit developed from the blossom of gratification. How could it be understood? Even on earth the Occident fails to understand the Orient, and in turn the Orient is just as incapable of appreciating the Occident; and if this is true between flesh and flesh, how can it be otherwise when the flesh is taxed to comprehend the things of the spirit? The perfect beauty of anything can only be seen in its native haunt. Love is essentially the lily of Heaven, and only as we near its native region can the beauty of emblem-blossom be found in anything approaching a suggestion of its unspeakable perfection.

God sighed in His love for earth; that sigh was Christ. We too shall love, when looking on the world of sin we sigh for its deliverance, and in that sigh the Christ shall live again in us. But until then the song of Heaven cannot be sung in the land of exile! Let it be understood, then, that in my progress of one degree nearer to the kingdom of love, I found the restored Vaone to be far more to me than my earth-hunger had taught me to expect. When you reach those who are passed on before they will not be less, but infinitely more than they were. Be assured of this. But when I became acclimatized to the condition, and learned to understand something of the law and order of my new sphere of life, I discovered that my love for Christ was incomparably greater than my love of mother! It was the same love differing rather in degree than quality, for its God-likeness is found in its being an infinite unit.

I had climbed to the peak of my first aspiration to find another far more majestic and sublime towering between myself and God, and I was willing, if need be, to leave the one that I might attain to the indescribable splendour of the other.
And then-!

Chapter 25 — Au Revoir

Here I must pause! 'Neither death, nor life, nor angels, nor principalities, nor powers, nor things present, nor things to come, nor height, nor depth, nor any other creature,' can enable us to understand what lies in that beyond, until we are blended in that union with Christ which will enable us to see the Father by reason of our likeness to Him.

It will be remembered that in speaking of the home in which I joined Vaone, I mentioned that the valley was singularly lacking in energizing influences. Its location is just across the border where the last earth-condition can be felt, and might fairly be spoken of as representing the capillaries of spiritual life, being the nearest approach to stagnation, where the only active desire of the soul is for rest. Many reach the condition direct from earth, many after being buffeted about and winning their way through the preparatory ordeals of various earth-conditions, and many more after liquidating the debts and paying the penalties of hell. For all tempest-tossed, tempted, tried and distressed souls, from wherever they come, it is a haven of refuge, and the desire to rest and be content is easily to be understood.

Vaone had known, as only sensitive, timorous souls can feel, the stress of storm and tempest, shipwreck of hopes and the horrors of loneliness; hence the lull she found from the sorrows of the past was in the nature of her ideas of Heaven with which she had remained satisfied.

And my own ideal of the after-life had been to find and be with her. This was my one goal and aspiration, and in accordance with the spiritual law that 'he who seeks shall find,' we came together. But Heaven had led me to her by a way I knew not. My soul had been awakened to other ideals before I met her, that afterwards I might be able to minister to her advancement. She might be content to remain, and my coming would have further confirmed her in the desire, but after what I had seen and learned, for me to sit still was an impossibility. I must go forward, and the love she had for me would compel her to come after, and thus constrain her to rise into a higher life.

So Heaven works out its scheme of ultimate redemption. Vaone's listless attitude surprised me from the first, and, as I knew her better, I wondered more and more. I could not rest. The gate of Heaven had been thrown open before me, and its inhabitants, its palaces, its ceaseless employments, its victories and rewards, its Christ, its God, called to me in such melodious irresistible voices that even the love I had once estimated as supreme could not hold me back. Even though I had to leave it, I must move forward.

But what is once attained can never be lost again beyond the tomb. I had scarcely arrived at the conscious recognition of this at the time of which I speak; but it is so, and I note it here, if perchance it may serve to save a pang of doubt.

Was I sorrowful when at length I knew that this difference in temperament was about to cause our separation? No! I knew the strength of our love for each other, and that my going would soon stimulate her desire to follow and rejoin me; therefore, when the intimation came, I gathered her very tenderly in my arms and spoke to her of what was about to take place.

"I thought so much of Heaven was too much to continue," she said resignedly as she drew me to her with ever-tightening embrace. "But you will sometimes come back to me?"

"Yes, I will come back frequently, for a little while. Now that we have found each other, we must not part again."

"Only for a little while?" she pleaded.

"Only for a little while; there will be no need for more; then you will come to me."

She lifted her head from my breast, her eyes bright with the light of a new inspiration, and her voice ringing musically with a suddenly acquired determination.

"I had not thought of that!" she exclaimed. "Yes, I will come to you! Whom God hath joined, naught is able to divide, and, after the long waiting, the Father in His love has brought you and me together. You must go, but in the going you have aroused my wish to be nearer to Him. Even so, He mercifully ordains that the lesser love shall be instrumental in guiding me to the greater."

"When shall we be able to solve the depth of His wonderful workings?" I asked, in my joyous astonishment at this new development. "While I was in the lower life, God was working through you to prepare a home for me, now He chooses me to go on to the next stage that by me He may prepare for your advance into His nearer presence: 'Even so, Father, for so it seemeth good unto Thee.' Keep Thou firm grip of our hands, and in Thine own way lead us nearer to Thyself:

'Not where we would, but where Thou seest best,
Whether o'er hill or vale, by torrent or by rill,
Guide us and lead us on and on, until
We reach Thy goal and on Thy bosom rest.

We nothing know; but, Lord, thou knowest all,
Life's new developments must all arise in Thee;
Work Thine own will, and when we do not see,
Still lead us on till at Thy feet we fall.

We trust but Thee; Father, to Thee we come!
Grant that our souls be lost in Thee for aye!
Let naught disturb our commune by the way!
Be Thou our all; our Christ, our Heaven, our home!'

* * *

THE LIFE ELYSIAN

*There breaks the soul from every weight away
And for itself beholds and understands!
In that clear dawn of life's true morning light
It turns, reviews, and then must needs accept
Whate'er results from yesternight's wild rush
And feverish greed, within the robing-room of earth.*

*'Tis then it learns how cherished ignorance
False guide has been, and led the soul astray,
Appraising tinsel at the price of gold,
And teaching how base metal and true wealth were one,
That, also, all the wild array of masquerade,
Which fools had brought together for their revels,
Were robes, insignia, orders and rewards
Provided by the King, that all His sons
Might dress and grace the marriage feast!*

*There comes the Truth, and all the false array
In which we strutted forth, lordly and envied,
Must then be thrown aside and left behind,
As worse than useless-we have to pay their cost
Ere we can forward pass. Each soul with painful rue
There doffs its mantle of hypocrisy, to find
Its royal lustre and its richness vanished with the night,
Leaving but sign of poverty behind.*

*Then sighs the soul to learn its bankrupt state,
For till that moment none can ever know
The price it pays for such a treacherous robe,
And false deceitful outfit;-
We don it in expediency and haste,
We doff it in the searching light of God.*

Where is laid bare all bruises, scars and wounds
We felt not when received in maddened rush
To save the object of our choice from other hands.
But in our passage to the feast we have to pause,
Consider, and discharge th' account for what we thought
Was free to those who could secure and keep!
And this is painful reckoning.

When this is o'er, then breaks the soul away
And learns it has another role than masquerade
To play on life's eternal stage. It throws aside
All relics of the brute, the savage and barbaric tastes,
And making restoration with a pure repentance
Steps to life's mark clad but in freedom's garb,
With naught to weight, to hinder or retard
Its course, and as a man starts on the race
Which has its goal and destiny in God.

'Tis of this race I sing, and now I bid you come
And see how it is run on God's own course-

The Life Elysian!

* * *

A BRIEF BIOGRAPHY OF ROBERT JAMES LEES

Robert James Lees was born in Leicestershire, England on August 12, 1849. He was better known as James and was a Spiritualist, a healer, a preacher, a philanthropist and a writer.

James believed that his psychic abilities were with him from the moment of his birth. He wrote very little about his childhood experiences, but he describes in Volume Two - "The Life Elysian" how, even as a very small child, he was aware of 'visitors from across the border'.

His first employment was with the Manchester Guardian and soon became involved in several London-based publications. He was a man who, having virtually no formal education, wrote fascinating works which continued to sell many years after his death. James wrote several books, which were dictated to him by friends from the spirit realm, of which the most well-known three-volume series being "Through the Mists", "The Life Elysian" and "The Gate of Heaven". "The Heretic" was written as his only autobiographical novel which was a record of his many years in London.

James was a loving and caring man. He, along with many other philanthropists of that time, worked hard to lift the less-fortunate of London's poorest areas towards self-respect and self-determination.

James' fame and prestige grew quickly in parts of Britain and he soon made his acquaintance with high-ranking philosophers, theologians and Prime Ministers. He claimed to have been present when Edison first experimented with recording sound and had the privilege of assisting the late Mr. W. E. Gladstone in the production of "The Impregnable Rock of Holy Scripture". He was also a close friend of the late Mr. W. T. Stead, the famous journalist who died in the Titanic disaster. However, many unsubstantiated claims have been made about James. For instance, it is claimed that he was involved in the arrest of Jack the Ripper, the Whitechapel Murderer of 1888. It is further claimed that he assisted in the arrest of the Irish Fenian terrorists. However, James spoke very little about his eventful life and until further research is made into these claims, they will remain a mystery.

James had sixteen children of which ten survived. His daughter, Evelyn Amy Florence (Eva Lees), was born on November 14, 1879 in Surrey, Kent, and always lived with her father. In her father's later years, she was his caregiver, housekeeper, counsellor and friend and continued to publish her father's books for many years after his death. She was also a devout spiritualist and was very active in the spiritualist circles of Leicester. She died in 1968 in Leicester.

Robert James Lees passed away in Leicester, England on January 11, 1931. He was 81 years old. He was cremated at Gilroes Cemetery and prior to the ceremony, a short spiritualist service was held in his study. His ashes were placed in Ilfracombe Cemetery, in the same grave as his late loving wife, Sarah.

**PRINTING HISTORY of
"The Life Elysian"**

Original Hardback Book Printed by
William Cross, Leicester in 1905

1976 to 2005 Book out of print

Republished 1st Impression spiral bound book
Printed in 2006 by McKay Publishing,
Calgary, Alberta, Canada
www.revealingthesilence.com

This Paperback edition
Printed in 2008 by

Sanders & Co UK Ltd.,
Northampton NN1 4HU England
Tel: 01604 630 195 Email: sandersltd@aol.com